Accessing the Clinical Genius of Winnicott

Donald Winnicott, psychoanalyst and pediatrician, is viewed by many in the psychodynamic field as the "other genius" in the history of psychodynamic theory and practice, along with Freud. This book selects and explores twelve of his most influential clinical papers.

Winnicott's works have been highly valued in the decades since they were first published, and are still relevant today. Winnicott's writings on the goals and techniques of psychodynamic psychotherapy have been foundational, in that he recast Freudian- and Kleinian-influenced thinking in the direction of the more relational schools of psychotherapy that define current 21st-century psychodynamic practice. Winnicott's writings help us to understand the maturational processes of children, certainly. But more than that, they help us to understand how best to intervene when the enterprise of childhood leads to compromises of psychological health in later years. Yet, despite Winnicott's influence and continuing relevance, his writings, while at some level simple, are elusive to modern readers. For one thing, he writes in the psychoanalytic genre of the 1930s–1960s, whose underlying theoretical assumptions and vocabulary are obscure in the present day and, for another, his writing often reflects primary process thinking, which is suggestive, but not declarative. In this work, Teri Quatman provides explanations and insight, in an interlocution with Winnicott's most significant papers, exploring both his language and concepts, and enabling the clinician to emerge with a deep and reflective understanding of his thoughts, perspectives, and techniques.

Engaging and accessible, *Accessing the Clinical Genius of Winnicott* will be of great use to anyone encountering Winnicott for the first time, particularly in psychodynamic psychotherapeutic training, and in the teaching of relational psychotherapies.

Teri Quatman is an Associate Professor of Counseling Psychology in the Graduate Department of Counseling Psychology at Santa Clara University, California, USA. She earned her Ph.D. from Stanford University in 1990, and has studied, practiced, and taught psychodynamic psychotherapy to graduate students for the past 28 years. She has also maintained a private psychotherapy practice from 1992 to the present.

Accessing the Clinical Genius of Winnicott

A Careful Rendering of Winnicott's Twelve Most Influential Clinical Papers

Teri Quatman

Routledge
Taylor & Francis Group

LONDON AND NEW YORK

First published 2020
by Routledge
2 Park Square, Milton Park, Abingdon, Oxon OX14 4RN

and by Routledge
52 Vanderbilt Avenue, New York, NY 10017

Routledge is an imprint of the Taylor & Francis Group, an informa business

© 2020 Teri Quatman

British Library Cataloguing-in-Publication Data
A catalogue record for this book is available from the British Library

Library of Congress Cataloging-in-Publication Data
Names: Quatman, Teri., author.
Title: Accessing the clinical genius of Winnicott: a careful rendering of Winnicott's 12 most influential clinical papers / Teri Quatman.
Description: Abingdon, Oxon; New York, NY: Routledge, 2020. |
Includes bibliographical references and index.
Identifiers: LCCN 2019056440 (print) | LCCN 2019056441 (ebook) |
ISBN 9780367859268 (hbk) | ISBN 9780367859244 (pbk) |
ISBN 9781003015819 (ebk)
Subjects: LCSH: Winnicott, D. W. (Donald Woods), 1896–1971. |
Psychoanalysis. | Developmental psychology.
Classification: LCC BF109.W55 Q38 2020 (print) |
LCC BF109.W55 (ebook) | DDC 150.19/5092–dc23
LC record available at https://lccn.loc.gov/2019056440
LC ebook record available at https://lccn.loc.gov/2019056441

ISBN: 978-0-367-85926-8 (hbk)
ISBN: 978-0-367-85924-4 (pbk)
ISBN: 978-1-003-01581-9 (ebk)

Typeset in Bembo
by Newgen Publishing UK

Contents

Foreword   vi
Acknowledgments   vii
Credits   viii

1 Mind and its relation to the psyche-soma (1949)   1

2 Primitive emotional development (1945)   24

3 Hate in the counter-transference (1949)   51

4 Transitional objects and transitional phenomena: a study of the
   first not-me possession (1953)   71

5 The antisocial tendency (1956)   97

6 Primary maternal preoccupation (1956)   117

7 Ego distortion in terms of True and False Self (1960)   133

8 The aims of psycho-analytical treatment (1962)   160

9 Notes on ego integration in child development (1962)   170

10 Mirror-role of mother and family in child development (1967)   190

11 The use of an object (1969)   203

12 Fear of breakdown (1974)   221

Author references   242
Index   245

Foreword

The chapters that follow include twelve of Winnicott's most important clinical papers. Each chapter is named by the title of the Winnicott paper to be discussed. I provide a brief one-paragraph introduction to each paper, and then proceed, in antiphonal style, to alternate Winnicott's words, paragraph by paragraph, with my translations and explications. I replicate the entire text of each of Winnicott's papers in boxes, with my comments interspersed. My words are, perhaps—hopefully—the beginning of your own dialogue with Winnicott—certainly (and again, hopefully) not the end. I hope that in presenting my "translations" of Winnicott's writings, he might reach you—might touch you—might cause you to ponder, and, upon reflection, to say "Yes! He's right! I've seen it. I know it. He's right on!" And there, at that moment, you will have come alive to the genius of Winnicott. So, this is my wish for you in this work: that he might touch you, and, in touching you, might transform something in you. Because that is who he is, and that is what he does.

Acknowledgments

In my first book, *Essential Psychodynamic Psychotherapy*, I acknowledged the village that stood at the perimeters of that work. In this book, I want to acknowledge the smaller circle.

First and foremost, there is Dr. Mardy Ireland, who agreed at the very start of things to lend her deep knowledge of Winnicott in particular, and psychodynamic thinkers in general, to the birthing of this work. She did that—carefully and consistently over time. For that I deeply thank her. Without her bracketing, I would not have had the courage to speak the impressions, thoughts, and offerings of Winnicott's words that came as I wrote this piece. I owe her a deep debt of thanks.

Secondly, I want to acknowledge Dr. Mel Marshark, who passed quietly from us in October of 2010. We had university life in common, and also our love for Winnicott in common—you, his patient and student; I, your friend and learner. You told me so many stories about D. W., but most of all, that Winnicott was the best among all of your multiple psychoanalysts. Of course. You truly made him come to life for me.

Thirdly, I want to acknowledge Dr. Tom Ogden, whose weekly seminar I attended every week for seven years in the 1990s and early 2000s, and who has been an ongoing guiding light to me in my growth in the psychodynamic world. Thank you, Tom, for your careful, well-crafted writings (which I routinely assign in my advanced classes) and for your gracious and generous support to me over time, without which I'd never have written.

And lastly, I want to acknowledge Dr. Johanna Mayer. She was my first psychodynamic supervisor at the Palo Alto Veterans Administration Hospital, and continues to be a model for me, given her extraordinary gifts as therapist and mentor. I aspire always to walk in her footsteps.

Credits

Winnicott, D. W. (1960). Ego distortion in terms of true and false self. In *The maturational processes and the facilitating environment: Studies in the theory of emotional development* (pp. 140–152). London: Karnac, 1990.

Winnicott, D. W. (1962). The aims of psycho-analytical treatment. In *The maturational processes and the facilitating environment: Studies in the theory of emotional development* (pp. 166–170). London: Karnac, 2007.

Winnicott, D. W. (1962). Notes on ego integration in child development. In *The maturational processes and the facilitating environment: Studies in the theory of emotional development* (pp. 56–63). London: Karnac, 2007. "id"

Winnicott, D. W. (1949). Hate in the counter-transference. *International Journal of Psycho-Analysis*, 30, 69–74.

Winnicott, D. W. (1953). Transitional objects and transitional phenomena—A study of the first not-me possession. *International Journal of Psycho-Analysis*, 34, 89–97.

Winnicott, D. W. (1969). The use of an object. *International Journal of Psycho-Analysis*, 50, 711–716.

Winnicott, D. W. (1974). Fear of breakdown. *International Review of Psycho-Analysis*, 1: 103–107.

1 Mind and its relation to the psyche-soma

(1949)[1]

Winnicott, D. W. (1949). Mind and its relation to the psyche-soma (rev. 1954). In: *Through paediatrics to psycho-analysis: Collected papers* (pp. 243–254). Levittown, PA: Brunner Mazel, 1992.

This Winnicott chapter is one of the cornerstones of this thinking process about the foundational elements of our being as humans. His central thesis is that our thinking apparatus as adults—our mind—is designed to be nested-in and infused with the ground of somatic experience. He says that the very first sense of our own psyche as infants is our experiencing of ourselves as physical beings. There is the physical experience, and then there is the imaginative elaboration of that experience. These, in interplay, are the initial building blocks of the human psyche. He asserts that when a baby has to adapt to certain kinds and degrees of maternal failure that *exceed* the growing baby's psyche-soma's capacities, the mind—the baby's not-yet-ready thinking process—has to step up and take over, and *prematurely* organize the care of the baby's own psyche-soma—something that the maternal environment was meant to do. This early maladaptation affects all subsequent stages of development, causing among other things an over-reliance on the (disembodied) mind, and a strong tendency to become the caretaker in intimate relationships, which comes with their having a difficult time allowing themselves to be the recipient of care in such relationships.

I've tried to follow Winnicott step by step here, bringing us carefully along as Winnicott weaves his thoughts for us. It's slow and careful, but I don't want us to miss any of the elegance of Winnicott's contributions contained in this piece.

He begins with a quote from Scott (1949):

> To ascertain what exactly comprises the irreducible mental elements, particularly those of a dynamic nature, constitutes in my opinion one of our most fascinating final aims. These elements would necessarily

[1] A paper read before the Medical Section of the British Psychological Society, 14 December, 1949, and revised October, 1953. *British Journal of Medical Psychology*, Vol. XXVII, 1954.

have a somatic and probably a neurological equivalent, and in that way we should by scientific method have closely narrowed the age-old gap between mind and body. I venture to predict that then the antithesis which has baffled all the philosophers will be found to be based on an illusion. In other words, I *do not think that the mind really exists as an entity*—possibly a startling thing for a psychologist to say [my italics]. When we talk of the mind influencing the body or the body influencing the mind we are merely using a convenient short-hand for a more cumbrous phrase....

(Jones, 1946)

This quotation by Scott (1949) stimulated me to try to sort out my own ideas on this vast and difficult subject. The body schema with its temporal and spatial aspects provides a valuable statement of the individual's dia-gram of himself, and in it I believe there is no obvious place for the mind. Yet in clinical practice we do meet with the mind as an entity localized somewhere by the patient; a further study of the paradox that 'mind does not really exist as an entity' is therefore necessary.

OK. So far, Winnicott is giving us the context for why he became interested in this question. He's intrigued with what the mind is, and where it belongs.

Mind as a function of psyche-soma

To study the concept of mind one must always be studying an individual, a total individual, and including the development of that individual from the very beginning of psychosomatic existence. If one accepts this dis-cipline then one can study the mind of an individual as it specializes out from the psyche part of the psyche-soma.

Winnicott is saying here that to study the mind of an individual—meaning our thinking apparatus—we must take that person's development from his first days into consideration. Winnicott is saying that the mind "specializes out"— or, develops out—from the psyche part of the psyche-soma. He will explain this further, but he is positing that the very instrument we use for taking in the world around us—our mind—is, or more properly, should be intimately grounded in the psyche, which, he will explain, is intimately nested in the phys-ical body. The word "psyche" (from the Greek word for breath, life, soul) here means to Winnicott the elaboration—via the infant's imagination—of bodily (somatic) parts, feelings, and functions; that is, the imaginative elaboration of the infant's physical aliveness.

He continues:

> The mind does not exist as an entity in the individual's schema of things provided the individual psyche-soma or body scheme has come satisfactorily through the very early developmental stages; mind is then no more than a special case of the function of the psyche-soma.

Winnicott is hinting at something here, but he has not explained himself fully yet. He's hinting that when the psyche-soma (which he has not clearly defined yet) comes successfully through its very early developmental stages, then what we think of as "the mind" is simply a by-product of the development of the psyche-soma.

He continues:

> In the study of a developing individual the mind will often be found to be developing a *false entity*, and a *false localization*. A study of these abnormal tendencies must precede the more direct examination of the mind-specialization of the healthy or normal psyche.

OK. Now he's asserting that somehow it is an abnormality for the mind to develop an awareness of itself and a location of itself. He thinks this is necessary to understand before we understand how the normal psyche-soma specializes out a "mind." In this way, his thinking process is similar to Freud's: he wants first to understand the abnormality, the pathology, before exploring normal development.

He continues:

> We are quite used to seeing the two words mental and physical opposed and would not quarrel with their being opposed in daily conversation. It is quite another matter, however, if the concepts are opposed in scientific discussion.

OK. Mental versus physical. These terms should not be thought of as opposed to one another. Here, Winnicott (in 1949) was prescient. We now know, for instance, that both the stomach and the heart—definitely parts of the body—have neurons that are in constant dynamic interplay with the emotional parts of the brain. Additionally, *neuro*transmitters that are manufactured by the body's immune system are found throughout the body. Furthermore, *neuro*peptides which are secreted by the immune and endocrine systems have receptors in the brain (Pert, 1997). We're following him here regarding "mental versus physical."

The use of these two words physical and mental in describing disease leads us into trouble immediately. The psychosomatic disorders, half-way between the mental and the physical, are in a rather precarious position. Research into psychosomatics is being held up, to some extent, by the muddle to which I am referring (MacAlpine, 1952). Also, neuro-surgeons are doing things to the normal or healthy brain in an attempt to alter or even improve mental states. These "physical" therapists are completely at sea in their theory; curiously enough they seem to be leaving out the importance of the physical body, of which the brain is an integral part.

Here he's decrying as a muddle the opposing of the physical versus the mental. He will take up more of this argument later in the paper. He continues:

Let us attempt, therefore, to think of the developing individual, starting at the beginning. Here is a body, and the psyche and the soma are not to be distinguished except according to the direction from which one is looking. One can look at the developing body or at the developing psyche. I suppose the word psyche here means the *imaginative elaboration of somatic parts, feelings, and functions*, that is, of physical aliveness. We know that this imaginative elaboration is dependent on the existence and the healthy functioning of the brain, especially certain parts of it. The psyche is not, however, felt by the individual to be localized in the brain, or indeed to be localized anywhere.

He speaks here of the very beginning hours of an infant's life. He defines the word "psyche" as indicating the imaginative elaboration of somatic parts, feelings, and functions, that is, of physical aliveness. So he is saying that the very first sense of our own psyche as infants is our experiencing of ourselves as physical beings. There is the physical experience, and then there is the imaginative elaboration of that experience. These, in interplay, are the initial building blocks of the human psyche. He also observes that the psyche, while dependent, in part, on the brain's functioning, is more than and different from the brain, and is not generally thought of by people as being located in the brain.

Gradually the psyche and the soma aspects of the growing person become involved in a process of mutual interrelation. The interrelating of the psyche with the soma constitutes an early phase of individual development (see Chapter XII). At a later stage the live body, with its limits, and with an inside and an outside, is *felt by the individual* to form the core for the imaginative self.

Gradually, the physical experience and the imaginative elaboration of that physical experience become, in Winnicott's words, "interrelated." Notice that "imaginative elaboration" is not the same as thinking. It *precedes* thinking. It is the use of something of the spirit or core of the emerging human to appreciate what s/he is experiencing in a purely physical sense—comfort, discomfort, restfulness, urgency, touch, warmth, holding, movement. Gradually, over time, the individual gains an awareness of the inside versus the outside of his/her body, but this is a developmental accomplishment. The body is felt by the individual to be core to or the core of the imaginative self. Winnicott is saying here that the experience of the body is the ground of our being. He continues:

> The development to this stage is extremely complex, and although this development may possibly be fairly complete by the time a baby has been born a few days, there is a vast opportunity for distortion of the natural course of development in these respects. Moreover, whatever applies to very early stages also applies to some extent to all stages, even to the stage that we call adult maturity.

In other words, the first hours and days, which are foundational, afford a "vast opportunity" for compromises of what *should be* the natural course of development.

And then he makes this riveting statement: "whatever applies to very early stages also applies to some extent to all stages, even to the stage that we call adult maturity." He's saying that in each successive developmental stage, there is a natural course of development, but also that there are vast opportunities for what should be happening *not* to happen, and therefore, developmental (and often permanent) compromises ensue.

Theory of mind

On the basis of these preliminary considerations I find myself putting forward a theory of mind. This theory is based on work with analytic patients who have needed to regress to an extremely early level of development in the transference. In this paper I shall only give one piece of illustrative clinical material, but the theory can, I believe, be found to be valuable in our daily analytic work.

OK. So Winnicott is suggesting here that, although he is writing about early, early development, it may also be found to be valuable in work with adult patients in psychotherapy. He says he'll illustrate this with a piece of clinical material later in the paper, but he asserts that what he has to say in this paper can be valuable in our daily work as clinicians. He has our attention. He continues:

> Let us assume that health in the early development of the individual entails *continuity of being.* The early psyche-soma proceeds along a certain line of development provided its *continuity of being is not disturbed;* in other words, for the healthy development of the early psyche-soma there is a need for a *perfect* environment. At first the need is absolute.

OK. Winnicott is here introducing a new concept: "continuity of being." The psyche-soma proceeds well in its developmental trajectory as long as its "continuity of being" is not disturbed, and for this, the newborn requires "absolute" attunement. What is "continuity of being"? The words he chooses have a certain poetic sound to them. They suggest a lack of disturbance, the presence of comfort, of being protected, of being OK. He emphasizes this. He says, "At first the need is absolute," and should be absolutely protected—the infant's need for this undisturbed "continuity of being." He then explains:

> The perfect environment is one which *actively adapts* to the needs of the newly formed psyche-soma, that which we as observers know to be the infant at the start.

Ah. So this crucial, at first, "perfect" environment is one wherein some person—usually the mother—makes this active adaptation to the needs of the newborn happen.

> A bad environment is bad because by failure to adapt it becomes an *impingement* to which the psyche-soma (i.e. the infant) *must react.* This reacting disturbs the continuity of the going-on-being of the new individual.

And the "bad" environment is one that forces the infant to react to it, i.e., impinges on the infant in such a way that the infant's "continuity of being" is disturbed or disrupted. OK. We can certainly imagine this in its extremes, which indeed some infants must endure. Also, in his language usage, he tells us to be aware that what we see from the outside as an infant, plus whatever we project upon that infant's thinking process or sense of awareness, the newborn is in truth a somatic-experiencing-being rather than a thinking being.

> In its beginnings the good (psychological) environment is a physical one, with the child in the womb or being held and generally tended;

This is important to understand. At first the need is a physical one: the need of the infant to be, in Winnicott's lovely words, "held and generally tended." He continues:

> Only in the course of time does the environment develop a new characteristic which necessitates a new descriptive term, such as emotional or psychological or social.

Not at first, but with passing time—days to weeks, perhaps—the environment needs to become an *emotionally* or *psychologically attuned* one. He uses the word "environment" to mean the maternal environment, the "environment" that seamlessly provides for the infant's needs.

> Out of this emerges the ordinary good mother with her ability to make active adaptation to her infant's needs arising out of her devotion, made possible by her narcissism, her imagination, and her memories, which enable her to know through identification what are her baby's needs.

"Out of this emerges the ordinary good mother…" This is a Winnicottian use of language which conjures a kind of initial caretaking haze from which the mother eventually emerges. He will call this in another paper "primary maternal preoccupation." He then suggests that the mother's ability to make active adaptation to her infant's needs comes primarily through her *identification with the infant*—her ability to use her own intuition to remember, by use of both her imagination and her implicit memory, what it's like to *be* that infant and what s/he might need moment-to-moment. He cites mother's narcissism as well. There is a necessary narcissistic investment in the survival and well-being of the dependent infant.

OK. Winnicott continues:

> The need for a good environment, which is absolute at first, rapidly becomes relative. The *ordinary good mother is good enough*. If she is *good enough* the infant becomes able to allow for her deficiencies by mental activity.

He's said a lot in this sentence: first, that the need for a "good"—meaning "*perfect*" environment which is 100%-attuned to the newborn's physical needs—rapidly attenuates, at which point ordinary maternal attunement to infant need is "good enough." (Winnicott becomes known for the phrase, "good enough mother," which provides psychic relief from the onus of needing to be "perfect" as a new mother.) He also begins to develop the thought that what frees her from the need to be perfect is the fact that the infant will progressively develop the ability to compensate for her shortfalls via his/her own mental activity—within certain limits, as Winnicott will explain.

This applies to meeting not only instinctual impulses but also all the most primitive types of ego need, even including the need for negative care or an alive neglect. The mental activity of the infant turns a *good-enough* environment into a perfect environment, that is to say, turns relative failure of adaptation into adaptive success. What releases the mother from her need to be near-perfect is the infant's understanding. In the ordinary course of events the mother tries not to introduce complications beyond those which the infant can understand and allow for; in particular she tries to insulate her baby from coincidences and from other phenomena that must be beyond the infant's ability to comprehend. In a general way she keep the world of the infant as simple as possible.

OK. He's developing this thought—that the infant's gradually developing capacity to understand or "grok" his environment makes the infant progressively able to tolerate slight maternal delays and misreads. But there is a substantial limit to what the infant can understand and allow for. The mother must be vigilant, even to prevent—his odd choice of words—"coincidences"—accidental happenings, chance events that exceed the infant's ability to comprehend them. Also, he's used the phrase "the need for negative care or an alive neglect." This pertains to the mother's attuned but graduated attenuation of up-to-the moment care, and also to the infant's need for times of formless quiescence in which the most caring thing is to allow the infant his own space and time (while still being present to him).

He continues:

The mind, then, has as one of its roots a variable functioning of the psyche-soma, one concerned with the threat to continuity of being that follows any failure of (active) environmental adaptation. It follows that mind-development is very much influenced by factors not specifically personal to the individual, including chance events.

Hmmmm. What's this? The mind—our thinking apparatus—has, as one of its roots (roots is a metaphor Winnicott uses in describing fundamental, enduring points of inception—foundational elements) the psyche-soma's vigilance with respect to failures of adaptation. This means that, when things break through the protections that a good-enough mother provides to her infant, there develops a kind of bodily based, imaginatively elaborated vigilance at the very foundations of the mind, or the way that one eventually comes to think. It is one of the deep roots of our thinking process: to watch out for the possibility that things might go wrong, especially if they did go wrong.

> In infant care it is vitally important that mothers, at first physically, and soon also imaginatively, can start off by supplying this active adaptation, but also it is a characteristic maternal function to provide *graduated failure of adaptation*, according to the growing ability of the individual infant to allow for relative failure by mental activity, or by understanding. Thus there appears in the infant a tolerance in respect of both ego need and instinctual tension.

OK. So the infant uses his/her gradually developing powers of understanding to tolerate less-than-perfect adaptation, both with respect to instinctual tensions (by which are meant hungers and other physical tensions), and also ego needs (by which are meant those aspects of the psychosomatic being of the infant that gradually organize and integrate, and over time gather the infant into a "me").

> It could perhaps be shown that mothers are released slowly by infants who are eventually found to have a low I.Q. On the other hand, an infant with an exceptionally good brain, eventually giving a high I.Q., releases the mother earlier.

Winnicott puts this observation out tentatively, as though he's not yet sure of this part, although it's likely in his practice as a pediatrician that he's observed this correlation.

> According to this theory then, in the development of every individual, the mind has a root, perhaps its most important root, in the need of the individual, at the core of the self, for a perfect environment. In this connection, I might refer to my view of psychosis as an environmental deficiency disease (see Chapter XVII). There are certain developments of this theory which seem to me to be important. Certain kinds of failure on the part of the mother, especially erratic behaviour, produce over-activity of the mental functioning. Here, in the overgrowth of the mental functioning reactive to erratic mothering, we see that there can develop an opposition between the mind and the psyche-soma, since in reaction to this abnormal environmental state the thinking of the individual begins to take over and organize the caring for the psyche-soma, whereas

> in health it is the function of the environment to do this. In health the mind does not usurp the environment's function, but makes possible an understanding and eventually a making use of its relative failure.

OK. Now we have a second "root" of the mind. In Winnicott's thinking, perhaps its most important root: a root in vigilance and a root in perfection. This is an important thesis: that in the very foundation of our minds—our thinking apparatus—our being reaches backward into the need for a perfect environment at the start. This is in the foundational bedrock of our thinking process. It's part of our humanness to look for perfection. I'll put aside for the moment his reference to psychosis and continue.

He then asserts that when a baby has to adapt to certain kinds and degrees of maternal failure that *exceed* the growing baby's psyche-soma's capacities, the mind—the baby's not-yet-ready thinking process—has, in essence, to step up and take over *prematurely*. He points especially to erratic mothering. But more generally, when the environmental failures are too great, the thinking part of the baby has to take over and organize the care of the baby's own psyche-soma—something that the maternal environment was meant to do. This is a developmental compromise of the *first order*, because instead of the mind being used to understand the emerging self-experience of the baby, it is instead co-opted into the task of doing what the environment (the mother) should be doing. As a by-product, there can develop an opposition between the mind and bodily based experience, which should be the whole of the initial world of the infant.

This next statement is a straightforward re-stating of the above:

> The gradual process whereby the individual becomes able to care for the self belongs to later stages in individual emotional development, stages that must be reached in due course, at the pace that is set by natural developmental force.

Then he continues:

> To go a stage further, one might ask what happens if the strain that is put on mental functioning organized in defence against a tantalizing early environment is greater and greater?

Fairbairn, writing in 1944, would use the word "tantalizing" to describe a maternal environment wherein, if the mother is too frustrating, given the infant's absolute need of her, she becomes infinitely desirable but at the same time infinitely frustrating (Fairbairn, 1944). He observed that there would then be erected a defensive structure to make such a mother safer to the infant. So Winnicott is now asking, what happens to the thinking apparatus under such strain?

He posits:

> One would expect confusional states, and (in the extreme) mental defect of the kind that is not dependent on brain-tissue deficiency. As a more common result of the lesser degrees of tantalizing infant care in the earliest stages we find *mental functioning becoming a thing in itself*, practically replacing the good mother and making her unnecessary.

OK, this is a wow! Mental functioning—the thinking apparatus of the developing infant—fills in for the erratic or absent caretaking of the mother. This would not seem a tragedy if we allow ourselves to be unaware that the development of the thinking process *is designed to be nested in the psyche-soma*, and that if it is called upon too early in development, there will be inevitable negative consequences. He will next begin to elaborate these.

> Clinically, this can go along with dependence on the actual mother and a false personal growth on a compliance basis. This is a most uncomfortable state of affairs, especially because the psyche of the individual gets "seduced" away into this mind from the intimate relationship which the psyche originally had with the soma. The result is a mind-psyche, which is pathological.

OK. Stay with him here. He's saying that an infant can do both—can depend on the actual mother but also can fill in with a hypertrophied mental apparatus when the mother is unable to provide a good-enough maternal environment. In this latter case, the mind-psyche, de-nested from the infant's body/soma, figures out how to be compliant with mother's needs, moods, erraticness, which is a betrayal of actually being a baby.

> A person who is developing in this way displays a distorted pattern affecting all later stages of development. For instance, one can observe a tendency for easy identification with the environmental aspect of all relationships that involve dependence, and a difficulty in identification with the dependent individual. Clinically one may see such a person develop into one who is a *marvellously good mother to others* for a limited period; in fact a person who has developed along these lines may have almost magical *healing properties* because of an extreme capacity to make active adaptation to primitive needs.

OK. This early maladaptation affects all subsequent stages of development, so this adaptation is neither inconsequential nor temporary. Winnicott provides one example of how it distorts human development. He says that it eventuates in "a tendency for easy identification with the environmental aspect of all relationships that involve dependence, and a difficulty in identification with the dependent individual." By the "environmental aspect of all relationships" he means the caretaking/caregiving/maternal provision aspects of intimate relationships. So this individual, in adulthood, easily takes the caretaking role in his/her intimate relationships. Likewise, s/he has a difficult time allowing him/herself to be cared for and about in such relationships. Winnicott says that these individuals can be very, very adept at reading even the most psychologically primitive and hard-to-discern needs of the other, but that this capacity has a limited usefulness, so to speak.

He continues:

> The falsity of these patterns for expression of the personality, however, becomes evident in practice. Breakdown threatens or occurs, because what the individual is all the time needing is to *find someone else* who will make real this "good environment" concept, so that the individual may return to the dependent psyche-soma which forms the only place to live from. In this case "without mind" becomes a desired state.

OK. Here's a really important punchline! This consummately caretaking individual is all the time operating with a tacit agenda of finding someone who will take over the caretaking role toward him/her, and allow him/her to relax from the constant use of his mind to surveil the need of the other, and to be allowed to *himself* sink into the early dependency of living solely from the basis of his own psyche-soma. Winnicott does not say this explicitly, but we can easily infer his thinking that this pursuit is bound not to go well…

He now leaves this topic temporarily, and moves on to questions of the perceived physical location of the mind or thinking apparatus, which was part of what arrested him in the first place.

> There cannot of course be a direct partnership between the mind-psyche and the body of the individual. But the *mind-psyche* is localized by the individual, and is placed either inside the head or outside it in some special relation to the head, and this provides an important source for headache as a symptom.

Keep in mind that the phrase "mind-psyche" is what Winnicott is describing as an aberrant development. Notice that he's inventing a quasi-poetic term which switches the order of development from soma-to-psyche-to-mind to mind-to-psyche, in that order, leaving out the soma entirely. Proper development would be the aged maturing of the psyche's interrelationship with the soma, and, following that, the development of the thinking apparatus as a natural outgrowth of the psyche-soma. The psyche-soma is the trunk of the tree; the mind is/should be a branch.

OK, so Winnicott is now making the observation that people who have had to develop the branch apart from the tree trunk tend to describe that branch, the "mind-psyche," as located in the head.

He goes on:

> The question has to be asked why the head should be the place inside which the mind tends to become localized by the individual, and I do not know the answer. I feel that an important point is the individual's need to localize the mind because it is an enemy, that is to say, for control of it. A schizoid patient tells me that the head is the place to put the mind because, *as the head cannot be seen by oneself*, it does not obviously exist as part of oneself. Another point is that the head has special experiences during the birth process, but in order to make full use of this latter fact I must go on to consider another type of mental functioning which can be specially activated during the birth process. This is associated with the word "memorizing".

Winnicott will now make use of his vast experience as both a pediatrician and a psychoanalyst. He'll speak of the concept of a newborn in the process of birth "memorizing" parts and pieces exactly. Notice as he explains this that he is not speaking of the kind of memorizing we do when mastering the text of a speech. That kind of explicit memory does not come on board in a developing human until approximately age three. He's speaking instead of a process which we now know as "implicit" memory—which captures the somatic, behavioral, and emotional aspects of an experience without encoding them as something "remembered" or as narrative memory (Nelson, 1995, as cited in Cordon et al., 2004). Nelson observes, "under some circumstances even very young infants are capable of long-term remembering" (Cordon et al., 2004; see also Hildreth, Sweeny, & Rovee-Collier, 2003; Rovee-Collier, Hartshorn, & DiRubbo, 1999; and Hartshorn et al., 1998; as cited in Cordon et al., 2004).

Winnicott continues:

> As I have said, the continuity of being of the developing psyche-soma (internal and external relationships) is disturbed by reactions to environmental impingements, in other words by the results of failures of the environment to make active adaptation. By my theory a rapidly increasing amount of reaction to impingement disturbing continuity of

psyche-soma becomes expected and allowed for according to mental capacity. Impingements demanding *excessive* reactions (according to the next
part of my theory) cannot be allowed for. All that can happen apart from
confusion is that the reactions can be *catalogued*.[1]

1   Cf. Freud's theory of obsessional neurosis (1909).

OK, so reactions to excessive impingements can cause confusional states in
babies. One set of responses available to a baby is to "catalogue" those experiences
in what we now know to be implicit memory. Again, this is not the kind of
memory we have about our high school graduation or even the first day or first
grade. Implicit memory captures the bodily, behavioral, and emotional aspects
of an experience without encoding them as something "remembered." So it's
possible for a baby to hold permanently, in his/her body, the exact sensations
that s/he experienced in moments of excessive impingement.

He continues:

Typically at birth there is apt to be an excessive disturbance of continuity
because of reactions to impingements, and the mental activity which I am
describing at the moment is that which is concerned with exact memorizing during the birth process. In my psycho-analytic work I sometimes
meet with regressions fully under control and yet going back to prenatal
life. Patients regressed in an ordered way go over the birth process again
and again, and I have been astonished by the convincing proof that I have
had that an infant during the birth process not only memorizes every
reaction disturbing the continuity of being, but also appears to memorize
these in the correct order. I have not used hypnosis, but I am aware of the
comparable discoveries, less convincing to me, that are achieved through
use of hypnosis. Mental functioning of the type that I am describing,
which might be called memorizing or cataloguing, can be extremely
active and accurate about the time of a baby's birth. I shall illustrate this by
details from a case, but first I want to make clear my point that *this type of
mental functioning is an encumbrance to the psyche-soma,* or to the individual's
continuity of being which constitutes the self. The individual may be able
to make use of it to relive the birth process in play or in a carefully controlled analysis. But this cataloguing type of mental functioning acts like a
foreign body if it is associated with environmental adaptive failure that is
beyond understanding or prediction.

OK. Keep in mind that Winnicott is not talking about explicit, narrative
memory, but about bodily based, emotional states that he has witnessed being

replayed by adults in his practice. He has here taken us into territory that very few clinicians will have experienced. That said, Winnicott is reporting on phenomena that he has himself witnessed in a subset of his psychoanalytic patients, to his astonishment. So we'll hear him out on this. He will now present us with a clinical case of this kind of "memorizing" of the details of the birth experience from his practice.

Clinical illustration

The following fragment of a case history is given to illustrate my thesis. Out of several years' intensive work it is notoriously difficult to choose a detail; nevertheless, I include this fragment in order to show that what I am putting forward is very much a part of daily practice with patients.

A woman[2] who is now 47 years old had made what seemed to others but not to herself to be a good relationship to the world and had always been able to earn her own living. She had achieved a good education and was generally liked; in fact I think she was never actively disliked. She herself, however, felt completely dissatisfied, as if always aiming to find herself and never succeeding. Suicidal ideas were certainly not absent but they were kept at bay by her belief which dated from childhood that she would ultimately solve her problem and find herself. She had had a so-called "classical" analysis for several years but somehow the core of her illness had been unchanged. With me it soon became apparent that this patient must make a very severe regression or else give up the struggle. I therefore followed the regressive tendency, letting it take the patient wherever it led; eventually the regression reached the limit of the patient's need, and since there has been a natural progression with the true self instead of a false self in action.

2   Case referred to again in another paper (see Chapter XXII, pp. 279–280).

Just a couple of comments before he continues. Winnicott says he followed the regressive tendency. By this he means that he stayed close to the patient's emotional material, not needing her to resist her growing dependency on him as her analyst, and not needing her to only act like the adult they both knew her to be, in other words, allowing her unabridged, unimpinged-upon "continuity of being." He then introduces us to the language of "true self" versus "false self," which he will elaborate explicitly elsewhere. Just for clarification, when Winnicott speaks of the early development of the psyche-soma, he says explicitly (elsewhere) that there is no consciousness of the self at first. There are only psychically elaborated somatic experiences. The emergence of a self is a developmental achievement.

OK. Here comes a long case example which is perfectly clear in its writing, less clear perhaps in its understanding. But Winnicott is known to be a clinical genius, and so in part we can witness with him the goings-on in his therapies, and the meanings he ascribes to them. Here comes the case example.

For the purpose of this paper I choose for description one thing out of an enormous amount of material. In the patient's previous analysis there had been incidents in which the patient had thrown herself off the couch in an hysterical way. These episodes had been interpreted along ordinary lines for hysterical phenomena of this kind. In the deeper regression of this new analysis light was thrown on the meaning of these falls. In the course of the two years of analysis with me the patient has repeatedly regressed to an early stage which was certainly prenatal. The birth process had to be relived, and eventually I recognized how this patient's unconscious need to relive the birth process underlay what had previously been an hysterical falling off the couch.

A great deal could be said about all this, but the important thing from my point of view here is that evidently every detail of the birth experience had been retained, and not only that, but the details had been retained in the exact sequence of the original experience. A dozen or more times the birth process was relived and each time the reaction to one of the major external features of the original birth process was singled out for re-experiencing.

Incidentally, these relivings illustrated one of the main functions of acting out; by acting out the patient informed herself of the bit of psychic reality which was difficult to get at the moment, but of which the patient so acutely needed to become aware. I will enumerate some of the acting-out patterns, but unfortunately I cannot give the sequence which nevertheless I am quite sure was significant.

The breathing changes to be gone over in most elaborate detail.

The constrictions passing down the body to be relived and so remembered.

The birth from the fantasy inside of the belly of the mother, who was a depressed, unrelaxed person.

The changeover from not feeding to feeding from the breast, and then from the bottle.

The same with the addition that the patient had sucked her thumb in the womb and on coming out had to have the fist in relation to the breast or bottle, thus making continuity between object relationship within and without.

The severe experience of pressure on the head, and also the extreme of awfulness of the release of pressure on the head; during which phase, unless her head were held, she could not have endured the re-enactment.

There is much which is not yet understood in this analysis about the bladder functions affected by the birth process.

The changeover from pressure all round (which belongs to the intra-uterine state). Pressure if not excessive means love. After birth therefore she was loved on the under side only, and unless turned round periodically became confused.

Here I must leave out perhaps a dozen other factors of comparable significance.

Gradually the re-enactment reached the worst part. When we were nearly there, there was the anxiety of having the head crushed. This was first got under control by the patient's identification with the crushing mechanism. This was a dangerous phase because if acted out outside the transference situation it meant suicide. In this acting-out-phase the patient existed in the crushing boulders or whatever might present, and the gratification came to her then from *destruction* of the head (including mind and false psyche) which had lost significance for the patient as part of the self.

Ultimately the patient had to accept annihilation. We had already had many indications of a period of blackout or unconsciousness, and convulsive movements made it likely that there was at some time in infancy a minor fit. It appears that in the actual experience there was a loss of consciousness which could not be assimilated to the patient's self until accepted as a death. When this had become real the word death became wrong and the patient began to substitute "a giving-in", and eventually the appropriate word was "a not-knowing".

In a full description of the case I should want to continue along these lines for some time, but development of this and other themes must be made in future publications. Acceptance of not-knowing produced tremendous relief. "Knowing" became transformed into "the analyst knows", that is to say, "behaves reliably in active adaptation to the patient's needs". The patient's whole life had been built up around mental functioning which had become falsely the place (in the head) from which she lived, and her life which had rightly seemed to her false had been developed out of this mental functioning.

Perhaps this clinical example illustrates what I mean when I say that I got from this analysis a feeling that the cataloguing of reactions to environmental impingements belonging to the time around about birth had been exact and complete; in fact I felt that the only alternative to the success of this cataloguing was absolute failure, hopeless confusion and mental defect.

But the case illustrates my theme in detail as well as generally. I quote again from Scott (1949):

> Similarly when a patient in analysis loses his mind in the sense that he loses the illusion of needing a psychic apparatus which is separate

from all the which has called his body, his world, etc., etc., this loss is equivalent to the gain of all that conscious access to and control of the connections between the superfices and the depths, the boundaries and solidity of his Body Scheme—its memories, its perceptions, its images, etc., etc., which he had given up at an earlier period in his life when the duality soma-psyche began.

Not infrequently in a patient whose first complaint is of fear of "losing his mind"—the desire to lose such a belief and obtain a better one soon becomes apparent.

At this point of not-knowing in this analysis there appeared the memory of a bird that was seen as "quite still except for the movement of the belly which indicated breathing". In other words, the patient had reached, at 47 years, the state in which physiological functioning in general constitutes living. The psychical elaboration of this could follow. The psychical elaboration of physiological functioning is quite different from the intellectual work which so easily becomes artificially a thing in itself and falsely a place where the psyche can lodge.

Naturally only a glimpse of this patient can be given, and even if one chooses a small part, only a bit of this part can be described. I would like, however, to pursue a little the matter of the gap in consciousness. I need not describe the gap as it appeared in more "forward" terms, the bottom of a pit, for instance, in which in the dark were all sorts of dead and dying bodies. Just now I am concerned only with the most primitive of the ways in which the gap was found, by the patient, by the reliving processes belonging to the transference situation. The gap in continuity, which throughout the patient's life had been actively denied, now became something urgently sought. We found a need to have the head broken into, and violent head-banging appeared as part of an attempt to produce a blackout. At times there was an urgent need for the destruction of the mental processes located by the patient in the head. A series of defences against full recognition of the desire to reach the gap in continuity of consciousness had to be dealt with before there could be acceptance of the not-knowing state. It happened that on the day on which this work reached its climax the patient stopped writing her diary.[3] This diary had been kept throughout the analysis, and it would be possible to reconstruct the whole of her analysis up to this time from it. There is little that the patient could perceive that has not been at least indicated in this diary. The meaning of the diary now became clear—it was a projection of her mental apparatus, and not a picture of the true self, which, in fact, had never lived till, at the bottom of the regression, there came a new chance for the true self to start.

The results of this bit of work led to a temporary phase in which there was no mind and no mental functioning. There had to be a temporary phase in which the breathing of her body was all. In this way the patient became able to accept the not-knowing condition because I was holding her and keeping a continuity by my own breathing, while g; it could not be any good, however, if I held her and maintained my own continuity of life if she were dead. What made my part operative was that I could see and hear her belly moving as she breathed (like the bird) and therefore I knew that she was alive.

Now for the first time she was able to have a psyche, an entity of her own, a body that breathes and in addition the beginning of fantasy belonging to the breathing and other physiological functions.

We as observers know, of course, that the mental functioning which enables the psyche to be there enriching the soma is dependent on the intact brain. But we do not place the psyche anywhere, not even in the brain on which it depends. For this patient, regressed in this way, these things were at last not important. I suppose she would now be prepared to locate the psyche wherever the soma is alive.

The patient has made considerable progress since this paper was read. Now in 1953 we are able to look back on the period of the stage I have chosen for description, and to see it in perspective. I do not need to modify what I have written. Except for the violent complication of the birth process body-memories, there has been no major disturbance of the patient's regression to a certain very early stage and subsequent forward movement towards a new existence as a real individual who feels real.

3   The diary was resumed at a later date, for a time, with a looser function, and a more positive aim including one day using her experiences more profitably.

Winnicott has offered us a detailed case illustration of his work with a woman who, despite much social approbation, did not feel real to herself. His work illustrates the extent to which he as therapist could tolerate what her psyche knew to do in the analysis—where it needed to go in order to re-capture something very much lost to her as a human being. She re-experienced a great deal of psychic (and physical) pain on her psyche's journey to restore to her the real ground of her being. This is what Winnicott is aiming at as he discusses the psyche-soma as the ground of all that follows in development. Now he'll zero in on the issue of the false localization of the mind.

Mind localized in the head

I now leave my illustration and return to the subject of the localizing of the mind in the head. I have said that the imaginative elaboration of body parts and functions is not localized. There may, however, be localizations which are quite logical in the sense that they belong to the way in which the body functions. For instance, the body takes in and gives out substances. An inner world of personal imaginative experience therefore comes into the scheme of things, and shared reality is on the whole thought of as outside the personality. Although babies cannot draw pictures, I think that they are capable (except through lack of skill) of depicting themselves by a circle at certain moments in their first months. Perhaps if all is going well, they can achieve this soon after birth; at any rate we have good evidence that at six months a baby is at times using the circle or sphere as a diagram of the self. It is at this point that Scott's body scheme is so illuminating and especially his reminder that we are referring to time as well as to space. In the body scheme as I understand it there seems to me to be no place for the mind, and this is not a criticism of the body scheme as a diagram; it is a comment on the falsity of the concept of the mind as a localized phenomenon.

Just a note here: in the drawings of young children, the circle is universally one of the earliest things a person can draw as a self-representation—or house for the emergent self.

In trying to think out why the head is the place where either the mind is localized, or else outside which it is localized, I cannot help thinking of the way in which the head of the human baby is affected during birth, the time at which the mind is furiously active cataloguing reactions to a specific environmental persecution.

Cerebral functioning tends to be localized by people in the head in popular thought, and one of the consequences of this deserves special study. Until quite recently surgeons could be persuaded to open the skulls of mentally defective infants to make possible further development of their brains which were supposed to be constricted by the bones of the skull. I suppose the early trephining of the skull was for relief of *mind* disorders, i.e. for cure of persons whose mental functioning was their enemy and who had falsely localized their mental functioning in their heads.

(Trephining is a surgical procedure referring to burring holes in the skull to relieve pressure. Evidence of this procedure dates back to the Neolithic Age.)

At the present time the curious thing is that once again in medical scientific thought the brain has got equated with the mind, which is felt by a certain kind of ill person to be an enemy, and a thing in the skull. The surgeon who does a leucotomy would at *first* seem to be doing what the patient asks for, that is, to be relieving the patient of mind activity, the mind having become the enemy of the psyche-soma.

Leucotomy is another name for lobotomy. The Portuguese neurologist António Egas is credited with having invented the lobotomy in 1935, for which he was awarded the Nobel Prize for Physiology or Medicine in 1949. Lobotomies were widely performed for more than two decades as a treatment for such severe mental disorders as schizophrenia and manic-depressive disorder, among other psychiatric illnesses. The operation involved severing most of the connections between the brain's prefrontal cortex and other parts of the brain. The procedure resulted in a general diminshing of both personality and intellect. Its side-effects included apathy, lethargy, uncontrolled hunger, and a lack of spontaneity and awareness. About 40,000 lobotomies were performed in the United States during the two decades between 1935 and 1955, and another 17,000 in England. The practice started to subside in the mid-1950s, as scientists developed antipsychotic and antidepressant medications that were much more effective ("Lobotomy," n.d.).

Nerverthless, we can see that the surgeon is caught up in the mental patient's false localization of the mind in the head, with its sequel, the equating of mind and brain. When he has done his work he has failed in the second half of his job. The patient wants to be relieved of the *mind activity* which has become a threat to the psyche-soma, but the patient next needs the full-functioning brain tissue *in order to be able to have psyche-soma existence*. By the operation of leucotomy with its irreversible brain changes the surgeon has made this impossible. The procedure has been of no use except through what the operation means to the patient. But the imaginative elaboration of somatic experience, the psyche, and for those who use the term, the soul, depend on the intact brain, as we know. We do not expect the *unconscious* of anyone to know such things, but we feel the neuro-surgeon ought to be *to some extent* affected by intellectual considerations.

Winnicott is writing in 1949, the same year in which Egas received the Nobel Prize for developing the lobotomy procedure. Winnicott had it right, despite the fact that this was clearly a currently lauded surgical procedure. He then turns briefly to psychosomatic symptoms:

In these terms we can see that one of the aims of *psychosomatic illness* is to draw the psyche from the mind back to the original intimate association with the soma. It is not sufficient to analyse the hypochondria of the psycho-somatic patient, although this is an essential part of the treatment. One has also to be able to see the *positive value of the somatic disturbance* in its work of counteracting a "seduction of the psyche into the mind". Similarly, the aim of physiotherapists and the relaxationists can be understood in these terms. They do not have to know what they are doing to be successful psychotherapists. In one example of the application of these principles, if one tries to teach a pregnant woman how to do all the right things one not only makes her anxious, but one feeds the tendency of the psyche to lodge in the mental processes. *Per contra*, the relaxation methods at their best enable the mother to become body-conscious, and (if she is not a mental case) these methods help her to a continuity of being, and enable her to live as a psyche-soma. This is essential if she is to experience child-birth and the first stages of mothering in a natural way.

He posits briefly that psychosomatic illness might actually have the implicit (unconscious) goal of drawing the psyche back to its grounding in the soma.

Summary

1. The true self, a continuity of being, is in health based on psyche-soma growth.
2. Mental activity is a special case of the functioning of the psyche-soma.
3. Intact brain functioning is the basis for psyche-being as well as for mental activity.
4. There is no localization of a mind self, and there is no thing that can be called mind.
5. Two distinct bases for normal mental functioning can already be given, viz,: (a) conversion of good enough environment into perfect (adapted) environment, enabling minimum of reaction to impingement, and maximum of natural (continuous) self-development; and (b) cataloguing of impingements (birth trauma, etc.) for assimilation at later stages of development.
6. It is to be noted that psyche-soma growth is universal and its complexities are inherent, whereas mental development is somewhat dependent on variable factors such as the quality of early environmental factors, the chance phenomena of birth and of management immediately after birth, etc.
7. It is logical to oppose psyche and soma and therefore to oppose the emotional development and the bodily development of an individual. It is not logical, however, to oppose the mental and the physical as these are not of the same stuff. Mental phenomena are complications of variable importance in psyche-soma continutity of being, in that which adds up to the individual's "self".

Winnicott's summary includes some unelaborated, perhaps assumed assertions. For one, that there is no thing that can be called mind. He's pointing out that the thinking apparatus is embedded in the body and the imagination, so can't be assigned a specific location. Another assertion in his summary is that he newly offers two bases for normal mental (mind) functioning, the second of which he did not offer explicitly in his text: (1) the experiencing of a good-enough early environment and (2) the cataloging of impingements for later assimilation. He is normalizing the cataloging of impingements in a way he did not truly do in his text, and making this process one of two bases for normal mental functioning. It is part of our work as therapists to make use of the need for cataloging—for finding a way to represent the things that were "un-representable" but were indeed somatically and psychically experienced in our earliest days—to reclaim the unclaimed raw material from which humanness is meant to be formed. Finally, he asserts newly in his summary that psyche-soma growth is inherent whereas mental development is more experience-dependent.

There are so many take-aways in this small offering from Winnicott. Some of what he says in passing is very valuable; some of what he elaborates in detail may be out of reach for most practicing therapists. His central thesis though, that our thinking apparatus as adults is designed to be nested-in and infused with the ground of somatic experience—that we are meant to be "minded-bodies"—helps to frame what it is to be truly human, and helps to define our task as we work with patients in our own practices.

References

Cordon, I., Pipe, M., Sayfan, L., Melinder, A., & Goodman, G. (2004). Memory for traumatic experiences in early childhood. *Developmental Review*, 24(1): 101–132.

Fairbairn, W. R. D. (1944). Endopsychic structure considered in terms of object-relationships. *International Journal of Psychoanalysis*, 25, 70–93.

2　Primitive emotional development

(1945)[1]

Winnicott, D. W. (1945). Primitive emotional development. In *Through paediatrics to psycho-analysis: Collected papers* (pp. 145–156). Levittown, PA: Brunner Mazel, 1992.

This paper is Winnicott's earliest major theoretical contribution to psycho-analysis. It contains the seeds of virtually all the major theoretical contributions that Winnicott would ultimately offer to the field during the next 26 years of his professional life. He discusses such wide-ranging topics as the patient's fantasies about his inner organization; the depressed patient and that patient's requiring an understanding of the therapist's own depression; hate in psychotherapy; the vital role of the frame in containing both the patient and the therapist; the infant's earliest sensory experiences; the earliest processes of infant development, including integration, personalization, and the realization of time and space; the infant's experience of environmental failures as retaliatory attacks; the development of a reality orientation in the baby; and moments of illusion that undergird the development of creativity.

As I begin this attempt to render this Winnicott paper, I wish to quote Thomas Ogden's (2001) comment on this paper, that Winnicott's writing "is extraordinarily resistant to paraphrase." It is. And to understand Winnicott, one must wade into him (as I have done), and then stand back from him, as Ogden has done. So I refer anyone truly attempting to understand what Winnicott offers to us in this extraordinary paper to do both: wade in, via this chapter, and then stand back to make (more) sense, via Ogden's (2001) thoughtful chapter, "Reading Winnicott."

It will be clear at once from my title that I have chosen a very wide subject. All I can attempt to do is to make a preliminary personal statement, as if writing the introductory chapter to a book.

1 Read before the British Psycho-Analytical Society, November 29, 1945. *International Journal of Psycho-Analysis*, Vol. XXVI, 1945.

I shall not first give an historical survey and show the development of my ideas from the theories of others, because my mind does not work that way. What happens is that I gather this and that, here and there, settle down to clinical experience, form my own theories and then, last of all, interest myself in looking to see where I stole what. Perhaps this is as good a method as any. About primitive emotional development there is a great deal that is not known or properly understood, at least by me, and it could well be argued that this discussion ought to be postponed five or ten years. Against this there is the fact that misunderstandings constantly recur in the Society's [British Psychoanalytical Society's] scientific meetings, and perhaps we shall find we do know enough already to prevent some of these misunderstandings by a discussion of these primitive emotional states.

Primarily interested in the child patient, and the infant, I decided that I must study psychosis in analysis. I have had about a dozen psychotic adult patients, and half of these have been rather extensively analysed. This happened in the war, and I might say that I hardly noticed the blitz, being all the time engaged in analysis of psychotic patients who are notoriously and maddeningly oblivious of bombs, earthquakes, and floods.

As a result of this work I have a great deal to communicate and to bring into alignment with current theories, and perhaps this paper may be taken as a beginning.

By listening to what I have to say, and criticizing, you help me to take my next step, which is the study of the sources of my ideas, both in clinical work and in the published writings of analysts. It has in fact been extremely difficult to keep clinical material out of this paper, which I wished nevertheless to keep short so that there might be plenty of time for discussion.

First I must prepare the way. Let me try to describe different types of psycho-analysis. It is possible to do the analysis of a suitable patient taking into account almost exclusively that person's personal relation to people, along with the conscious and unconscious fantasies that enrich and complicate these relationships between whole persons. This is the original type of psycho-analysis. In the last two decades we have been shown how to develop our interest in fantasy, and how the patient's own fantasy about his inner organization and its origin in instinctual experience is important as such.[1]

1 Chiefly through the work of Melanie Klein.

Winnicott here is speaking of the "original type of psycho-analysis," which is the product of Sigmund Freud, and took as its point of entry the kinds of conflicts that arose both intra- and inter-personally because of how the id and superego were in inherent conflict, and because of the divisions between conscious and unconscious life. Then, Winnicott explicitly credits Melanie Klein's thoughts and writings on fantasy—which Klein renamed "phantasy." According to Klein, phantasy is the medium for the earliest system of meaning in the psyche—in essence, how the baby primitively "thinks" about his experience. Klein thought phantasy was the psychic representation of bodily experience/instinct, and that it occurred from birth onward. Klein posited that when the infant felt painful need or intolerable anxiety, coming either from his own body or from the external frustration of bodily needs, his psyche would produce a particular phantasy. In Klein's thinking, phantasy emanates from within but also imagines what is without. It links feelings to part and whole human objects, thereby progressively creating the world of imagination. Klein also thought that, through such primitive defenses as splitting and projection, the infant would re-locate "bad" or threatening objects outside him/herself into the external world. The infant would also preserve the "good" objects, both within him/herself (and also externally), by keeping them safely split off from their bad or threatening counterparts. Klein viewed the infant's efforts to manage these primitive anxieties as the central psychological struggle of the beginning months of life. She also felt that these efforts were foundational to all subsequent psychological development, and that these very primitive defenses of early infancy were preserved and remained active in severely disturbed children, adolescents, and adults.

So Winnicott is giving credit to Klein for influencing psychoanalysts to be interested in patients' fantasies about their inner organization and its root systems in instinctual experience. Ultimately, though, he agreed with Freud concerning Freud's view that fantasy is a developmental achievement and is not present from birth.

So now, back to Winnicott:

> We have been shown further that in certain cases it is this, the patient's fantasy about his inner organization, that is vitally important, so that the analysis of depression and the defences against depression cannot be done on the basis only of consideration of the patient's relations to real people and his fantasies about them. This new emphasis on the patient's fantasy of himself opened up the wide field of analysis of hypochondria in which the patient's fantasy about his inner world includes the fantasy that this is localized inside his own body. It became possible for us to relate, in analysis, the qualitative changes in the individual's inner world to his instinctual experiences. The quality of these instinctual experiences accounted for the good and bad nature of what is inside, as well as for its existence.

OK. So the patient's fantasies about his inner organization become important in Winnicott's thinking. He asserts that, in the analysis of depression, we must think beyond the kinds of struggles (and fantasies, conscious and unconscious) that humans have in their relationships with "real people." He suggests that an emphasis on the patient's fantasies of his internal world moves us more productively into the terrain of depression and the defenses against depression, which he will explain later.

He also observes that sometimes a patient's fantasy about his internal world can be "localized," or given material existence, inside his own body. So Winnicott is saying that fantasy can be re-located into the body, and that we encounter this in hypochondriasis.

He says further that, because instincts give rise to the inner world of fantasy and perception, it has become possible to link aspects of an individual's inner world to the quality of their (very early, and therefore, primitive) instinctual experience. This opens the door for Winnicott to examine the formation of early fantasy based upon the quality of the infant's real early experience, which, in Winnicott's words, "account[s] for the good and bad nature of what is inside, as well as for its existence." This reference to the quality of early experience is a stepping-off point in Winnicott's thinking and writing which will seed all of his later writings. It is also worth noting that this is where Winnicott differs from Klein, who values real early experience as much less important than what the infant brings to that experience on the basis of instinct and phantasy.

> This work was a natural progression in psycho-analysis; it involved new understanding but not new technique. It quickly led to the study and analysis of still more primitive relationships, and it is these that I wish to discuss in this paper. The existence of these more primitive types of object relationship has never been in doubt.

OK. So Winnicott is saying that Klein's influence and insights led to the study and analysis of more primitive—meaning earlier—relationships, including ones dating back to infancy, but that this is a "natural progression in psycho-analysis," rather than a radical departure (which in many ways, it is).

> I have said that no modification in Freud's technique was needed for the extension or analysis to cope with depression and hypochondria. It is also true, according to my experience, that the same technique can take us to still more primitive elements, provided of course that we take into consideration the changes in the transference situation inherent in such work.

So here Winnicott is saying that Freud's technique of listening to and interpreting patients' free associations was adequate to taking on "still more primitive elements," provided that the analyst knows that there would be a required change in his awareness of and openness to the psychic transmissions between analyst and patient—the transference–countertransference as we now call it.

The following paragraph is quite dense, so I will take it step by step:

> I mean by this that a patient needing analysis of ambivalence in external relationships has a fantasy of his analyst and the analyst's work that is different from that of one who is depressed. In the former case the analyst's work is thought of as done out of love for the patient, hate being deflected on to hateful things.

Here he contrasts a patient who is feeling ambivalent about his current or past relationships with a patient who is depressed. He asserts that a patient who is coming to therapy due to conflict and ambivalence in external (real) relationships feels/imagines that his therapist holds him in a set of good feelings—empathy, love, respect, etc., leading to the offering of accurate-enough interpretations. He does not typically imagine hateful feelings held toward him by the therapist. Hate, in his mind, is reserved for hateful things.

> The depressed patient requires of his analyst the understanding that the analyst's work is to some extent his effort to cope with his own (the analyst's) depression, or shall I say guilt and grief resultant from the destructive elements in his own (the analyst's) love.

Here Winnicott asserts that, in contrast to the ambivalent patient, the depressed patient needs something radically different: that to do this work, the therapist must become aware of the therapist's own depression. He then expands what he means: that the therapist must become aware of the dark sides of his own efforts to love—that love inevitably involves a demand on the person one loves which unavoidably at times exerts strain on the loved object. Recognizing these destructive elements inherent in one's efforts to love leads to feelings of guilt and grief. So the depressed patient needs the therapist to have done the work of coping with the mix of love *plus* guilt and grief which is the hallmark of the depressive position described by Klein.

> To progress further along these lines, the patient who is asking for help in regard to his primitive, pre-depressive relationship to objects needs his analyst to be able to see the analyst's undisplaced and co-incident love and hate of him.

OK. Winnicott just went a step further, or, shall we say, backward. The patient who is asking for help with his "pre-depressive position" relationship to loved objects needs to be able also to perceive in the analyst the analyst's understanding of the analyst's own pre-depressive position ways of loving, which involve love and hate toward the loved/hated object.

Let me explain. In this thought, Winnicott is drawing on the Kleinian concept of "pre-depressive position love," which Winnicott calls later in this paper "ruthless" love. The "pre-depressive" (paranoid-schizoid) Kleinian position is a mental constellation normally experienced from birth through about the six-month point. In this position, there are felt by the infant to be two separate maternal objects: the ideal/loved object, and the persecuting/hated object. These are held entirely separately in the infant's mind. During this primitive period, the infant's main anxiety concerns his own survival, which leads to his ruthless need of and treatment of his maternal object. As a person progresses from Klein's paranoid-schizoid to the depressive position, he begins to understand that his ruthlessness has an impact on the loved maternal object, in response to which he experiences guilt and grief. Winnicott goes on to say that when a therapist (analyst) is treating a depressed patient, there are quite early, pre-depressive feelings at play—in both directions—in the transference and the countertransference. The therapist is interacting with a primitive part of the patient which transacts in unbridled love *and* hate, both in fantasy and in reality. So, the patient needs the therapist to be able to see these pre-depressive elements in *himself* in order for the therapist to hold and truly resonate with them in the patient. In such cases, the therapist would need to experience his own "undisplaced and co-incident love and hate" of the patient—in other words, to become conscious of the elements of both love and hate in his feelings toward the patient.

OK, so now Winnicott continues:

In such cases the end of the hour, the end of the analysis, the rules and regulations, these all come in as important expressions of hate, just as the good interpretations are expressions of love, and symbolical of good food and care. This theme could be developed extensively and usefully.

Winnicott is saying that in such cases, the frame of the therapy takes on an extra measure of importance because it is a safe vehicle of expression for the therapist's hate, which is expressed in the protective structures of the therapy. The adherence to the starting and ending times of therapy, the fee, and the therapist's restricted availability to the patient are all important expressions of the therapist's capacity to own his own hate right next to ("co-incident" with) his own empathic love. Winnicott is saying that, as therapists, we have to be conscious of both the loving and hating elements of being in the therapeutic relationship with such a patient.

He continues:

> Before embarking directly on a description of primitive emotional development I should also like to make it clear that the analysis of these primitive relationships cannot be undertaken except as an extension of the analysis of depression.

OK, so he is now shifting gears just a bit in order to get over to his more general treatment of the main topic: primitive emotional development. He asserts that the analysis of primitive relationships should be undertaken in a way that is congruent with and perhaps an extension of the analysis of depression as just described (which includes the therapist's awareness of his own primitivity).

> It is certain that these primitive types of relationship, so far as they appear in children and adults, may come as a flight from the difficulties arising out of the next stages, after the classical conception of regression.

OK, now he says that it is certain that these primitive types of relationship (which he has yet to define) may represent a "regression"—a going backward to a less mature, younger stage of development.

> It is right for a student analyst to learn first to cope with ambivalence in external relationships and with simple repression and then to progress to the analysis of the patient's fantasy about the inside and outside of his personality, and the whole range of his defences against depression, including the origins of the persecutory elements. These latter things the analyst can surely find in any analysis, but it would be useless or harmful for him to cope with principally depressive relationships unless he was fully prepared to analyse straightforward ambivalence.

Here Winnicott is describing what he feels should be the normal course of the training of a new therapist:

First, coping with ambivalence in external relationships, meaning the simultaneous existence of contradictory feelings toward the same object.

Next, understanding simple repression—the conflict between conscious and unconscious elements in the psyche, causing a person to (unconsciously) hide from himself certain troubling motives, wishes, or desires.

Next, analyzing a patient's fantasy about the insides versus the outsides of his personality.

Next, understanding the range of a patient's defenses against depression (manic defenses such as control, contempt, and triumph) but also more primitive defenses including the primitive fantasies which are expressed in self-hatred, self-criticism, self-blame, and persecutory elements—paranoia about threats toward oneself by external objects.

> It is likewise true that it is useless and even dangerous to analyse the primitive pre-depressive relationships, and to interpret them as they appear in the transference, unless the analyst is fully prepared to cope with the depressive position, the defenses against depression, and the persecutory ideas which appear for interpretation as the patient progresses.

OK. So here Winnicott is commenting further that a therapist who is working with someone's pre-depressive relationships has to be ready to handle the emergence of the depressive position in his patient, which brings along with it the kinds of defenses available in the paranoid-schizoid armamentarium: control (of the therapist), contempt (for the therapist), and triumph over the therapist-object. In addition there will come some of the paranoia (persecutory ideas) that is left over as a retreat into the paranoid-schizoid position. One has to be ready to understand and endure all of these as a therapist.

OK. So now with these thoughts as background and context, he shifts to other topics.

> I have more preparatory remarks to make. It has often been noted that, at five to six months, a change occurs in infants which makes it more easy than before for us to refer to their emotional development in the terms that apply to human beings generally. Anna Freud makes rather a special point of this and implies that in her view the tiny infant is concerned more with certain care aspects than with specific people. Bowlby recently expressed the view that infants before six months are not particular, so that separation from their mother does not affect them in the same way as it does after six months. I myself have previously stated that infants reach something at six months, so that whereas many infants of five months grasp an object and put it to the mouth, it is not till six months that the average infant starts to follow this up by deliberately dropping the object as part of his play with it.

OK. So Winnicott is here marking the six-month marker as developmentally significant, recognized by such luminaries and colleagues in his field as Anna Freud and John Bowlby.

> In specifying five to six months we need not try to be too accurate. If a baby of three or even two months or even less should reach the stage of development that it is convenient in general description to place at five months, no harm will be done.

Now he modifies the rigidity of the six-month marker. It may be two or three months, depending upon the child.

> In my opinion the stage we are describing, and I think one may accept this description, is a very important one. To some extent it is an affair of physical development, for the infant at five months becomes skilled to the extent that he grasps an object he sees, and can soon get it to his mouth. He could not have done this earlier. (Of course he may have wanted to. There is no exact parallel between skill and wish, and we know that many physical advances such as the ability to walk, are often held up till emotional development releases physical attainment. Whatever the physical side of the matter, there is also the emotional.) We can say that at this stage a baby becomes able in his play to show that he can understand he has an inside, and that things come from outside. He shows he knows that he is enriched by what he incorporates (physically and psychically). Further, he shows that he knows he can get rid of something when he has got from it what he wants from it. All this represents a tremendous advance. It is at first only reached from time to time, and every detail of this advance can be lost as a regression because of anxiety.

OK, so a baby at five to six months can understand he has an inside, and that things come from outside. He knows that he can get rid of something when he has gotten from it what he wants from it. And all of this developmental advance can be lost via regression due to anxiety.

> The corollary of this is that now the infant assumes that his mother also has an inside, one which may be rich or poor, good or bad, ordered or muddled. He is therefore starting to be concerned with the mother and her sanity and her moods. In the case of many infants there is a relationship as between whole persons at six months. Now, when a human being feels he is a person related to people, he has already travelled a long way in primitive development.

OK. So at this stage—six months or so—the infant is able to appreciate that the mother has an inside also, and is beginning to understand her psychic state—"her sanity and her moods." Also around this same time, the infant may have the capacity to have a whole-person-to-whole-person relationship with his mother. Here, Winnicott is referring to what Klein named the "depressive position," and which he re-named the "stage of concern." Central to this position is the achievement of ambivalence—the realization of holding both loving and hateful feelings (and fantasies) about one and the same loved maternal object. So love and hate can now coexist in the same psyche, and are no longer required to be held in separate (non-interpenetrating) spaces inside. Both people in the relationship can now be "whole."

> Our task is to examine what goes on in the infant's feelings and personality before this stage which we recognize at five to six months, but which may be reached later or earlier.

OK, So Winnicott is going to look at the stage *before* six months—the pre-depressive (paranoid-schizoid) position.

> There is also this question: how early do important things happen? For instance, does the unborn child have to be considered? And if so, at what age after conception does psychology come in? I would answer that if there is an important stage at five to six months there is also an important stage round about birth. My reason for saying this is the great differences that can be noticed if the baby is premature or post-mature. I suggest that at the end of nine months gestation an infant becomes ripe for emotional development, and that if an infant is post-mature he has reached this stage in the womb, and one is therefore forced to consider his feelings before and during birth. On the other hand a premature infant is not experiencing much that is vital till he has reached the age at which he should have been born, that is to say some weeks after birth. At any rate this forms a basis for discussion.

Winnicott is here posing a central question (which he will answer again and again through his writings): How early do psychologically important things happen? He discusses pre- and post-maturity of infants. He observes that a premature infant is not experiencing much that is vital till he has reached the age at which he should have been born, that is to say some weeks after birth.

> Another question is: psychologically speaking, does anything *matter*, before five to six months? I know that the view is quite sincerely held in some quarters that the answer is "No". This view must be given its due, but it is not mine. The main object of this paper is to present the thesis that the early emotional development of the infant, before the infant

> knows himself (and therefore others) as the whole person that he is (and that they are), is vitally important: indeed that here are the clues to the psychopathology of psychosis.

So Winnicott believes, contrary to many of his peers, that the first six months of a child's life are unequivocally and lastingly important in terms of psychological development.

Early developmental processes

There are three processes which seem to me to start very early: (1) integration, (2) personalization, and (3), following these, the appreciation of time and space and other properties of reality, in short, realization.

OK. Winnicott has just said a lot. He names three processes that start early: (1) integration; (2) personalization; and (3) realization of time and space (and other realities).

> A great deal that we tend to take for granted had a beginning and a condition out of which it developed. For instance, many analyses sail through to completion without time being ever in dispute. But a boy of nine who loved to play with Ann, aged two, was acutely interested in the expected new baby. He said: "When the new baby's born will he be born before Ann?" For him time-sense is very shaky. Again, a psychotic patient could not adopt any routine because if she did she had no idea on a Tuesday whether it was last week, or this week, or next week.

So, he starts with the concept of (3) realization (of time). He observes that the realization of time is, or can become, absent for some people. This has become part of our modern Mental Status Exam of mental functioning: orientation to time: "What day/month/year is it?"

> The localization of self in one's own body is often assumed, yet a psychotic patient in analysis came to recognize that as a baby she thought her twin at the other end of the pram was herself. She even felt surprised when her twin was picked up and yet she remained where she was. Her sense of self and other-than-self was undeveloped.

Localization of self in one's own body—(2) "personalization"—includes the sense that one lives in one's own body. Winnicott refers to his psychotic patient who did not have this sense when she was little.

> Another psychotic patient discovered in analysis that most of the time she lived in her head, behind her eyes. She could only see out of her eyes as out of windows and so was not aware of what her feet were doing, and in consequence she tended to fall into pits and to trip over things. She had no "eyes in her feet". Her personality was not felt to be localized in her body, which was like a complex engine that she had to drive with conscious care and skill. Another patient, at times, lived in a box 20 yards up, only connected with her body by a slender thread. In our practices examples of these failures in primitive development occur daily, and by them we may be reminded of the importance of such processes as integration, personalization, and realization. It may be assumed that at the theoretical start the personality is unintegrated, and that in regressive disintegration there is a primary state to which regression leads. We postulate a primary unintegration.

He here gives other examples of several patients who did not truly inhabit their own bodies, which illustrates both a sense of depersonalization and that of unintegration. He posits that at the start the personality is (1) unintegrated, and that it is possible to regress to this point of unintegration in life beyond infancy, at which point it is more properly referred to as "disintegration."

> Disintegration of personality is a well-known psychiatric condition, and its psychopathology is highly complex. Examination of these phenomena in analysis, however, shows that the primary unintegrated state provides a basis for disintegration, and that delay or failure in respect of primary integration predisposes to disintegration as in regression, or as a result of failure in other types of defence.

According to Winnicott in other writings, the primary unintegrated state must be held by the mother's ego support in order for the infant to feel the sense of going-on-being, which Winnicott views to be crucial to healthy development. Unintegration means that the things about our being and thinking that normally act in concert (our five senses, our voluntary control of our bodies, etc.) are allowed to rest in unrelated bits and pieces. Given mother's ego support, normal unintegration can occur, and appears to represent a resting state for an infant. The task of integration depends directly on both qualities inherent in the infant—a tendency to integrate—and qualities of the maternal holding environment—consistency, responsivity, sensitivity, attunement to bodily need states, etc. Delay or failure with respect to the early developmental task of integration (which is experienced as a falling apart that is catastrophic to the infant) predisposes an individual to later disintegration. This "falling apart" of the child, adolescent, or adult personality is a well-known psychiatric condition.

> Integration starts right away at the beginning of life, but in our work we can never take it for granted. We have to account for it and watch its fluctuations.

We can't take psychic integration for granted, no matter what we assume to be a patient's level of functioning. The assumption that the task of integration has been completely accomplished is a common error among clinicians. Therapists have to be aware and alert to the fact that integration may fluctuate—much more than we may commonly assume.

> An example of unintegration phenomena is provided by the very common experience of the patient who proceeds to give every detail of the week-end and feels contented at the end if everything has been said, though the analyst feels that no analytic work has been done. Sometimes we must interpret this as the patient's need to be known in all his bits and pieces by one person, the analyst. To be known means to feel integrated at least in the person of the analyst. This is the ordinary stuff of infant life, and an infant who has had no one person to gather his bits together starts with a handicap in his own self-integrating task, and perhaps he cannot succeed, or at any rate cannot maintain integration with confidence.

OK. This is an important Winnicottian statement. There is the instance of the patient who proceeds to give every detail of his weekend and feels contented at the end. This represents the patient's need to be known and held in all his bits and pieces by one person, the analyst. To be known means to feel integrated at least in the person of the analyst. Winnicott offers this as an example of "account[ing] for" the task of integration, and "watch[ing] for its fluctuations."

> The tendency to integrate is helped by two sets of experience: the technique of infant care whereby an infant is kept warm, handled and bathed and rocked and named, and also the acute instinctual experiences which tend to gather the personality together from within. Many infants are well on the way toward integration during certain periods of the first twenty-four hours of life. In others the process is delayed, or setbacks occur, because of early inhibition of greedy attack. There are long stretches or

time in a normal infant's life in which a baby does not mind whether he is many bits or one whole being, or whether he lives in his mother's face or in his own body, provided that from time to time he comes together and feels something. Later I will try to explain why disintegration is frightening, whereas unintegration is not.

The tendency to integrate is helped by two sets of experiences from without and from within: without, the technique of infant care whereby an infant is kept warm, handled, bathed, rocked, and named; within, the acute instinctual experiences which tend to gather the personality together from within. Delays or setbacks can occur when the infant's early "greedy attack[s]" are prevented from reaching gratification. Here Winnicott is emphasizing that the everyday stuff of infant care has so much to do with everything psychic that develops—or does not develop.

In regard to environment, bits of nursing technique and faces seen and sounds heard and smells smelt are only gradually pieced together into one being to be called mother. In the transference situation in analysis of psychotics we get the clearest proof that the psychotic state of unintegration had a natural place at a primitive stage of the emotional development of the individual.

Here Winnicott shows his attunement to babies in his pediatric practice: "bits of nursing technique and faces seen and sounds heard and smells smelt." His very language conveys the feeling of the initial phase of unintegration—of bits and pieces needing to be woven into a whole. And he links this to his understanding of psychotic process: the psychotic state of unintegration had a natural place at a primitive stage of the emotional development of the individual. Unintegration is not frightening to the infant; later disintegration is indeed frightening.

It is sometimes assumed that in health the individual is always integrated, as well as living in his own body, and able to feel that the world is real. There is, however, much sanity that has a symptomatic quality, being charged with fear or denial of madness, fear or denial of the innate capacity of every human being to become unintegrated, depersonalized, and to feel that the world is unreal. Sufficient lack of sleep produces these conditions in any one.[2]

2   Through artistic expression we can hope to keep in touch with our primitive selves, whence the most intense feelings and even fearfully acute sensations derive, and we are poor indeed if we are only sane.

Winnicott asserts the innate capacity of every human being to become unintegrated, depersonalized, and derealized—to feel that the world is unreal, for example, when sleep-deprived, but also when in fear or denial of aspects of madness within.

> Equally important with integration is the development of the feeling that one's person is in one's body. Again it is instinctual experience and the repeated quiet experiences of body-care that gradually build up what may be called satisfactory personalization. And as with disintegration so also the depersonalization phenomena of psychosis relate to early personalization delays.

Winnicott asserts that in psychotic process the feeling that one's person inhabits one's body can be lost. He relates this to delays in the early process of personalization.

> Depersonalization is a common thing in adults and in children; it is often hidden for instance in what is called deep sleep and in prostration attacks with corpse-like pallor: "She's miles away", people say, and they are right.

He cites the examples of depersonalization that occur in deep sleep and prostration attacks—the need to lie down for a long period of time due to migraine or other causes.

> A problem related to that of personalization is that of the imaginary companions of childhood. These are not simple fantasy constructions. Study of the future of these imaginary companions (in analysis) shows that they are sometimes other selves of a highly primitive type. I cannot here formulate a clear statement of what I mean, and it would be out of place for me to explain this detail at length now. I would say, however, that this very primitive and magical creation of imaginary companions is easily used as a defence, as it magically by-passes all the anxieties associated with incorporation, digestion, retention, and expulsion.

Imaginary companions: Winnicott comments that they are sometimes related to highly primitive experiences—meaning very early experiences—and to the anxieties related to the bodily processes of ingestion and expulsion.

This is followed by such a notable footnote from Winnicott: "We are poor indeed if we are only sane." He means by this that our primitive selves carry our most intense feelings and acute sensations, and that our capacity to touch these parts of ourselves is enlivening. Winnicott includes this in a footnote here, but he will develop this theme more in later papers.

Dissociation

Out of the problem of unintegration comes another, that of dissociation. Dissociation can usefully be studied in its initial or natural forms. According to my view there grows out of unintegration a series of what are then called dissociations, which arise owing to integration being incomplete or partial. For example, there are the quiet and the excited states. I think an infant cannot be said to be aware at the start that while feeling this and that in his cot or enjoying the skin stimulations or bathing, he is the same as himself screaming for immediate satisfaction, possessed by an urge to get at and destroy something unless satisfied by milk. This means that he does not know at first that the mother he is building up through his quiet experiences is the same as the power behind the breasts that he has in his mind to destroy.

This is such a lovely paragraph wherein Winnicott is presenting the very, very early experience of the infant. The infant has quiet states; he has excited states. Winnicott asserts that dissociations grow out of, or come from, times of unintegration, developmentally. So as the infant is coming together into an integrated being with integrated sensations, he is still not entirely together. He is not the same to himself in quiet and excited states—these states are "dissociated" in the infant, and his mother is not the same to him in quiescent and hungry states.

Also I think there is not necessarily an integration between a child asleep and a child awake. This integration comes in the course of time. Once dreams are remembered and even conveyed somehow to a third person, the dissociation is broken down a little; but some people never clearly remember their dreams, and children depend very much on adults for getting to know their dreams. It is normal for small children to have anxiety dreams and terrors. At these times children need someone to help them to remember what they dreamed. It is a valuable experience whenever a dream is both dreamed *and* remembered, precisely because of the breakdown of dissociation that this represents. However complex such a dissociation may be in child or adult, the fact remains that it can start in the natural alternation of the sleeping and awake states, dating from birth.

Winnicott is giving voice here to a kind of dissociation almost anyone can relate to: the difference between our awake self and our dreaming self, and how important it is to a child to have a parent audience their dream self and link it to their awake self.

In fact the waking life of an infant can be perhaps described as a gradually developing dissociation from the sleeping state.

Artistic creation gradually takes the place of dreams or supplements them, and is vitally important for the welfare of the individual and therefore for mankind.

Winnicott believed that our creative expressions were a source of true human vitality, both individually and collectively—for mankind.

Dissociation is an extremely widespread defence mechanism and leads to surprising results. For instance urban life is a dissociation, a serious one for civilization. Also war and peace. The extremes in mental illness are well known. In childhood dissociation appears for instance in such common conditions as somnambulism, incontinence of faeces, in some forms of squinting, etc. It is very easy to miss dissociation when assessing a personality.

Winnicot felt that our multiple selves—selves that differ according to context—were examples of dissociation. He was born in 1896 in England. He witnessed two world wars. He knew firsthand that people thought and behaved differently during war versus peace. He names three childhood conditions that he felt derived from dissociation: sleep-walking, encopresis, and some forms of squinting.

Reality adaptation

Let us now assume integration. If we do, we reach another enormous subject, the primary relation to external reality. In ordinary analyses we can and do take for granted this step in emotional development, which is highly complex and which, when it is made, represents a big advance in emotional development, yet is never finally made and settled. Many cases that we consider unsuitable for analysis are unsuitable indeed if we cannot deal with the transference difficulties that belong to an essential lack of true relation to external reality. If we allow analysis of psychotics, we find that in some analyses this essential lack of true relation to external reality is almost the whole thing.

Here Winnicott is speaking about our relation to external reality and to the thought espoused by Freud and his followers that some cases were not appropriate for psychoanalysis, including those with psychotic disorders. He states here that a part of that mindset comes from analysts not being able to deal with the *transference* difficulties inherent in working with someone who truly lacks a relation to external reality, meaning that it introduces bizarre elements into the patient's ways of perceiving and relating to the therapist.

Before I comment further, I will now let Winnicott paint a picture of some of the details of our early development of our relationship to external reality.

> I will try to describe in the simplest possible terms this phenomenon as I see it. In terms of baby and mother's breast (I am not claiming that the breast is essential as a vehicle of mother-love) the baby has instinctual urges and predatory ideas. The mother has a breast and the power to produce milk, and the idea that she would like to be attacked by a hungry baby. These two phenomena do not come into relation with each other till the mother and child *live an experience together.* The mother being mature and physically able has to be the one with tolerance and understanding, so that it is she who produces a situation that may with luck result in the first tie the infant makes with an external object, an object that is external to the self from the infant's point of view.
>
> I think of the process as if two lines came from opposite directions, liable to come near each other. If they overlap there is a moment of *illusion*—a bit of experience which the infant can take as *either* his hallucination *or* a thing belonging to external reality.
>
> In other language, the infant comes to the breast when excited, and ready to hallucinate something fit to be attacked. At that moment the actual nipple appears and he is able to feel it was that nipple that he hallucinated. So his ideas are enriched by actual details of sight, feel, smell, and next time this material is used in the hallucination. In this way he starts to build up a capacity to conjure up what is actually available. The mother has to go on giving the infant this type of experience. The process is immensely simplified if the infant is cared for by one person and one technique. It seems as if an infant is really designed to be cared for from birth by his own mother, or failing that by an adopted mother, and not by several nurses.

Let me recap. Winnicott is describing the initial steps of the process of our developing a relationship to external reality. He leads with a disclaimer for those who cannot breast feed their child: he is *not* saying that breast feeding is essential to successful parenting. But he uses the initial encounters of the infant with the mother's breast to explain our first contact with external reality. He uses highly imaginative language to speak about the early experience of the infant–mother couple, putting out the scene in frame-by-frame-like 16-millimeter film. From the infant's side of things, the infant has instinctual urges. He comes to the breast, excited and feeling "predatory." At that exact moment, he is met by the actual nipple. Being utterly unacquainted with external reality, he feels initially that this must be the nipple that he *created*, that he conjured up, that he hallucinated. This is a moment of illusion for the baby, which, in other writings of Winnicott he refers to as a moment of omnipotence. The baby and mother "live" an experience together—both must bring their aliveness to this encounter in order for them to live an experience together. The experience is enhanced by details of sight, feel, and smell which are used to elaborate and anticipate subsequent "hallucinatory" moments. With repeated experience, the infant starts to build up a capacity to conjure up what is actually available. With "luck," this process will in time result in the dawning realization in the infant of something external to him. Thus is his gradual introduction to the world of external reality. From the mother's side of this process, she has to be in sync with her infant, and to offer herself in well-timed attunement to her infant's need states, with tolerance and understanding, and to go on giving the infant this type of experience, over, over, over again.

> It is especially at the start that mothers are vitally important, and indeed it is a mother's job to protect her infant from complications that cannot yet be understood by the infant, and to go on steadily providing the simplified bit of the world which the infant, through her, comes to know. Only on such a foundation can objectivity or a scientific attitude be built. All failure in objectivity at whatever date relates to failure in this stage of primitive emotional development. Only on a basis of monotony can a mother profitably add richness.

So Winnicott sees this process of need-anticipated-by-and-met-by-the-mother-repeatedly as vitally important to the eventual development of a solid reality orientation (objectivity) in the developing person. It is her job to steadily present simplified bits of the world to the infant, and to prevent complications that the infant cannot yet understand and that would disrupt the necessarily gradual taking-in of the outside world by the infant. He then adds a startling statement: "All failure in objectivity at whatever date relates to failure in this stage of primitive emotional development." This process of mother-mediated early infant integration cannot be jeopardized without doing damage to this future person's grasp on objective reality. (Wow, what a statement by Winnicott!)

> One thing that follows the acceptance of external reality is the advantage to be gained from it. We often hear of the very real frustrations imposed by external reality, but less often hear of the relief and satisfaction it affords.

Real milk is satisfying as compared with imaginary milk, but this is not the point. The point is that in fantasy things work by magic: there are no brakes on fantasy, and love and hate cause alarming effects. External reality has brakes on it, and can be studied and known, and, in fact, fantasy is only tolerable at full blast when objective reality is appreciated well. The subjective has tremendous value but is so alarming and magical that it cannot be enjoyed except as a parallel to the objective.

Operating in reality has real advantages. Without the acceptance of external reality, we operate in a psychic world with no brakes on it. He could not have said this better! Reality and fantasy have to be in balance with one another. Fantasy at first is what propels us into the world and to the creation of illusion with an attuned mother. Objective reality follows upon this and in large measure comes in to establish a limit to fantasy.

It will be seen that fantasy is not something the individual creates to deal with external reality's frustrations. This is only true of fantasying. Fantasy is more primary than reality, and the enrichment of fantasy with the world's riches depends on the experience of illusion.

Winnicott departs from Freud's view that fantasy is used principally as a tool to deal with external reality's frustrations. He feels that fantasy precedes reality in our development, and that the enriching role of fantasy in humans depends on the monotony of primary care that provides the repeated experience of illusion for an infant. Only on the basis of that monotony can a mother build up the world of illusion in her early infant, and thereby profitably add the richness of well-anchored fantasy to her infant's present and future experience.

It is interesting to examine the individual's relation to the objects in the self-created world of fantasy. In fact there are all grades of development and sophistication in this self-created world according to the amount of illusion that has been experienced, and so according to how much the self-created world has been unable or able to use perceived external world objects as material. This obviously needs a much more lengthy statement in another setting.

The self-created world of fantasy objects is a point of fascination for Winnicott. He believes that the richness of this self-created world is correlated with the amount of illusion one has been allowed to experience as a baby, and how much one has been able to use external world objects to enrich that world.

> In the most primitive state, which may be retained in illness, and to which regression may occur, the object behaves according to magical laws, i.e. it exists when desired, it approaches when approached. It hurts when hurt. Lastly it vanishes when not wanted.

Winnicott here is speaking of human objects. He's saying that at the most primitive time of an infant's development, the laws of reality do not pertain. Instead, there are the magical laws of fantasy: objects exist when I desire them to exist; they go away when I desire them to go away. This state, while completely developmentally appropriate to a tiny infant, can be replicated in adulthood via periods of regression or states of mental illness (doing damage to real external relationships).

> This last is most terrifying and is the only true annihilation. To not want, as a result of satisfaction, is to annihilate the object. This is one reason why infants are not always happy and contented after a satisfactory feed. One patient of mine carried this fear right on to adult life and only grew up from it in analysis, a man who had had an extremely good early experience with his mother and in his home.[3] His chief fear was of satisfaction.
>
> 3 I will just mention another reason why an infant is not satisfied with satisfaction. He feels fobbed off. He intended, one might say, to make **a** cannibalistic attack and he has been put off by an opiate, the feed. At best he can postpone the attack.

Why would satisfaction and not wanting be terrifying and "the only true annihilation"? It seems that he is saying that if an object vanishes (in fantasy) when it is not wanted (because of satisfaction), then the infant may be left, dropped, no longer held, no longer ego–supported, which brings about the experience of annihilation for the infant. Another possibility for satisfaction not to be satisfying to the infant is mentioned in the footnote: that the infant was not allowed to stir within himself, to desire a feed, to "attack" the breast and thus to complete his moment of illusion. This sequence is stolen from the infant by a premature feed, the feed being done on the basis of someone else's timing.

> I realize that this is only the bare outline of the vast problem of the initial steps in the development or a relation to external reality, and the relation of fantasy to reality. Soon we must add ideas of incorporation. But at the start a simple *contact* with external or shared reality has to be made, by the infant's hallucinating and the world's presenting, with moments of illusion for the infant in which the two are taken by him to be identical, which they never in fact are.

For this illusion to be produced in the baby's mind a human being has to be taking the trouble all the time to bring the world to the baby in understandable form, and in a limited way, suitable to the baby's needs. For this reason a baby cannot exist alone, psychologically or physically, and really needs one person to care for him at first.

The subject of illusion is a very wide one that needs study; it will be found to provide the clue to a child's interest in bubbles and clouds and rainbows and all mysterious phenomena, and also to his interest in fluff, which is most difficult to explain in terms of instinct direct. Somewhere here, too, is the interest in breath, which never decides whether it comes primarily from within or without, and which provides a basis for the conception of spirit, soul, anima.

These moments of illusion for an infant, wherein he conjures up and receives just the right satisfaction at just the right time—these moments become the building blocks for his ability, eventually, to meet and welcome objective reality, which is the only basis from which he can eventually enjoy the rich benefits of creative, imaginative, enlivening fantasy. (Sometimes, as therapists, when we see an excess of fascination with these things of infancy, it represents a striving to redo the transition from fantasy to objective reality in a more satisfactory way.)

Primitive ruthlessness (stage of pre-concern)

We are now in a position to look at the earliest kind of relationship between a baby and his mother.

If one assumes that the individual is becoming integrated and personalized and has made a good start in his realization, there is still a long way for him to go before he is related as a whole person to a whole mother, and concerned about the effect or his own thoughts and actions on her.

(You'll recognize here that Winnicott is referring backward to his discussion of integration, personalization, and realization, and forward to the progression from the paranoid-schizoid world to the depressive position world of whole objects and the child's realization of his impact on his mother. In the next paragraph, he will re-name the depressive position the stage of "concern.")

We have to postulate an early ruthless object relationship. This may again be a theoretical phase only, and certainly no one can be ruthless after the concern stage except in a dissociated state.

(When Winnicott says dissociated state, he is referring to the state in which we are not quite "ourselves"—when we "lose" it.)

> But ruthless dissociation states are common in early childhood, and emerge in certain types of delinquency, and madness, and must be available in health. The normal child enjoys a ruthless relation to his mother, mostly showing in play, and he needs his mother because only she can be expected to tolerate his ruthless relation to her even in play, because this really hurts her and wears her out. Without this play with her he can only hide a ruthless self and give it life in a state of dissociation.[4]
>
> 4   There is in mythology a ruthless figure—Lilith—whose origin could be usefully studied.

Winnicott seems to be saying here that without being able to play out his ruthlessness with his mother in play, it will emerge more readily—perhaps later in life—in states of dissociation.

> I can bring in here the great fear of disintegration as opposed to the simple acceptance of primary unintegration. Once the individual has reached the stage of concern he cannot be oblivious to the result of his impulses, or to the action or bits of self such as biting mouth, stabbing eyes, piercing yells, sucking throat, etc., etc. Disintegration means abandonment to impulses, uncontrolled because acting on their own; and, further, this conjures up the idea of similarly uncontrolled (because dissociated) impulses directed towards himself.[5]
>
> 5   Crocodiles not only shed tears when they do not feel sad—pre-concern tears; they also readily stand for the ruthless, primitive self.

Winnicott is now talking about a step further on the ruthlessness spectrum—that of abandonment to uncontrolled impulses, one in which a person is oblivious to the result of his impulses, which happens in the extreme state of disintegration. Similarly, one can direct such uncontrolled impulses in the context of harming oneself.

> ## Primitive retaliation
>
> To go back half a stage: it is usual, I think, to postulate a still more primitive object relationship in which the object acts in a retaliatory way. This is prior to a true relation to external reality. In this case the object, or the

environment, is as much part of the self as the instinct is which conjures it up.[6]

6   This is important because of our relationship to Jung's analytical psychology. We try to reduce everything to instinct, and the analytical psychologists reduce everything to this part or the primitive self which looks like environment but which arises out of instinct (Archetype). We ought to modify our view to embrace both ideas, and to see (if it is true) that in the earliest theoretical primitive state the self has its own environment, self-created, which is as much the self as the instincts that produce it. This is a theme which requires development.

This is important so I'll interject mid-paragraph. When an infant is still in the very early stage wherein he imagines no one and nothing external to him, the mother/object and the environment which she mediates to the infant is not perceived to be separate from him. To quote Winnicott, "the object, or the environment, is as much part of the self as the instinct is which conjures it up." So, during this time, if there is not a perfect syncing up of infant need with maternal response, it is felt by the infant as though the object/environment is actively attacking him, acting in a retaliatory way.

In introversion of early origin and therefore of primitive quality the individual lives in this environment which is himself, and a very poor life it is. There is no growth because there is no enrichment from external reality.

In those who are primitive in their introversion, the (perhaps schizoid) individual lives in this encapsulated environment, un-enriched by external reality, which is a no-growth proposition.

To illustrate the application of these ideas I add a note on thumb-sucking (including fist- and finger-sucking). This can be observed from birth onwards, and therefore can be presumed to have a meaning which develops from the primitive to sophistication, and it is important both as a normal activity and as a symptom or emotional disturbance.

We are familiar with the aspect of thumb-sucking covered by the term autoerotic. The mouth is an erotogenic zone, specially organized in infancy, and the thumb-sucking child enjoys pleasure. He also has pleasurable ideas.

So far, he is talking about thumb-sucking as an entirely normal, pleasurable infant activity.

Hate is also expressed when the child damages his fingers by too vigorous or continuous sucking, and in any case he soon adds nail-biting to cope with this part of his feelings. He is also liable to damage his mouth. But it is not certain that all the damage that may be done to a finger or mouth in this way is part of hate. It seems that there is in it the element that something must suffer if the infant is to have pleasure: the object of primitive love suffers by being loved, apart from being hated.

His final sentence carries his meaning: a child who damages himself via thumb or finger sucking may not be enacting self-hatred. He may be enacting his primitive understanding that something or someone has to suffer in order for love to happen.

We can see in finger-sucking, and in nail-biting especially, a turning-in of love and hate, for reasons such as the need to preserve the external object or interest.

So, in finger sucking and nail biting, there may be an element of wanting to preserve or protect the external loved object from the burden of the child, so there can be a taking over of loving and hating impulses via the activity of finger sucking or nail biting.

Also we see a turning-in to self, in face of frustration in love of an external object.

We also might see these activities as a turning to the self for comfort when frustrated by the external object.

The subject is not exhausted by this kind of statement and deserves further study.

I suppose anyone would agree that thumb-sucking is done for consolation, not just pleasure; the fist or finger is there instead of the breast or mother, or someone. For instance, a baby of about four months reacted to the loss or his mother by a tendency to put his fist right down his throat, so that he would have died had he not been physically prevented from acting this way.

Clearly to Winnicott, thumb sucking is done for consolation as well as pleasure.

> Whereas thumb-sucking is normal and universal, spreading out into the use of the dummy, and indeed to various activities of normal adults, it is also true that thumb-sucking persists in schizoid personalities, and in such cases is extremely compulsive. In one patient of mine it changed at 10 years into a compulsion to be always reading.

Some schizoid persons use thumb sucking into adulthood.

> These phenomena cannot be explained except on the basis that the act is an attempt to localize the object (breast, etc.), to hold it half-way between in and out. This is either a defence against loss of object in the external world or in the inside of the body, that is to say, against loss of control over the object.

Winnicott surmises that these activities may be an attempt to replicate having the breast, either as a defense against its actual loss in the external world or its loss in terms of fantasied internal control.

> I have no doubt that normal thumb-sucking has this function too.
> The auto-erotic element is not always clearly of paramount importance and certainly the use of dummy and fist soon becomes a clear defence against insecurity feelings and other anxieties of a primitive kind.

In essence then, the auto-erotic satisfaction of the oral erogenous zone is not always the chief motivation for thumb sucking; it (and other sucking activities, including fists and dummies) also functions to quell insecurities and primitive anxieties.

> Finally, every fist-sucking provides a useful dramatization of the primitive object relationship in which the object is as much the individual as is the desire for an object, because it is created out of the desire, or is hallucinated, and at the beginning is independent of co-operation from external reality.
> Some babies put a finger in the mouth while sucking the breast, thus (in a way) holding on to self-created reality while using external reality.

To summarize more fully here, the object is as much the individual as is the desire for an object—in the beginning, the infant is creating all of it—need, desire, object, satisfaction—because at the very beginning to the infant, there is no external reality. Some babies put a finger in their mouth while sucking the breast, illustrating that they are wanting to be the author of the experience while they simultaneously use external reality.

Summary

An attempt has been made to formulate the primitive emotional processes which are normal in early infancy, and which appear regressively in the psychoses.

Winnicott's one-sentence summary in no way gathers up all the topics he has introduced in this paper. It will take him 26 years of thinking and writing to render fully what he has begun to think about with us in this paper.

3   Hate in the counter-transference

(1949)

Winnicott, D. W. (1949). Hate in the counter-transference. *International Journal of Psycho-Analysis*, 30, 69–74.

Winnicott here discusses the work we as therapists do with the full range of patients, including psychotic and antisocial patients, but also personality-disordered patients or patients with psychotic anxieties. According to Winnicott, therapists must be able to recognize, own, and study the range of their emotional and countertransferential reactions to their patients. He simply adds: "These will include hate." He discusses the source and significance of hateful feelings in therapy. In addition, and quite significantly, he places the range of reactions a therapist has to a patient at the center of what might be important to understand in the therapy. He says that these countertransferential reactions "will at times be the most important things in the analysis."

Summary

An analyst has to display all the patience and tolerance and reliability of a mother devoted to her infant, has to recognize the patient's wishes as needs, has to put aside other interests in order to be available and to be punctual, and objective, and has to seem to want to give what is really only given because of the patient's needs.

There may be a long initial period in which the analyst's point of view cannot be (even unconsciously) appreciated by the patient.

Acknowledgment cannot be expected because at the primitive root of the patient that is being looked for there is no capacity for identification with the analyst, and certainly the patient cannot see that the analyst's hate is often engendered by the very things the patient does in his crude way of loving.

In the analysis (research analysis) or in ordinary management of the more psychotic type of patient, a great strain is put on the analyst (psychiatrist, mental nurse) and it is important to study the ways in which anxiety of psychotic quality and also hate are produced in those who work with severely ill psychiatric patients.

Only in this way can there be any hope of the avoidance of therapy that is adapted to the needs of the therapist rather than to the needs of the patient.

In this paper I wish to examine one aspect of the whole subject of ambivalency, namely, hate in the counter-transference.

OK, so Winnicott has launched his paper with a summary. He's addressing the work with severely ill psychotic psychiatric patients by analysts, psychiatrists, and mental nurses (and, in today's language, psychotherapists) but this requires a clarification. The reader should bear in mind that members of the British School of Object Relations at the time Winnicott was writing often used the term "psychotic" to apply to what we now think of as borderline or other severe personality disorders. In addition, five years before this paper, he expressed a caveat in his "Primitive emotional development" (1945) paper, as follows:

It is sometimes assumed that in health the individual is always integrated, as well as living in his own body, and able to feel that the world is real. There is, however, much sanity that has a symptomatic quality, being charged with fear or denial of madness, fear or denial of the innate capacity of every human being to become unintegrated, depersonalized, and to feel that the world is unreal.

To this he adds in "The effect of psychosis on family life" (1965): "Psychosis is much more down to earth and concerned with the elements of human personality and existence than is psychoneurosis, and (to quote myself!) we are poor indeed if we are only sane."

So, even though in this paper Winnicott is explicitly addressing severe (psychotic) emotional illness, his work may indeed be applicable to a much broader spectrum of those who seek psychotherapy, and certainly to the experience of those who treat patients in psychodynamic therapies. His thoughts apply particularly well to our work with patients whose developmental histories make them at some times, in some ways psychotic (which may include all of us, if we are to take Winnicott at his word). His thoughts in this paper, therefore, are valuable to all who do psychodynamic work.

He continues:

I believe that the task of the analyst (call him a research analyst) who undertakes the analysis of a psychotic is seriously weighted by this phenomenon, and that analysis of psychotics becomes impossible unless the analyst's own hate is extremely well sorted-out and conscious. This is

> tantamount to saying that an analyst needs to be himself analysed, but it also asserts that the analysis of a psychotic is irksome as compared with that of neurotic, and inherently so.
>
> Apart from psycho-analytic treatment, the management of a psychotic is bound to be irksome.

OK. So Winnicott is using terminology to differentiate types of patients that we no longer commonly use. Neurosis in Winnicott's language refers to psychological disorders that still let the sufferer remain in contact with reality. A neurosis is the formation of behavioral or psychosomatic symptoms such as acute or chronic anxiety, depression, obsessive–compulsive disorders, phobias, that are out of proportion to the circumstances of a person's life. In general, according to Freudian thought, these represent instances where the ego's efforts to deal with its desires through such defenses as repression and displacement, and so on, fail, and symptoms emerge. Psychotic disorders, on the other hand, represent a more severe break with reality.

Winnicott continues:

> From time to time I have made acutely critical remarks about the modern trends in psychiatry, with the too easy electric shocks and the too drastic leucotomies. Because of these criticisms that I have expressed I would like to be foremost in recognition of the extreme difficulty inherent in the task of the psychiatrist, and of the mental nurse in particular. Insane patients must always be a heavy emotional burden on those who care for them. One can forgive those who do this work if they do awful things. This does not mean, however, that we have to accept whatever psychiatrists and neuro-surgeons do as sound according to principles of science.

When Winnicott was writing this article (1949), he was decrying current techniques for treating the severely emotionally ill, in particular, leucotomies (lobotomies). For perspective, at the time of the writing of this article, anti-psychotic medications did not exist. The range of common interventions in asylums included electroconvulsive therapy, metrazol therapy (which induced seizures), insulin shock therapy (which induced "deep sleep" comas in patients), fever therapy (raising body temperature up to 105 degrees), hydrotherapy (a full-body wrap with a cold, wet sheet wrapped tightly around the patient, or, alternatively, a continuous warm bath), and lobotomy (Grob, 1994). Professionals hoped that these treatments would help the mentally ill patient.

The leucotomy (lobotomy) was introduced in 1946, and had been developed by Portuguese neurologist António Egas Moniz. This procedure achieved rapid acceptance due to widespread publicity in the late 1940s and the belief that it was effective in controlling psychotic behavior. The procedure was performed using a modified ice pick–like device, transnasally, severing the pre-frontal cortex from other regions of the brain. While lobotomies did serve to tranquilize some agitated patients, they also deprived many of their motivation, intelligence, social skills, judgment, and the "spark" of personality. In 1949, Moniz received the Nobel Prize in Physiology and Medicine for his development of this procedure. In the United States, 5,000 lobotomies were performed in 1949 (Grob, 1994).

Antipsychotic medications were discovered serendipitously as an extension of a surgical anesthesia drug in the early 1950s (initially, chlorpromazine), and antipsychotic medication soon supplanted the use of many other extant techniques, including the lobotomy (Grob, 1994). The last true transorbital lobotomy in the United States was performed by Dr. Walter Freeman in 1967.

Now we follow Winnicott, who was a practicing psychiatrist during this period, and knew well the harsh treatments that were visited upon the severely mentally ill.

Therefore although what follows is about psycho-analysis, it really has value to the psychiatrist, even to one whose work does not in any way take him into the analytic type of relationship to patients.

To help the general psychiatrist the psycho-analyst must not only study for him the primitive stages of the emotional development of the ill individual, but also must study the nature of the emotional burden which the psychiatrist bears in doing his work. What we as analysts call the counter-transference needs to be understood by the psychiatrist too. However much he loves his patients he cannot avoid hating them, and fearing them, and the better he knows this the less will hate and fear be the motive determining what he does to his patients.

OK. So this is a moving statement from Winnicott. The psychoanalyst must not only come to understand the emotional development of his patient, but he must study and communicate the emotional burden borne by the hospital-based psychiatrist (and other staff workers) in doing their work.

He now proceeds to the crux of his argument:

Statement of theme

One could classify counter-transference phenomena thus:

(Winnicott will now present a list of three kinds of countertransference.)

> 1. Abnormality in counter-transference feelings, and set relationships and identifications that are under repression in the analyst. The comment on this is that the analyst needs more analysis, and we believe this is less of an issue among psycho-analysts than among psychotherapists in general.

This is what has been historically thought of as countertransference, introduced by Freud in 1910 in his paper, "The future prospects of psycho-analytic theory." The therapist has his own set of developmentally acquired relational templates (set relationships) and has assimilated certain aspects of his parental models (identifications) that are under repression (unconscious to him) and that may come up in and interfere with his work with his patients. These, according to Freud (1910), should be "recognized and overcome" via the therapist's own therapy.

Now Winnicott will describe the second variant of countertransference:

> 2. The identifications and tendencies belonging to an analyst's personal experiences and personal development which provide the positive setting for his analytic work and make his work different in quality from that of any other analyst.

This is a different meaning of the word "countertransference." Winnicott is modernizing "countertransference" here to include the whole of a therapist's reactions and responses to a patient, not only his unresolved issues. The whole of the therapist's personal, developmental, and professional experience, in Winnicott's view, leads him to have a unique relationship with and reactions to his patient, providing a "positive setting" for the work of the therapy.

> 3. From these two I distinguish the truly objective counter-transference, or if this is difficult, the analyst's love and hate in reaction to the actual personality and behaviour of the patient, based on objective observation.

OK. Winnicott is here proposing a *third variant* of countertransference: reactions by the therapist to the objective impact of the patient's personality and behavior on him. These include both love and hate. He is suggesting that there are effects of working with a particular patient that would impact *anyone* working with him, and that these effects would be highly similar across various therapists.

> I suggest that if an analyst is to analyse psychotics or anti-socials he must
> be able to be so thoroughly aware of the counter-transference that he can
> sort out and study his objective reactions to the patient. These will include
> hate. Counter-transference phenomena will at times be the important
> things in the analysis.

Winnicott is shockingly frank as he begins this discussion. A therapist working
with psychotic patients or patients with antisocial personalities (here we should
include the full range of personality-disordered patients or patients with psychotic anxieties) must be able to recognize, own, and study the range of his emotional and countertransferential reactions to his patient. And then, his simple
statement: "*These will include hate.*" In addition, he places these reactions at the
center of what might be important to understand: these countertransferential
reactions "will at times be the important things in the analysis."

> ## The motive imputed to the analyst by the patient
>
> I wish to suggest that the patient can only appreciate in the analyst what
> he himself is capable of feeling.

OK. Right. If there is a range of feelings unfamiliar to a patient, or perhaps more to the point, a set of feelings that the patient is restricted to in his
truncated emotional world, then he will project these on to the therapist, and
see exhibited in his therapist only those feelings that are familiar to the patient.
Winnicott now gives us a range of examples.

> In the matter of motive, the obsessional will tend to be thinking of the
> analyst as doing his work in a futile obsessional way.

Obsessional patients will, via projection, see the therapist as obsessional.

> A hypo-manic patient who is incapable of being depressed, except in a
> severe mood swing, and in whose emotional development the depressive
> position has not been securely won, who cannot feel guilt in a deep way,
> or a sense of concern or responsibility, is unable to see the analyst's work
> as an attempt on the part of the analyst to make reparation in respect of
> his own (the analyst's) guilt feelings.

A hypo-manic (bipolar II) patient who has not achieved the Kleinian developmental position of the depressive position, and cannot feel guilt or concern

or responsibility, cannot imagine a sense of guilt and the desire to make reparation in the therapist.

> A neurotic patient tends to see the analyst as ambivalent towards the patient, and to expect the analyst to show splitting of love and hate; this patient, when in luck, gets the love, because someone else is getting the analyst's hate.

A psychotic patient (or, again, a borderline patient) is not able to have loving and hating feelings toward the same object at the same time. He is not able to background the negative feelings and foreground the positive ones or vice versa. He feels 100% one way or the other. Black is black. White is white, emotionally and cognitively. There is no gray-zone. Winnicott calls this "coincident love and hate." Ambivalence, in contrast, is the capacity to hold and integrate opposing feelings of love and hate toward the same object. It is a developmental achievement (that some people never achieve). In neurosis, the patient is able to tolerate the coexistence of these two opposite feelings, and sees the therapist as having both in potential toward the patient, but hopes to receive the love side of this ambivalence from the therapist.

> Would it not follow that if a psychotic is in a "coincident love–hate" state of feeling he experiences a deep conviction that the analyst is also only capable of the same crude and dangerous state of coincident love–hate relationship?

Here Winnicott poses a question in parallel with his foregoing observations: if a psychotic patient only experiences "coincident love and hate" toward his object, would that person not also perceive the same crude emotions—love and hate, coincident with one another—in his therapist?

OK, before we follow Winnicott further, let's slow down and reconsider what "coincident love and hate" means to Winnicott. This is a reference to primitive, infantile feeling states of loving and hating the same object (the mother) that are not yet integrated with one another. In this initially omnipotent state, there is no connection between emotional events. There is no self- or other-integration. The child who cries feels that he has no relation to the child who coos; in the baby's eyes, the mother who feeds has no relation to the mother who frustrates. Loving and hating feeling states exist, unencumbered by reason or perspective. They fill the entire subjective reality field. They exist out of the meter of ordinary linearly experienced time. They can turn on a dime.

> Should the analyst show love he will surely at the same moment kill the patient.

In the patient's mind, should the therapist show love, he most certainly in the next moment might potentially want to murder the patient. Thus, the level of perceived danger for the patient is extremely high.

> This coincidence of love and hate is something that characteristically recurs in the analysis of psychotics, giving rise to problems of management which can easily take the analyst beyond his resources.

With psychosis comes this primitive psychic organization wherein love and hate are held in full force toward the same object at the same time. This coincidence of love and hate in the patient, and the perceived coincidence of love and hate in the therapist, make the therapy with psychotic patients quite difficult and, to use a Winnicottian word, "irksome."

> This coincidence of love and hate to which I am referring is something which is distinct from the aggressive component complicating the primitive love impulse and implies that in the history of the patient there was an environmental failure at the time of the first object-finding instinctual impulses.

Winnicott distinguishes the love and hate in psychotic/borderline patients from the ruthless love of an infant, wherein the infant cares for nothing but his own desires and will attack his environment (including his mother) in a wild rage if he doesn't get his way. Ruthless love hurts its recipient, but it does not intend to hurt, as there is no distinction in the infant at this stage between self and other. Coincident love and hate—love and hate that overlay one another and can shift seamlessly from one to the other—are different from ruthless infantile love, and are indicative of early environmental failure at the first "object-finding." This refers to the time when the infant is developmentally ready to move from his own omnipotently created world to his discovering the world of external objects and beginning to experience external reality. If, instead, he finds the external object unable to survive this process of infant discovery, the infant goes back, developmentally, to the more primitive arrangement of coincident love and hate. Winnicott is saying here that the understanding of this distinction is critical in the treatment of psychotic/borderline patients.

> If the analyst is going to have crude feelings imputed to him he is best forewarned and so forearmed, for he must tolerate being placed in that position. Above all he must not deny hate that really exists in himself. Hate that is justified in the present setting has to be sorted out and kept in storage and available for eventual interpretation.

The therapist should know in advance that he might have crude feelings imputed to him, and to keep them in storage. Winnicott will explain what "kept in storage" means.

> If we are to become able to be the analysts of psychotic patients we must have reached down to very primitive things in ourselves, and this is but another example of the fact that the answer to many obscure problems of psycho-analytic practice lies in further analysis of the analyst. (Psychoanalytic research is perhaps always to some extent an attempt on the part of an analyst to carry the work of his own analysis further than the point to which his own analyst could get him.)

Winnicott firmly believed that we have to have plumbed the depths of our own primitive emotions via our own therapies in order to do the work with primitive patients. We have to have felt our own coincident loving and hating feelings.

> A main task of the analyst of any patient is to maintain objectivity in regard to all that the patient brings, and a special case of this is the analyst's need to be able to hate the patient objectively.

Here Winnicott is making reference to this third category of countertransference, explained above: "the analyst's love and hate in reaction to the actual personality and behaviour of the patient." Hating the patient "objectively" means acknowledging that with primitive patients (psychotic, sociopathic, borderline, personality-disordered), some of their behaviors and feelings inflicted on to us and installed into us as therapists are objectively irksome, upsetting, and disturbing, and disequilibrating.

> Are there not many situations in our ordinary analytic work in which the analyst's hate is justified? A patient of mine, a very bad obsessional, was almost loathsome to me for some years. I felt bad about this until the analysis turned a corner and the patient became lovable, and then I realized that his unlikeableness had been an active symptom, unconsciously determined. It was indeed a wonderful day for me (much later on) when I could actually tell the patient that I and his friends had felt repelled by him, but that he had been too ill for us to let him know. This was also an important day for him, a tremendous advance in his adjustment to reality.

OK, so here Winnicott experienced a loathsomeness in his patient and he recognized his feeling in response to that in himself. He thought about it, and, even in as talented a therapist as Winnicott, he could not overcome it and he felt badly about it. It was only as the patient turned a corner and became "lovable" that Winnicott was able to piece together what had been happening the whole way—that the patient's unlikeableness was indeed a part of his symptom complex, and that others would also have been repelled by these aspects of this man. Winnicott held this feeling in him for some years. As the man became more psychologically healthy, Winnicott could share with him the degree to which his now attenuated loathsomeness had affected Winnicott and no doubt his other friends and associates.

> In the ordinary analysis the analyst has no difficulty with the management of his own hate. This hate remains latent. The main thing, of course, is that through his own analysis he has become free from vast reservoirs of unconscious hate belonging to the past and to inner conflicts.

This is a clear reference to the previously explained source of counter-transference that needs to be dealt with in the therapist in advance through his own therapy. He says it above as follows: "Abnormality in counter-transference feelings, and set relationships and identifications that are under repression in the analyst." He also makes the statement that a therapist's hate is not stimulated in a prominent way by the course of an ordinary therapy. Ordinarily, the therapist's hate remains latent and to a large extent unfelt.

He now moves to reasons why, in the ordinary course of doing therapy with non-psychotic patients, a therapist does not struggle with hateful feelings toward his patients:

> There are other reasons why hate remains unexpressed and even unfelt as such:
>
> 1. Analysis is my chosen job, the way I feel I will best deal with my own guilt, the way I can express myself in a constructive way.
> 2. I get paid, or I am in training to gain a place in society by psycho-analytic work.
> 3. I am discovering things.
> 4. I get immediate rewards through identification with the patient, who is making progress, and I can see still greater rewards some way ahead, after the end of the treatment.
> 5. Moreover, as an analyst I have ways of expressing hate. Hate is expressed by the existence of the end of the "hour".
>
> I think this is true even when there is no difficulty whatever, and when the patient is pleased to go. In many analyses these things can be

> taken for granted, so that they are scarcely mentioned, and the analytic work is done through verbal interpretations of the patient's emerging unconscious transference. The analyst takes over the role of one or other of the helpful figures of the patient's childhood. He cashes in on the success of those who did the dirty work when the patient was an infant.

Here Winnicott has enumerated some of the satisfactions (and mollifiers) of the ordinary work of therapy. He goes on to say that the work then consists of functioning as a continuation of the psychically positive relationship the patient had with one or the other of his caregiving figures. The patient sees the therapist through the lens of his experience with these positive childhood relationships. Always the pediatrician, he reminds us that successful parenting of infants and children always involves dirty work.

> These things are part of the description of ordinary psycho-analytic work, which is mostly concerned with patients whose symptoms have a neurotic quality.
> In the analysis of psychotics, however, quite a different type and degree of strain is taken by the analyst, and it is precisely this different strain that I am trying to describe.

Again, keep in mind that Winnicott is including the whole range of personality disorders in his reference to psychotic patients. This is important, because while many therapists today do not have the experience of working with psychotic patients, most if not all do have the experience of working with the range of personality disturbances and the psychotic anxieties described by Winnicott. He now takes us to an example from his own practice.

> **Illustration of counter-transference anxiety**
>
> Recently for a period of a few days I found I was doing bad work. I made mistakes in respect of each one of my patients. The difficulty was in myself and it was partly personal but chiefly associated with a climax that I had reached in my relation to one particular psychotic (research) patient.

(When Winnicott uses the modifier "research patient," he means that he is observing and studying the case as he would a case study.)

The difficulty cleared up when I had what is sometimes called a "healing" dream. (Incidentally I would add that during my analysis and in the years since the end of my analysis I have had a long series of these healing dreams which, although in many cases unpleasant, have each one of them marked my arrival at a new stage in emotional development.)

On this particular occasion I was aware of the meaning of the dream as I woke or even before I woke. The dream had two phases. In the first I was in the gods in a theatre and looking down on the people a long way below in the stalls. I felt severe anxiety as if I might lose a limb.

This was associated with the feeling I have had at the top of the Eiffel Tower that if I put my hand over the edge it would fall off on to the ground below. This would be ordinary castration anxiety.

(Ordinary castration anxiety is the fear of the literal or metaphorical loss of the penis, symbolized in Winnicott's dream by his fear that he might lose a limb. Metaphorically, it refers to the idea of being made to feel dominated and/or insignificant, and to the defenses that are mounted to preserve one's self-esteem.)

In the next phase of the dream I was aware that the people in the stalls were watching a play and I was now related to what was going on on the stage through them. A new kind of anxiety now developed. What I knew was that I had no right side of my body at all. This was not a castration dream. It was a sense of not having that part of the body.

As I woke I was aware of having understood at a very deep level what was my difficulty at that particular time. The first part of the dream represented the ordinary anxieties that might develop in respect of unconscious fantasies of my neurotic patients. I would be in danger of losing my hand or my fingers if these patients should become interested in them. With this kind of anxiety I was familiar, and it was comparatively tolerable.

The second part of the dream, however, referred to my relation to the psychotic patient. This patient was requiring of me that I should have no relation to her body at all, not even an imaginative one; there was no body that she recognized as hers and if she existed at all she could only feel herself to be a mind. Any reference to her body produced paranoid anxieties because to claim that she had a body was to persecute her. What she needed of me was that I should have only a mind speaking to her mind. At the culmination of my difficulties on the evening before the dream I had become irritated and had said that what she was needing of me was little better than hair-splitting. This had had a disastrous effect and it took many weeks for the analysis to recover from my lapse. The essential thing, however, was that I should understand my own anxiety and this was represented in the dream by the absence of the right side of my body when I tried to get into relation to the play that the people in the stalls were watching. This right side of my body was the side related to this particular patient and was therefore affected by her need to deny absolutely even an imaginative relationship of our bodies. This denial was producing in me this psychotic type of anxiety, much less tolerable than ordinary castration anxiety.

Winnicott writes in other papers about the process of personalization—the process of inhabiting the body by a developing infant. He writes, too, about psychotic anxieties, one of which is depersonalization, or the frightening reverse of this process, the dis-inhabiting of one's body. His dream image of the absence of the right side of his body evoked what it was like for him to experience the psychotic anxiety of his patient's absence to her own body and denial of even an imaginative relationship to her own body or to his body.

Whatever other interpretations might be made in respect of this dream the result of my having dreamed it and remembered it was that I was able to take up this analysis again and even to heal the harm done to it by my irritability which had its origin in a reactive anxiety of a quality that was appropriate to my contact with a patient with no body.

We may note here that this woman's absence to her own body made Winnicott feel absent to his body, a feeling made explicit in his dream.

Winnicott used the dream to understand the deal that was being struck in the therapy: that she was insisting that he, too, dis-inhabit his body. Winnicott's realization softened his reactive anxiety, and he was able to heal the harm inflicted by his irritable comment to her.

Postponement of interpretation

The analyst must be prepared to bear strain without expecting the patient to know anything about what he is doing, perhaps over a long period of time. To do this he must be easily aware of his own fear and hate. He is in the position of the mother of an infant unborn or newly born. Eventually, he ought to be able to tell his patient what he has been through on the patient's behalf, but an analysis may never get as far as this.

Winnicott is saying here that we must be prepared to bear strain in the thera-peutic relationship—to experience fear, discomfort, etc. toward our patient, but to keep that to ourselves, sometimes for a long time.

There may be too little good experience in the patient's past to work on. What if there been no satisfactory relationship of early infancy for the analyst to exploit in the transference?

There is a vast difference between those patients who have had satisfac-tory early experiences which can be discovered in the transference, and those whose very early experiences have been so deficient or distorted that the analyst has to be the first in the patient's life to supply certain environmental essentials. In the treatment of the patient of the latter kind all sorts of things in analytic technique become vitally important that can be taken for granted in the treatment of patients of the former type.

OK. So here Winnicott is making explicit reference to a patient's earliest relational environment, and that, as therapists, we function through the medi-ation of and as beneficiaries of whatever early satisfying relationships our patient experienced. It is through aspects of their prior, formative relationships that our patients see and experience us. We call this their "transference," because they are transferring forward on to our relationship with them aspects of relationships they experienced in the past. If positive relationships were absent, and instead their "very early experiences have been so deficient or distorted that the analyst has to be the first in the patient's life to supply certain environmental essentials," certain aspects of analytic technique become crucially important.

I asked an analyst who confines his attention to neurotics whether he does analysis in the dark, and he said, "Why, no! Surely our job is to provide an ordinary environment, and the dark would be extraordinary." He was surprised at my question. He was orientated towards analysis of neurotics. But this provision and maintenance of an ordinary environment can be in itself a vitally important thing in the analysis of a psychotic, in fact it can be, at times, even more important than the verbal interpretations which also have to be given. For the neurotic the couch and warmth and com-fort can be symbolical of the mother's love; for the psychotic it would be more true to say that these things are the analyst's physical expression of love. The couch is the analyst's lap or womb, and the warmth is the live warmth of the analyst's body. And so on.

Here Winnicott emphasizes the importance of our providing the regular-ities and comforts of the therapeutic environment, which become vital to our patients with early deprivations and psychotic-level anxieties. The consistencies of the environment and of our behaviors can be more important to a patient than what we say to them.

Objective hate under test

There is, I hope, a progression in misstatement of my subject. The analyst's hate is ordinarily latent and is easily kept latent. In analysis of psychotics the analyst is under greater strain to keep his hate latent, and he can only do this by being thoroughly aware of it.

I'll pause him here. It's extremely important in our work with more psychically compromised patients that we recognize the hateful feelings that are aroused and engendered in us toward the patient. This is a different level of work from what we do with ordinary patients. With psychotic/borderline/severely compromised patients we must recognize and own the difficulties inherent in working with them in order to avoid subtle, unconscious intrusions of those negative feelings into our work with them.

Now I want to add that in certain stages of certain analyses the analyst's hate is actually sought by the patient, and what is then needed is hate that is objective. If the patient seeks objective or justified hate he must be able to reach it, else he cannot feel he can reach objective love.

This is an extraordinary observation by Winnicott: that some patients actually seek to find the therapist's hateful feelings toward them—not the countertransference that comes because they remind us of our disaffected older brother. No, they seek countertransference in us as therapists that is actually an appropriate, objective response to their noxious effect on us. He'll give us an example of what he means!

It is perhaps relevant here to cite the case of the child of the broken home, or the child without parents. Such a child spends his time unconsciously looking for his parents. It is notoriously inadequate to take such a child into one's home and to love him. What happens is that after a while child so adopted gains hope, and then he starts to test out the environment he has found, and to seek proof of his guardians' ability to hate objectively. It seems that he can believe in being loved only after reaching being hated.

Some patients seek our honest, objective response to their worst parts or to their worst treatment of us.

During the second world war a boy of nine came to a hostel for evacuated children, sent from London not because of bombs but because of truancy. I hoped to give him some treatment during his stay in the hostel, but his symptom won and he ran away as he had always done from everywhere since the age of six when he first ran away from home. However, I had established contact with him in one interview in which I could see and interpret through a drawing of his that in running away he was unconsciously saving the inside of his home and preserving his mother from assault, as well as trying to get away from his own inner world which was full of persecutors.

I was not very surprised when he turned up in the police station very near my home. This was one of the few police stations that did not know him intimately. My wife very generously took him in and kept him for three months, three months of hell. He was the most lovable and most maddening of children, often stark staring mad. But fortunately we knew what to expect. We dealt with the first phase by giving him complete freedom and a shilling whenever he went out. He had only to ring up and we fetched him from whatever police station had taken charge of him.

Soon the expected change-over occurred, the truancy symptom turned round, and the boy started dramatizing the assault on the inside. It was really a whole-time job for the two of us together, and when I was out the worst episodes took place. Interpretation had to be made at any minute of day or night, and often the only solution in a crisis was to make the correct interpretation, as if the boy were in analysis. It was the correct interpretation that he valued above everything. The important thing for the purpose of this paper is the way in which the evolution of the boy's personality engendered hate in me, and what I did about it.

Did I hit him? The answer is no, I never hit. But I should have had to have done so if I had not known all about my hate and if I had not let him know about it too. At crises I would take him by bodily strength, and without anger or blame, and put him outside the front door, whatever the weather or the time of day or night. There was a special bell he could ring, and he knew that if he rang it he would be readmitted and no word said about the past. He used this bell as soon as he had recovered from his maniacal attack.

The important thing is that each time, just as I put him outside the door, I told him something; I said that what had happened had made me hate him. This was easy because it was so true.

I think these words were important from the point of view of his progress, but they were mainly important in enabling me to tolerate the situation without letting out, without losing my temper and every now and again murdering him.

This boy's full story cannot be told here. He went to an Approved School. His deeply rooted relation to us has remained one of the few stable things in his life. This episode from ordinary life can be used to illustrate the general topic of hate justified in the present; this is to be distinguished from hate that is only justified in another setting but which is tapped by some action of a patient (child).

OK. This is an endearing story of Winnicott's struggle to re-parent a boy who aroused feelings of intense hatred in Winnicott. He confesses that his words to the boy ("what had happened had made me hate him") "were mainly important in enabling me to tolerate the situation without letting out, without losing my temper and every now and again murdering him." His honesty with respect to his own hateful feelings kept the relationship honest, which sustained both Winnicott and the boy.

A mother's love and hate

Out of all the complexity of the problem of hate and its roots I want to rescue one thing, because I believe it has an importance for the analyst of psychotic patients. I suggest that the mother hates the baby before the baby hates the mother, and before the baby can know his mother hates him. Before developing this theme I want to refer to Freud's remarks. In *Instincts and their Vicissitudes* (1915) (where he says so much that is original and illuminating about hate), Freud says:

> we might at a pinch say of an instinct that it "loves" the objects after which it strives for purposes of satisfaction, but to say that it "hates" an object strikes us as odd, so we become aware that the attitudes of love and hate cannot be said to characterize the relation of instincts to their objects, but are reserved for the relations of the ego as a while to objects...

This I feel is true and important. Does this not mean that the personality must be integrated before an infant can be said to hate? However early integration may be achieved perhaps integration occurs earliest at the height of excitement or rage there is a theoretical earlier stage in which whatever the infant does that hurts is not done in hate. I have used the word "ruthless love" in describing this stage. Is this acceptable? As the infant becomes able to feel a whole person, so does the word hate develop meaning as a description of a certain group of his feelings.

So the infant does not start with an initial capacity for hate. He must develop into a being—a whole person—mature enough to see the other as separate from himself—in order to both love and hate the other.

The mother, however, hates her infant from the word go. I believe Freud thought impossible that a mother may under certain circumstances have only love for her baby; but we may doubt this. We know about a mother's love and we appreciate its reality and power. Let me give some of the reasons why a mother hates her baby, even a boy.

A.   The baby is not her own (mental) conception.
B.   The baby is not the one of childhood play, father's child, brother's child, etc.
C.   The baby is not magically produced.
D.   The baby is a danger to her body in pregnancy and at birth.
E.   The baby is an interference with her private life, a challenge to preoccupation.
F.   To a greater or lesser extent a mother feels that her own mother demands a baby, so that her baby is produced to placate her mother.
G.   The baby hurts her nipples even by suckling, which is at first a chewing activity.
H.   He is ruthless, treats her as scum, an unpaid servant, a slave.
I.   She has to love him, excretions and all, at any rate at the beginning, till he has doubts about himself.
J.   He tries to hurt her, periodically bites her, all in love.
K.   He shows disillusionment about her.
L.   His excited love is cupboard love, so that having got what he wants he throws her away like orange peel.
M.   The baby at first must dominate, he must be protected from coincidences, life must unfold at the baby's rate and all this needs his mother's continuous and detailed study. For instance, she must not be anxious when holding him, etc.
N.   At first he does not know at all what she does or what she sacrifices for him. Especially he cannot allow for her hate.
O.   He is suspicious, refuses her good food, and makes her doubt herself, but eats well with his aunt.
P.   After an awful morning with him she goes out, and he smiles at a stranger, who says: "Isn't he sweet!"
Q.   If she fails him at the start she knows he will pay her out for ever.
R.   He excites her but frustrates; she mustn't eat him or trade in sex with him.

This is a hilarious list, which could only be written by Winnicott, the pediatrician. And it is so hilarious because it is so true.

I think that in the analysis of psychotics, and in the ultimate stages of the analysis, even of a normal person, the analyst must find himself in a position comparable to that of the mother of a new-born baby. When deeply regressed the patient cannot identify with the analyst or appreciate his point of view any more than the foetus or newly born infant can sympathize with the mother.

Yes, as therapists, we at times—sometimes for long times—have to tolerate the absence of room for our feelings and our perspectives as people regress to the more primitive parts of themselves. Winnicott is right to use the metaphor of a mother with a newborn. The infant for a long time has no capacity for empathy or appreciation of the mothering person; they are about a more preeminent task!

A mother has to be able to tolerate hating her baby without doing anything about it. She cannot express it to him. If, for fear of what she may do, she cannot hate appropriately when hurt by her child she must fall back on masochism, and I think it is this that gives rise to the false theory of a natural masochism in women. The most remarkable thing about a mother is her ability to be hurt so much by her baby and to hate so much without paying the child out, and her ability to wait for rewards that may or may not come at a later date.

Here we see Winnicott the pediatrician, once again, focusing our attention on how much hurt a mother absorbs as she does the job of loving her baby into existence.

Perhaps she is helped by some of the nursery rhymes she sings, which her baby enjoys but fortunately does not understand?

Rockabye Baby, on the tree top,
When the wind blows the cradle will rock,
When the bough breaks the cradle will fall,
Down will come baby, cradle and all.

I think of a mother (or father) playing with a small infant; the infant enjoying the play and not knowing that the parent is expressing hate in the words, perhaps in birth symbolism. This is not a sentimental rhyme. Sentimentality is useless for parents, as it contains a denial of hate, and sentimentality in a mother is no good at all from the infant's point of view.

> It seems to me doubtful whether a human child as he develops is capable of tolerating the full extent of his own hate in a sentimental environment.
> He needs hate to hate.
> If this is true, a psychotic patient in analysis cannot be expected to tolerate his hate of the analyst unless the analyst can hate him.

Winnicott is clear about our need to recognize what is irksome about working with some patients. He is unclear about how to discern which patients need to encounter our honest, well-timed, well-modulated expression of our hate toward them. He leaves that to our own discernment.

Practical problem of interpretation

If all this is accepted there remains for discussion the question of the interpretation of the analyst's hate to the patient. This is obviously a matter fraught with danger, and it needs the most careful timing. But I believe an analysis is incomplete if even towards the end it has not been possible for the analyst to tell the patient what he, the analyst, did unbeknown for the patient while he was in the early stages. Until the interpretation is made the patient is kept to some extent in the position of infant, one who cannot understand what he owes to his mother.

Winnicott ends his paper with the end of the story: that at some point, after all the careful, endless absorbing of the baby's/patient's behaviors, insensitivities, and projections, the story of it must be told in order for the patient to fully transition to the world of external reality. It is also a way in which the patient is not left with an illusion of over-idealizing the analyst as if there is such a human being who does not hate.

4 Transitional objects and transitional phenomena

A study of the first not-me possession

(1953)[1]

Winnicott, D. W. (1953). Transitional objects and transitional phenomena— A study of the first not-me possession. *International Journal of Psycho-Analysis*, 34, 89–97.

Many psychic developmental accomplishments lie "between the thumb and the teddy bear." In this paper, one that gained him significant recognition, Winnicott is carefully observing the process whereby a child comes to traverse the difference between a world that is entirely subjective—the new infant's world of omnipotence—and a world that consists of objects and occurrences external to the infant. He explores the meaning of an area that lies between objective and subjective realities in the life of the infant. The piece of blanket appears to be the vehicle of transit on this important journey. The infant's transitional object is neither internal nor external. The transitional object and transitional phenomena represent the infant's first foray into the realm of illusion and creativity beyond that which the maternal environment provided for him. This intermediate area of experience is the resting place between inner and outer reality. It is the prototype for the place of creativity, of freedom, of play, of imagination, of arts and religion where, in adulthood, reality does not constrain.

Introduction

It is well known that infants as soon as they are born tend to use fist, fingers, thumbs in stimulation of the oral erotogenic zone, in satisfaction of the instincts at that zone, and also in quiet union. It is also well known that after a few months infants of either sex become fond of playing with dolls, and that most mothers allow their infants some special object and expect them to become, as it were, addicted to such objects.

1 Based on a paper given at a Scientific Meeting of the British Psycho-Analytical Society on May 30, 1951. A shortened version was distributed to members beforehand, and Dr. Winnicott confined his remarks to the section "Illusion–disillusionment".

> There is a relationship between these two sets of phenomena that are separated by a time interval, and a study of the development from the earlier into the later can be profitable, and can make use of important clinical material that has been somewhat neglected.

OK, so Winnicott launches his famous paper on transitional objects in 1953. He begins with an observation: that infants tend to use fists and fingers to suck on at first. After a few months, they tend to choose another object—often a doll or stuffed animal—as their soothing object. He wants to study the transition between finger sucking and the choice of another soothing/stimulating object in infancy.

> ## The first possession
>
> Those who happen to be in close touch with mothers' interests and problems will be already aware of the very rich patterns ordinarily displayed by babies in their use of the first not-me possession.[1] These patterns, being displayed, can be subjected to direct observation.
>
> There is a wide variation to be found in a sequence of events which starts with the newborn infant's fist-in-mouth activities, and that leads eventually on to an attachment to a teddy, a doll or soft toy, or to a hard toy.
>
> 1   It is necessary to stress that the word used here is "possession" and not "object". In the typed version distributed to members I did in fact use the word "object" (instead of "possession") in one place by mistake, and this led to confusion in the discussion. It was pointed out that the first not-me *object* is usually taken to be the breast. The reader's attention is drawn to the use of the word "transitional" in many places by Fairbairn in *Psychoanalytic Studies of the Personality* (Tavistock Publications, 1952), notably p. 35. (Also in this Journal, 22.)

OK. So Winnicott is repeating his observation here: fist-in-mouth activities are eventually replaced by attachment to an object—a doll, a stuffed animal, or a toy, hard or soft. He emphasizes in his footnote that this "object" is not an object as we often use that word in Object Relations. Instead, it is the child's first "not-me" possession.

> It is clear that something is important here other than oral excitement and satisfaction, although this may be the basis of everything else. Many other important things can be studied, and they include:

1. The nature of the object.
2. The infant's capacity to recognize the object as "not-me".
3. The place of the object—outside, inside, at the border.
4. The infant's capacity to create, think up, devise, originate, produce an object.
5. The initiation of an affectionate type of object relationship.

OK. Winnicott is focusing us on various attributes of this first "not-me" possession. Perhaps notable among these attributes are the infant's capacity to recognize the object as not himself, and his capacity to create such an object and to imbue it with meaning. Also notable is the infant's capacity to initiate an affectionate relationship toward this self-chosen object.

> I have introduced the terms "transitional object" and "transitional phenomena" for designation of the intermediate area of experience, between the thumb and the teddy bear, between the oral erotism and true object-relationship, between primary creative activity and projection of what has already been introjected, between primary unawareness of indebtedness and the acknowledgement of indebtedness ("Say: ta!").

Winnicott is here locating transitional objects and transitional phenomena for us. So many psychic developmental accomplishments lie "between the thumb and the teddy bear." Winnicott enumerates some of the transitions that an infant must traverse: (1) moving beyond the baby's initial oral eroticism to an encounter with a beginning-to-be-real external other; (2) moving beyond the baby's primary creativity—his omnipotent "creation" of the ministrations he encounters—to his projections on to the outside of those things that have been taken in by the baby via introjection; and (3) moving beyond ruthless loving—which does not recognize the demands on the other—to an awareness of the contributions of the other and the attendant indebtedness to the other. These are the quite significant domains that are traversed via the use of transitional objects and transitional phenomena.

> By this definition an infant's babbling or the way an older child goes over a repertory of songs and tunes while preparing for sleep come within the intermediate area as transitional phenomena, along with the use made of objects that are not part of the infant's body yet are not fully recognized as belonging to external reality.

"Transitional phenomena," according to Winnicott, include a wide range of a child's behavior; for instance, the infant's babbling or the older child's singing, or the use an infant makes of objects that are not part of the infant's body, but are not yet recognized as belonging to external reality.

Inadequacy of usual statement

It is generally acknowledged that a statement of human nature in terms of interpersonal relationships is not good enough even when the imaginative elaboration of function and the whole of fantasy both conscious and unconscious, including the repressed unconscious, are allowed for. There is another way of describing persons that comes out of the researches of the past two decades. Of every individual who has reached to the stage of being a unit with a limiting membrane and an outside and an inside, it can be said that there is an *inner reality* to that individual, an inner world which can be rich or poor and can be at peace or in a state of war. This helps, but is it enough?

OK. So Winnicott is now asserting that there is more to humans than their interpersonal relationships—their Object Relations. Even if we add the concept of the unconscious—and the repressed unconscious, and the activity of fantasy—there is more to be accounted for. Winnicott points out that there is an inner reality in all individuals, once they have reached "unit status," which is the stage of recognizing the difference between their own insides and that which is outside.

My claim is that if there is a need for this double statement, there is also need for a triple one; the third part of the life of a human being, a part that we cannot ignore, is an intermediate area of *experiencing*, to which inner reality and external life both contribute. It is an area which is not challenged, because no claim is made on its behalf except that it shall exist as a resting-place for the individual engaged in the perpetual human task of keeping inner and outer reality separate yet inter-related.

OK, so in addition to internal reality and external reality Winnicott is positing a third territory—an intermediate area of experiencing—where inner and outer realities can meet, mix, coexist with, and co-influence one another. This area provides respite from the ongoing work of keeping inner and outer reality separate, yet related. Winnicott will explain this further.

It is usual to refer to "reality-testing", and to make a clear distinction between apperception and perception.

"Reality testing" is a term coined by Freud. It refers to the ability to compare one's emotion or thought against the evidence of external reality. "Perception" is the raw sensory input of the external world; "apperception" is the attachment of meaning to that input, colored by our past experiences and internal constructs. So Winnicott is asserting that it's usual in the thinking and writings of psychoanalysts to refer to inner versus outer reality, but to leave out the transitional space that he is sketching out in this paper.

I am here staking a claim for an intermediate state between a baby's inability and growing ability to recognize and accept reality,

OK—and I'm parsing Winnicott carefully now. He is staking a claim much as one would claim a physical plot of land: he believes that there is an intermediate territory between a baby's initial solipsism and his growing ability to recognize and accept external reality—a territory between inner and outer reality. He then continues:

and I am therefore studying the substance of *illusion*, that which is allowed to the infant, and which in adult life is inherent in art and religion, and yet becomes the hallmark of madness when an adult puts too powerful a claim on the credulity of others, forcing them to acknowledge a sharing of illusion that is not their own.

OK, so Winnicott is going to study illusion as it is present in the experience of developing infants and babies. This, he posits, is the territory between inner and outer reality. He acknowledges that illusion has a limit in mental health: that if we insist that others accept our illusion without recognizing it for what it is—illusion—we find ourselves (or another) occupying the arena of madness.

We can share a respect for *illusory experience*, and if we wish we may collect together and form a group on the basis of the similarity of our illusory experiences. This is a natural root of grouping among human beings.

Here he is acknowledging that adult humans sometimes form groups on the basis of their shared illusions, something that is common in both art and religion.

I hope it will be understood that I am not referring exactly to the little child's Teddy Bear nor to the infant's first use of the fist (thumb, fingers).

> I am not specifically studying the first object of object-relationships. I am concerned with the first possession, and with the intermediate area between the subjective and that which is objectively perceived.

OK, so Winnicott here emphasizes for us that he will be talking not about thumbs and teddy bears as objects, but rather as symbols carrying the meaning of an area that lies between objective and subjective realities. This is his unique observation and contribution in this paper.

Development of a personal pattern

There is plenty of reference in psychoanalytic literature to the progress from "hand to mouth" to "hand to genital", but perhaps less to further progress to the handling of truly "not-me" objects. Sooner or later in an infant's development there comes a tendency on the part of the infant to weave other-than-me objects into the personal pattern. To some extent these objects stand for the breast, but it is not especially this point that is under discussion.

OK, so now we have Winnicott, the pediatrician, offering his careful observation of infants. At some point they no longer confine themselves to their own bodies as objects for touch and exploration. They procure other-than-me objects.

> In the case of some infants the thumb is placed in the mouth while fingers are made to caress the face by pronation and supination movements of the forearm. The mouth is then active in relation to the thumb, but not in relation to the fingers. The fingers caressing the upper lip, or some other part, may be or may become more important than the thumb engaging the mouth. Moreover this caressing activity may be found alone, without the more direct thumb–mouth union.[2]
>
> 2 Cf. Freud: 'Case of Dora', *Collected Papers*, Vol. 3, pp. 63–64; also Hoffer, Willi: *The Psychoanalytic Study of the Child*, Vol. III–IV, p. 51.

Here he is making the simple point that little ones may do more than thumb or fist sucking along with their sucking behaviors. And in fact this ancillary activity may be more important to the infant than the auto-erotic pleasure of thumb sucking.

In common experience one of the following occurs, complicating an auto-erotic experience such as thumb-sucking: •

(1) with the other hand the baby takes an external object, say a part of a sheet or blanket, into the mouth along with the fingers;
or (2) somehow or other the bit of cloth[3] is held and sucked, or not actually sucked. The objects used naturally include napkins and (later) handkerchiefs, and this depends on what is readily and reliably available;
or (3) the baby starts from early months to pluck wool and to collect it and to use it for the caressing part of the activity.[4] Less commonly, the wool is swallowed, even causing trouble;
or (4) mouthing, accompanied by sounds of "mummum", babbling,[5] anal noises, the first musical notes and so on.

3 A recent example is the blanket-doll of the child in the film *A Child Goes to Hospital* by Robertson (Tavistock Clinic).
4 Here there could possibly be an explanation for the use of the term "wool-gathering", which means: inhabiting the transitional or intermediate area.
5 See W. C. M. Scott's recent paper on 'Blathering'.

OK. So now Winnicott, ever the careful infant observer, lists for us some of these ancillary activities, including both tactile and auditory elements.

One may suppose that thinking, or fantasying, gets linked up with these functional experiences. All these things I am calling *transitional* phenomena.

OK. This is worth pausing over. One may suppose that thinking or fantasying gets linked up with these functional experiences. Winnicott is suggesting that the infant begins to embellish these gestures with imaginative elaboration, or "proto-thinking," assigning the infant's own shades of psychological meaning to the experience. All of this comprises, for Winnicott, the area of intermediate experience via transitional phenomena.

Also, out of all this (if we study any one infant) there may emerge some thing or some phenomenon—perhaps a bundle of wool or the corner of a blanket or eiderdown, or a word or tune, or a mannerism, which becomes vitally important to the infant for use at the time of going to sleep,[6] and is a defence against anxiety, especially anxiety of depressive type.

6 See Illingworth, R. S., *B.M.J.*, 7 April, 1951, "Sleep Disturbances in Young Children".

Here Winnicott again uses his observations as a pediatrician to call our attention to this detail, which is that a little one will tend to seize upon and elevate a soft element or a tune or mannerism as an aid to help him/her in going to sleep, in order to allay the infant's anxiety, especially of the "depressive type" (where the infant feels concern about the loss of his maternal love object).

Perhaps some soft object or type of object has been found and used by the infant, and this then becomes what I am calling a *transitional object*. This object goes on being important. The parents get to know its value and carry it round when travelling. The mother lets it get dirty and even smelly, knowing that by washing it she introduces a break in continuity in the infant's experience, a break that may destroy the meaning and value of the object to the infant.

OK, here the "transitional object" makes its entry into Winnicott's paper. It might be a piece of wool or cloth or a soft object that has been found by the infant. So far we know that it has been found and used by the infant, that it goes on being important, and that parents get to know its value and ensure that the infant has access to it, even when travelling. They also know not to wash it.

I suggest that the pattern of transitional phenomena begins to show at about 4–6–8–12 months. Purposely I leave room for wide variations.

Here Winnicott does something he rarely does: he provides an actual age range: 4–12 months.

Patterns set in infancy may persist into childhood, so that the original soft object continues to be absolutely necessary at bed-time or at time of loneliness or when a depressed mood threatens. In health, however, there is a gradual extension of range of interest, and eventually the extended range is maintained, even when depressive anxiety is near. A need for a specific object or a behaviour pattern that started at a very early date may reappear at a later age when deprivation threatens.

Patterns set in infancy may persist into childhood, even though there tends to be an extension of the range of interest in a child and a relative diminution in the importance of the original transitional object. The child (at any age) may indeed revert to needing his original object at times of stress.

> This first possession is used in conjunction with special techniques derived from very early infancy, which can include or exist apart from the more direct autoerotic activities.

Winnicott describes this initial object as the infant's "first possession." A child treats this first possession with techniques carried over from very early infancy. This can include or exclude typical auto-erotic activity. Winnicott next speaks to the expansion of a child's range of possessions:

> Gradually in the life of an infant Teddies and dolls and hard toys are acquired. Boys to some extent tend to go over to use hard objects, whereas girls tend to proceed right ahead to the acquisition of a family. It is important to note, however, that *there is no noticeable difference between boy and girl in their use of the original not-me possession*, which I am calling the transitional object.

So Winnicott notices gender difference in preference in this expansion of the range of toys of interest—usually (but not always) for hard objects in boys, and the acquisition of "a family" in girls. He emphasizes, however, that there is no gender difference in the choice of the initial, original transitional object.

> As the infant starts to use organized sounds (mum, ta, da) there may appear a "word" for the transitional object. The name given by the infant to these earliest objects is often significant, and it usually has a word used by the adults partly incorporated in it. For instance, "baa" may be the name, and the "b" may have come from the adult's use of the word "baby" or "bear".

OK. So the transitional object often acquires a name within the child's developing phonetic repetoire. The name is given by the child.

> I should mention that sometimes there is no transitional object except the mother herself.

This point seems important. Sometimes there is no identifiable transitional object except the mother herself.

> Or an infant may be so disturbed in emotional development that the transition state cannot be enjoyed, or the sequence of objects used is broken. The sequence may nevertheless be maintained in a hidden way.

Winnicott poses two possibilities in the case of infants whose emotional development is severely disturbed: (1) that they have not been able to develop a transitional object or state because they are managing disturbance, impingement, annihilation; (2) that the sequence of objects used is "broken," which might happen if a child is removed from a home or if a parent misguidedly violates the child's attachment to the transitional object or to a succession of transitional objects by taking it/them away.

Summary of special qualities in the relationship

1. The infant assumes rights over the object, and we agree to this assumption. Nevertheless some abrogation of omnipotence is a feature from the start.
2. The object is affectionately cuddled as well as excitedly loved and mutilated.
3. It must never change, unless changed by the infant.
4. It must survive instinctual loving, and also hating, and, if it be a feature, pure aggression.
5. Yet it must seem to the infant to give warmth, or to move, or to have texture, or to do something that seems to show it has vitality or reality of its own.
6. It comes from without from our point of view, but not so from the point of view of the baby. Neither does it come from within; it is not an hallucination.
7. Its fate is to be gradually allowed to be decathected, so that in the course of years it becomes not so much forgotten as relegated to limbo. By this I mean that in health the transitional object does not "go inside" nor does the feeling about it necessarily undergo repression. It is not forgotten and it is not mourned. It loses meaning, and this is because the transitional phenomena have become diffused, have become spread out over the whole intermediate territory between "inner psychic reality" and "the external world as perceived by two persons in common", that is to say, over the whole cultural field.

This is Winnicott's summary of the special qualities of a transitional object. Some notable features in his list include that the infant assumes rights over the object, and that the adults somehow agree to this assumption. They know that the object has been deemed to be special to the infant, and they honor this. Also notable is that the object seems to the infant to give something—to have a reality of its own. Also, the object will be gradually de-cathected—gradually diminished in its special function. It loses its unique meaning gradually as transitional phenomena have been spread out on to a larger repertoire of objects.

> At this point my subject widens out into that of play, and of artistic cre-
> ativity and appreciation, and of religious feeling, and of dreaming, and also
> of fetishism, lying and stealing, the origin and loss of affectionate feeling,
> drug addiction, the talisman of obsessional rituals, etc.

OK, so Winnicott is now going to shift gears to widen the scope of his
observations.

> ### Relationship of the transitional object to symbolism
>
> It is true that the piece of blanket (or whatever it is) is symbolical of some
> part-object, such as the breast. Nevertheless the point of it is not its sym-
> bolic value so much as its actuality. Its not being the breast (or the mother)
> although real is as important as the fact that it stands for the breast (or
> mother).

OK. So the transitional object found and claimed and named by the child may
at some level be a symbolic stand-in for the mother's breast, but its importance
lies in the fact that it is also real, separate, and different from the mother's breast.

> When symbolism is employed the infant is already clearly distinguishing
> between fantasy and fact, between inner objects and external objects,
> between primary creativity and perception. But the term transitional
> object, according to my suggestion, gives room for the process of
> becoming able to accept difference and similarity. I think there is use for a
> term for the root of symbolism in time, a term that describes the infant's
> journey from the purely subjective to objectivity; and it seems to me
> that the transitional object (piece of blanket, etc.) is what we see of this
> journey of progress towards experiencing.

Wow. Winnicott is carefully observing the process whereby a child comes
to traverse the difference between a world that is entirely subjective—the
new infant's world of omnipotence—and a world that consists of objects and
occurrences external to the infant. The piece of blanket appears to be the
vehicle of transit on this important journey.

> It would be possible to understand the transitional object while not fully
> understanding the nature of symbolism. It seems that symbolism can only
> be properly studied in the process of the growth of an individual, and that

> it has at the very best a variable meaning. For instance, if we consider the wafer of the Blessed Sacrament, which is symbolic of the body of Christ. I think I am right in saying that for the Roman Catholic community it *is* the body, and for the Protestant community it is a *substitute*, a reminder, and is essentially not, in fact, actually the body itself. Yet in both cases it is a symbol.

Winnicott is exploring the root process that underlies our capacity for symbolization. He uses the example of the Catholic versus the Protestant view of the communion wafer, pointing out that symbolism can be more literal in some uses, less in others.

> A schizoid patient asked me, after Christmas, had I enjoyed eating her at the feast? And then, *had I really eaten her or only in fantasy?* I knew that she could not be satisfied with either alternative. Her split needed the double answer.

Here he illustrates via a case example the spectrum of literal versus figurative symbolism.

Clinical description of a transitional object

For anyone in touch with parents and children, there is an infinite quantity and variety of illustrative clinical material.[7] The following illustrations are given merely to remind readers of similar material in their own experiences.

7 There are excellent examples in the one article I have found on this same subject. Wulff ("Fetishism and Object Choice in Early Childhood", *Psychoanal. Quart.*, 1946, 15, p. 450) is clearly studying this same phenomenon, but he calls the objects "fetish objects". It is not clear to me that this term is correct, and I discuss this below. I did not actually know of Wulff's paper until I had written my own, but it gave me great pleasure and support to find the subject had already been considered worthy of discussion by a colleague. See also Abraham: case description in "The First Pregenital Stage of the Libido", Selected Papers (Hogarth Press), p. 267, and Lindner: Jahrbuch für Kinderheilkunde, *N.F.*, xiv.

Two brothers; contrast in early use of possessions

Two brothers; contrast in early use of possessions

(Distortion in use of transitional object.) X, now a healthy man, has had to fight his way towards maturity. The mother "learned how to be a mother" in her management of X when he was an infant and she was able to avoid certain mistakes with the other children because of what she learned with him. There were also external reasons why she was anxious at the time of her rather lonely management of X when he was born. She took her job as a mother very seriously and she breast-fed X for seven months. She feels that in his case this was too long and he was very difficult to wean. He never sucked his thumb or his fingers and when she weaned him "he had nothing to fall back on". He had never had the bottle or a dummy or any other form of feeding. He had a very strong and early *attachment to her herself*, as a person, and it was her actual person that he needed.

Here Winnicott is giving us a case example of a child whose transitional object was the mother herself.

From twelve months he adopted a rabbit which he would cuddle and his affectionate regard for the rabbit eventually transferred to real rabbits. This particular rabbit lasted till he was five or six years old. It could be described as a *comforter*, but it never had the true quality of a transitional object. It was never, as a true transitional object would have been, more important than the mother, an almost inseparable part of the infant. In the case of this particular boy the kind of anxieties which were brought to a head by the weaning at seven months later produced asthma, and only gradually did he conquer this. It was important for him that he found employment far away from the home town. His attachment to his mother is still very powerful, although he comes within the wide definition of the term normal, or healthy. This man has not married.

Winnicott is offering in this case example some extra detail on transitional objects: they become "more important than the mother, almost an inseparable part of the infant." He also links the boy's weaning process, given that his mother was indeed his transitional object, to later development of asthma. He now moves to a more typical use of a transitional object in X's younger brother.

(Typical use of transitional object.) X's younger brother, Y, has developed in quite a straightforward way throughout. He now has three healthy children of his own. He was fed at the breast for four months and then weaned without difficulty.[8] Y sucked his thumb in the early weeks and this again "made weaning easier for him than for his older brother". Soon after weaning at five to six months he adopted the end of the blanket where the stitching finished. He was pleased if a little bit of the wool stuck out at the corner and with this he would tickle his nose.

This very early became his "Baa"; he invented this word for it himself as soon as he could use organized sounds. From the time when he was about a year old he was able to substitute for the end of the blanket a soft green jersey with a red tie. This was not a "comforter" as in the case of the depressive older brother, but a "soother". It was a sedative which always worked. This is a typical example of what I am calling a *Transitional Object*. When Y was a little boy it was always certain that if anyone gave him his "Baa" he would immediately suck it and lose anxiety, and in fact he would go to sleep within a few minutes if the time for sleep were at all near. The thumb-sucking continued at the same time, lasting until he was three or four years old, and he remembers thumb-sucking and a hard place on one thumb which resulted from it. He is now interested (as a father) in the thumb-sucking of his children and their use of "Baas".

> 8 The mother had "learned from her first child that it was a good idea to give one bottle feed while breast feeding", that is, to allow for the positive value of substitutes for herself, and by this means she achieved easier weaning than with X.

Winnicott gives us in this vignette another piece of the transitional object profile: it confers not just "comfort" for the child, but "sooth[ing]," as would a sedative. It consistently brought soothing; the child could suck on it and could reliably be observed to lose anxiety. When sleep was near, it helped the child settle into sleep. This case also illustrates several other features of transitional objects that Winnicott has already mentioned: (1) that he swapped out his end-of-blanket for a soft jersey when he was about one; (2) that he continued to suck his thumb while using his transitional object.

The story of seven ordinary children in this family brings out the following points, arranged for comparison:

		Thumb.	Transitional object.			Type of child.
X Boy		O	Mother	.	.	. Rabbit (comforter)	Mother-fixated
Y Boy		+	'BAA'	.	.	. Jersey (soother)	Free
Twins { Girl		O	Dummy	.	.	. Donkey (friend)	Late maturity
{ Boy		O	'EE'	.	.	. EE (protective)	Latent psychopathic
...Girl		O	'BAA'	.	.	. Blanket (reassurance)	Developing well
...Girl		+	Thumb	.	.	. Thumb (satisfaction)	Developing well
...Boy		+	'Mimi's	.	.	. *Cult (company)	Developing well

Children of Y

* Innumerable similar soft objects distinguished by colour, length, width, and early subjected to sorting and classification.

Value in history-taking

In consultation with a parent it is often valuable to get information about the early techniques and possessions of all the children of the family. This starts the mother off on a comparison of her children one with another, and enables her to remember and compare their characteristics at an early age.

Winnicott here sketches out in schematic form the use of thumb plus transitional objects in the seven children in X's family. He provides no further elaboration, but urges clinicians to get information about this early stage of development from parents.

The child's contribution

Information can often be obtained from a child in regard to transitional objects; for instance, Angus (11 years 9 months) told me that his brother "has tons of teddies and things" and "before that he had little bears", and he followed this up with a talk about his own history. He said he never had teddies. There was a bell rope which hung down, a tag end of which he would go on hitting, and so go off to sleep. Probably in the end it fell, and that was the end of it. There was, however, something else. He was very shy about this. It was a purple rabbit with red eyes. "I wasn't fond of it. I used to throw it around." "Jeremy has it now. I gave it to him. I gave it to Jeremy because it was naughty. It *would* fall off the chest of drawers. *It still visits me. I like it to visit me.*" He surprised himself when he drew the purple rabbit. It will be noted that this eleven-year-old boy with the ordinary good reality-sense of his age spoke as if lacking in reality sense when describing the transitional object's qualities and activities. When I saw the mother later she expressed surprise that Angus remembered the purple rabbit. She easily recognized it from the coloured drawing.

What we see here is Winnicott's harvesting information from a boy just short of 12 years old. The boy had swapped out the bell rope tag (transitional object) for a purple rabbit, which he clearly had invested with human features. This well-adjusted, reality-oriented 11-year-old "spoke as if lacking in reality sense when describing the transitional object's qualities and activities," so profound and lasting was his relationship with his transitional object.

Ready availability of examples

I deliberately refrain from giving more case material here, particularly as I wish to avoid giving the impression that what I am reporting is rare. In practically every case history there is something to be found that is interesting in the transitional phenomena, or in their absence. (It is my intention to give other examples and to develop subsidiary themes in future work.)

Theoretical study

There are certain comments that can be made on the basis of accepted psycho-analytic theory.

1. The transitional object stands for the breast, or the object of the first relationship.
2. The transitional object antedates established reality-testing.
3. In relation to the transitional object the infant passes from (magical) omnipotent control to control by manipulation (involving muscle erotism and co-ordination pleasure).
4. The transitional object may eventually develop into a fetish object and so persist as a characteristic of the adult sexual life. (See Wulff's development of the theme.)
5. The transitional object may, because of anal erotic organization, stand for fæces (but it is not for this reason that it may become smelly and remain unwashed).

Winnicott's points from psychoanalytic theory are clear. I will comment on several.

1. He has already observed that the transitional object may stand and stand in for the mother's breast, but as importantly, it is different from the mother's breast, and comes to be imbued with its own characteristics.
2. The transitional object is chosen before the child has established his reality testing. Indeed, it is the transit vehicle that moves the child from complete subjectivity to the ability to perceive objects objectively.
3. Here, again, Winnicott provides more nuance about transitional objects: a child, in relation to his transitional object, at first exerts magical, omnipotent control over the object. But later, as time passes, he uses the object in more motoric ways, involving the pleasurable use of his own muscles and maturing sense of coordination.

4. Here Winnicott makes room for the observations of another writer, Wulff, who sees some aspects of a child's relationship to his transitional object reappear in adult sexual life in the context of fetishism.
5. The transitional object may come for some children, given their progression through psychosexual stages, to symbolize their own developing anal maturity and control, and so may stand for their feces (although, Winnicott points out, this ascription of meaning is not typically what soils the transitional object).

Relationship to internal object (Klein)

It is interesting to compare the transitional object concept with Melanie Klein's concept of the internal object. The transitional object is *not an internal object* (which is a mental concept)—it is a possession. Yet it is not (for the infant) an external object either.

The following complex statement has to be made. The infant can employ a transitional object when the internal object is alive and real and good enough (not too persecutory). But this internal object depends for its qualities on the existence and aliveness and behaviour of the external object (breast, mother figure, general environmental care). Badness or failure of the latter indirectly leads to deadness or to a persecutory quality of internal object. After a persistence of failure of the external object the internal object fails to have meaning to the infant, and then, and then only, does the transitional object become meaningless too. The transitional object may therefore stand for the "external" breast, but *indirectly*, through standing for an "internal" breast.

The transitional object is never under magical control like the internal object, nor is it outside control as the real mother is.

OK. So Winnicott is here comparing his concept of the transitional object with Klein's concept of an internal object. The transitional object is a possession of the infant, so not internal. It is physical rather than mental. Yet, it is not an external object to the infant either, because the infant imbues it with characteristics that would only pertain to it if they were assigned to it by the infant. So it is neither internal nor external.

In addition, Winnicott asserts that an infant can only choose and make use of a transitional object if the external object—the mother, the breast, the whole environment created for the infant—has allowed the infant to internalize a good-enough internal object. If the internal object is dead or persecutory or fails to have meaning for the infant, then there will be no meaning-infused transitional object. He finishes off by contrasting the transitional object to the internal object, which is under the infant's magical, omnipotent control, and also to the external object (the real mother), who is completely outside the infant's control. The transitional object is neither.

Illusion–disillusionment

In order to prepare the ground for my own positive contribution to this subject I must put into words some of the things that I think are taken too easily for granted in many psychoanalytic writings on infantile emotional development, although they may be understood in practice.

Winnicott is about to present some of his basic views on child development. I will withhold comment until he has made his points.

There is no possibility whatever for an infant to proceed from the pleasure-principle to the reality principle or towards and beyond primary identification (see Freud, *The Ego and the Id*, p. 14),[9] unless there is a good enough mother.[10] The good enough "mother" (not necessarily the infant's own mother) is one who makes active adaptation to the infant's needs, an active adaptation that gradually lessens, according to the infant's growing ability to account for failure of adaptation and to tolerate the results of frustration. Naturally the infant's own mother is more likely to be good enough than some other person, since this active adaptation demands an easy and unresented preoccupation with the one infant; in fact, success in infant-care depends on the fact of devotion, not on cleverness or intellectual enlightenment.

The good enough mother, as I have stated, starts off with an almost complete adaptation to her infant's needs, and as time proceeds she adapts less and less completely, gradually, according to the infant's growing ability to deal with her failure.

The infant's means of dealing with this maternal failure include the following:

1. The infant's experience, often repeated, that there is a time limit to frustration. At first, naturally, this time limit must be short.
2. Growing sense of process.
3. The beginnings of mental activity.
4. Employment of auto-erotic satisfactions.
5. Remembering, reliving, fantasying, dreaming; the integrating of past, present, and future.

If all goes well the infant can actually come to gain from the experience of frustration, since incomplete adaptation to need makes objects real, that is to say hated as well as loved. The consequence of this is that *if all goes well* the infant can be disturbed by a close adaptation to need that is continued too long, not allowed its natural decrease, since exact adaptation resembles magic and the object that behaves perfectly becomes no better than an hallucination. Nevertheless *at the start* adaptation needs to be almost exact, and unless this is so it is not possible for the infant to begin to develop a capacity to experience a relationship to external reality, or even to form a conception of external reality.

9   See also Freud: Group Psychology and the Analysis of the Ego, p. 65.
10 One effect, and the main effect, of failure of the mother in this respect at the start of an infant's life, is discussed clearly (in my view) by Marion Milner, in her paper appearing in the *Melanie Klein Birthday Volume*, Hogarth Press, 1952, also this Journal, **32** (1952), p. 181. She shows that because of the mother's failure there is brought about a premature ego-development, with precocious sorting out of a bad from a good object. The period of illusion (or my Transitional Phase) is disturbed. In analysis or in various activities in ordinary life an individual can be seen to be going on seeking the valuable resting-place of illusion. Illusion in this way has its positive value. See also Freud: *Aus den Anfängen der Psychoanalyse: Briefe an Wilhelm Fliess*. In 1895 Freud wrote (pp. 402 and 413) that only by outside help certain early functioning can proceed satisfactorily.

OK, so Winnicott has summarized some of his basics regarding parenting of an infant. He is very clear and straightforward in his language. At first, there is required primary maternal preoccupation, freely and unresentfully given to the infant. There must be nearly perfect adaptation to infant need at first. Gradually, that adaptation needs to attenuate, in synchrony with the infant's growing ability to tolerate frustration and to imagine frustration's time limit. This incomplete adaptation is required in order for objects to become real to the infant—and to have an external, objective existence. Winnicott says this succinctly: "the object that behaves perfectly becomes no better than an hallucination."

Illusion and the value of illusion

The mother, at the beginning, by almost 100 per cent adaptation affords the infant the opportunity for the *illusion* that her breast is part of the infant. It is, as it were, under magical control. The same can be said in terms of infant care in general, in the quiet times between excitements. Omnipotence is nearly a fact of experience. The mother's eventual task is gradually to disillusion the infant, but she has no hope of success unless at first she has been able to give sufficient opportunity for illusion.

OK. This is a central tenet in Winnicott's metapsychology: that the infant starts out in a place where there is no outside and no inside; there is only experience. That experience is construed by the infant as having been created by himself. He is hungry; the breast appears; he made it happen. He is uncomfortable (and wet); his diapers become dry; he made it happen. This is the initial state of illusion that an infant occupies. Thus, the infant exists for a while in an illusory state of omnipotence.

> In another language, the breast is created by the infant over and over again out of the infant's capacity to love or (one can say) out of need. A subjective phenomenon develops in the baby which we call the mother's breast.[11] The mother places the actual breast just there where the infant is ready to create, and at the right moment.
>
> 11   I include the whole technique of mothering. When it is said that the first object is the breast, the word "breast" is used, I believe, to stand for the technique of mothering as well as for the actual flesh. It is not impossible for a mother to be a good enough mother (in my way of putting it) with a bottle for the actual feeding. If this wide meaning of the word "breast" is kept in mind, and maternal technique is seen to be included in the total meaning of the term, then there is a bridge forming between the wording of Melanie Klein's statement of early history and that of Anna Freud. The only difference left is one of dates, which is in fact an unimportant difference which will automatically disappear in the course of time.

Let me use Winnicott's words again: "A subjective phenomenon develops in the baby which we call the mother's breast." In other words, the baby creates his conception of an internal object, the mother's breast, which represents to him the full spectrum of maternal care. Winnicott emphasizes in his footnote that "breast" is meant to stand in for the whole technique of mothering. The infant lives, initially, in a state of subjective illusion with respect to how this breast/ how this environmental provision came to be and under whose control it is.

> From birth therefore the human being is concerned with the problem of the relationship between what is objectively perceived and what is subjectively conceived of, and in the solution of this problem there is no health for the human being who has not been started off well enough by the mother. *The intermediate area to which I am referring is the area that is allowed to the infant between primary creativity and objective perception based on reality testing.* The transitional phenomena represent the early stages of the use of illusion, without which there is no meaning for the human being in the idea of a relationship with an object that is perceived by others as external to that being.

Winnicott frames this problem of what is subjective and illusory and what is objective reality as a central concern in every human being. He asserts that, if one has not been started well enough by a mother figure, there is no way that this problem (subjectivity versus objectivity) will be solved satisfactorily. An infant must be allowed the luxury of illusion and omnipotence at first in order to enjoy a sense of primary creativity. Transitional phenomena represent the infant's first foray into the realm of illusion and creativity beyond that which the maternal environment provided for him. In this way Winnicott situates creativity earlier in development than Klein, who situates creativity as a part of the infant's reparation efforts to the mother for infant aggression and hate. Winnicott illustrates the progression from subjectivity to transitionality in two figures to follow:

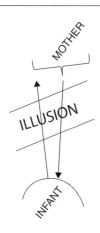

Fig. 1

The idea illustrated in **Fig. 1** is this: that at some theoretical point early in the development of every human individual an infant in a certain setting provided by the mother is capable of conceiving of the idea of something which would meet the growing need which arises out of instinctual tension. The infant cannot be said to know at first what is to be created. At this point in time the mother presents herself. In the ordinary way she gives her breast and her potential feeding urge. The mother's adaptation to the infant's needs, when good enough, gives the infant the illusion that there is an external reality that corresponds to the infant's own capacity to create. In other words, there is an overlap between what the mother supplies and what the child might conceive of. To the observer the child perceives what the mother actually presents, but this is not the whole truth. The infant perceives the breast only in so far as a breast could be created just there and then. There is no interchange between the mother and the infant. Psychologically the infant takes from a breast that is part of the infant, and the mother gives milk to an infant that is part of herself. In psychology, the idea of interchange is based on an illusion.

The infant is a completely naïve player in the initial scenes of his own life. He feels a need. He does not know at first what the need is. Mother adapts. The infant has the illusion that there is a satisfaction that he created. There is no interchange in the mind/experience of the infant; there is only creation.

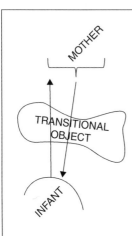

Fig. 2

In **Fig. 2** a shape is given to the area of illusion, to illustrate what I consider to be the main function of the transitional object and of transitional phenomena. The transitional object and the transitional phenomena start each human being off with what will always be important for them, i.e. a neutral area of experience which will not be challenged. Of the transitional object it can be said that it is a matter of agreement between us and the baby that we will never ask the question "Did you conceive of this or was it presented to you from without?" The important point is that no decision on this point is expected. The question is not to be formulated.

In Figure 2, we see that the transitional object is now between the mother/breast and the infant. It takes over some of the functions of the mother, which have been internalized in the infant and can now be projected into a transitional object. The point that Winnicott stresses about Figure 2 is that it is essential that the infant be allowed to operate with the illusion that he created that which he found. No one should ever raise the question to him: "Did you conceive of this or was it presented to you from the outside?" The transitional illusion is delicate. It cannot bear the scrutiny of reality testing yet.

This problem, which undoubtedly concerns the human infant in a hidden way at the beginning, gradually becomes an obvious problem on account of the fact that the mother's main task (next to providing opportunity for illusion) is disillusionment.

OK. Winnicott just said something important, so I'll interrupt him. He said that next to providing an infant the setting and opportunity for illusion, the mother's next main task is *disillusion*, a task that persists into the child's growing up years. Both are of enormous importance—the initial provision of illusion, and the gradual, deliberate, well-timed process of disillusion.

This is preliminary to the task of weaning, and it also continues as one of the tasks of parents and educators. In other words, this matter of *illusion* is one which belongs inherently to human beings and which no individual finally solves for himself or herself, although a *theoretical* understanding of it may provide a *theoretical* solution. If things go well, in this gradual disillusionment process, the stage is set for the frustrations that we gather together under the word weaning; but it should be remembered that when we talk about the phenomena (which Mrs. Klein has specifically illuminated) that cluster round weaning we are assuming the underlying process, the process by which opportunity for illusion and gradual disillusionment is provided. If illusion–disillusionment has gone astray the infant cannot get to so normal a thing as weaning, nor to a reaction to weaning, and it is then absurd to refer to weaning at all. The mere termination of breast feeding is not a weaning.

We can see the tremendous significance of weaning in the case of the normal child. When we witness the complex reaction that is set going in a certain child by the weaning process we know that this is able to take place in that child because the illusion–disillusionment process is being carried through so well that we can ignore it while discussing actual weaning.

Winnicott frames weaning as a natural part of the process of disillusionment. If the gradual process of disillusionment has not been enacted, there will be no meaningful weaning. There will only be the termination of breast feeding, for which the child will be unprepared.

Development of the theory of illusion–disillusionment

It is assumed here that the task of reality-acceptance is never completed, that no human being is free from the strain of relating inner and outer reality, and that relief from this strain is provided by an intermediate area of experience[12] which is not challenged (arts, religion, etc.). This intermediate area is in direct continuity with the play area of the small child who is "lost" in play.

12   Cf. Riviere: *Int. J. Psycho-Anal.*, 17 (1936), p. 399.

This intermediate area of experience is the resting place between inner and outer reality. It is the place of creativity, of freedom, of play, of imagination, of arts and religion where reality does not constrain. It is continuous with the experience of a child lost in play.

> In infancy this intermediate area is necessary for the initiation of a relationship between the child and the world, and is made possible by good enough mothering at the early critical phase. Essential to all this is continuity (in time) of the external emotional environment and of particular elements in the physical environment such as the transitional object or objects.
>
> The transitional phenomena are allowable to the infant because of the parents' intuitive recognition of the strain inherent in objective perception, and we do not challenge the infant in regard to subjectivity or objectivity just here where there is the transitional object.

It is important that parents recognize in their developing children the strain inherent in the perception of objective reality; it is likewise important that they not rob their children of the space of illusion.

> Should an adult make claims on us for our acceptance of the objectivity of his subjective phenomena we discern or diagnose madness. If, however, the adult can manage to enjoy the personal intermediate area without making claims, then we can acknowledge our own corresponding intermediate areas, and are pleased to find overlapping, that is to say common experience between members of a group in art or religion or philosophy.

It is also important that adults accord one another the freedom to occupy transitional space, except when these adults make claims on us for our acceptance of the objectivity of their subjective illusions. All adults need time in transitional/intermediate areas to bear the strain of the near constant effort to recognize what is me and not me, what is inner (fantasy) and what is outer (external reality).

Reference to Wulff's paper

I wish to draw particular attention to the paper by Wulff, referred to above, in which excellent clinical material is given illustrating exactly that which I am referring to under the heading of transitional objects and transitional phenomena. There is a difference between my point of view and that of Wulff which is reflected in my use of this special term and his use of the term "fetish object". A study of Wulff's paper seems to show that in using the word fetish he has taken back to infancy something that belongs in ordinary theory to the sexual perversions. I am not able to find in his article sufficient room for the consideration of the child's transitional object as a healthy early experience. Yet I do consider that transitional phenomena are healthy and universal. Moreover if we extend the use of the word fetish to cover normal phenomena we shall perhaps be losing some of the value of the term.

I would prefer to retain the word fetish to describe the object that is employed on account of a *delusion* of a maternal phallus. I would then go further and say that we must keep a place for the *illusion* of a maternal phallus, that is to say, an idea that is universal and not pathological. If we shift the accent now from the object on to the word illusion we get near to the infant's transitional object; the importance lies in the concept of illusion, a universal in the field of experience.

Following this, we can allow the transitional object to be potentially a maternal phallus but originally the breast, that is to say, the thing created by the infant and at the same time provided from the environment. In this way I think that a study of the infant's use of the transitional object and of transitional phenomena in general may throw light on the origin of the fetish object and of fetishism. There is something to be lost, however, in working backwards from the psycho-pathology of fetishism to the transitional phenomena which belong to the beginnings of experience and which are universal and inherent in healthy emotional development.

Winnicott finishes his paper with a brief argument with a paper by Wulff. They differ in how they frame the concept of adult fetishism. Winnicott objects to its being traced backward to the illusions of infancy. He wants it kept more strictly within the bounds of fetishism explored by Freud.

Summary

Attention is drawn to the rich field for observation provided by the earliest experiences of the healthy infant as expressed principally in the relationship to the first possession.

This first possession is related backwards in time to autoerotic phenomena and fist and thumb sucking, and also to the first soft animal or doll and to hard toys. It is related both to the external object (mother's breast) and to internal objects (magically introjected breast), but is distinct from each.

The transitional objects and transitional phenomena belong to the realm of illusion which is at the basis of initiation of experience. This early stage in development is made possible by the mother's special capacity for making adaptation to the needs of her infant, thus allowing the infant the illusion that what the infant creates really exists.

This intermediate area of experience, unchallenged in respect of its belonging to inner or external (shared) reality, constitutes the greater part of the infant's experience and throughout life is retained in the intense experiencing that belongs to the arts and to religion and to imaginative living, and to creative scientific work.

A positive value of illusion can therefore be stated.

An infant's transitional object ordinarily becomes gradually decathected, especially as cultural interests develop. In psychopathology: *Addiction* can be stated in terms of regression to the early stage at which the transitional phenomena are unchallenged;

Fetish can be described in terms of a persistence of a specific object or type of object dating from infantile experience in the transitional field, linked with the delusion of a maternal phallus;

Pseudologia and thieving can be described in terms of an individual's unconscious urge to bridge a gap in continuity of experience in respect of a transitional object.

Winnicott's summary introduces several extensions of his theory of transitional objects, namely, to the areas of addiction, fetishism, pseudologia (fantastical story-telling), and thieving. These are summary references, none of which he elaborates in his paper.

5   The antisocial tendency

(1956)[1]

Winnicott, D. W. (1956). The antisocial tendency. In C. Winnicott, R. Shepherd, & M. Davis (eds.), *Deprivation and delinquency* (pp. 120–131). London: Tavistock, 1984.

In this paper, Winnicott offers the hypothesis that those children and youth who exhibit an "antisocial tendency" (marked by stealing, destroying things, or engaging in a full range of "nuisance" behaviors) may in fact be exhibiting signs of deprivation in their earlier life. According to Winnicott, the child's subsequent period of antisocial behavior represents a surge of hope within the child—hope to access that of which s/he was formerly deprived. He believes that in the development of the antisocial tendency there was initial good care and connection that was, at some point, lost. The loss extended so long that it exceeded the child's capacity to keep the memory of good care and connection alive inside. He suggests that the two trends reflected by stealing and destruction may represent the child's bid for the restoring of the fusion between the libidinal/love and aggressive/motility drives.

The antisocial tendency provides psychoanalysis with some awkward problems, problems of a practical as well as a theoretical nature. Freud, through his introduction to Aichhorn's *Wayward Youth*, showed that psychoanalysis not only contributes to the understanding of delinquency, but it is also enriched by an understanding of the work of those who cope with delinquents.

I have chosen to discuss the antisocial tendency, not delinquency. The reason is that the organized antisocial defence is overloaded with secondary gain and social reactions which make it difficult for the investigator to get to its core. By contrast the antisocial tendency can be studied as it appears in the normal or near-normal child, where it is related to the difficulties that are inherent in emotional development.

---

1 A paper read before the British Psycho-analytic Society, 20 June, 1956.

OK, So Winnicott starts off clarifying his target: not delinquent youth or youth with an antisocial pattern already established, but those with an antisocial "tendency." His rationale is that he wants to study and understand the dynamics beneath this tendency without the confounders of secondary gain and societal reactions that can occur in more advanced cases. It seems important here also to clarify that the word "antisocial" as used in psychological nosology does not mean schizoid, but rather refers to those whose willful non-conformity to laws and norms of the culture (or the family) involves irresponsible or aggressive behavior that harms or abridges the rights of others, including people and animals.

Winnicott starts with two vignettes from his own experience.

I will start with two simple references to clinical material:

For my first child analysis I chose a delinquent. This boy attended regularly for a year and the treatment stopped because of the disturbance that the boy caused in the clinic. I could say that the analysis was going well, and its cessation caused distress both to the boy and to myself in spite of the fact that on several occasions I got badly bitten on the buttocks. The boy got out on the roof and also he spilt so much water that the basement became flooded. He broke into my locked car and drove it away in bottom gear on the self-starter. The clinic ordered termination of the treatment for the sake of the other patients. He went to an approved school.

I may say that he is now 35, and he has been able to earn his living in a job that caters for his restlessness. He is married, with several children. Nevertheless I am afraid to follow up his case for fear that I should become involved again with a psychopath, and I prefer that society should continue to take the burden of his management.

It can easily be seen that the treatment for this boy should have been not psychoanalysis but placement. Psychoanalysis only made sense if added after placement. Since this time I have watched analysts of all kinds fail in the psychoanalysis of antisocial children.

Here Winnicott is quite straightforward. It is his belief, based upon his own experience and also his observation of others' failed therapies, that psychoanalysis is not the treatment of choice for antisocial children. Instead, Winnicott recommends placement in an appropriate facility focused on management. He will clarify later in this paper what he means by management.

By contrast, the following story brings out the fact that antisocial tendency may sometimes be treated very easily if the treatment be adjunctive to specialized environmental care.

I was asked by a friend to discuss the case of her son, the eldest of a family of four. She could not bring John to me in an open way because of her husband who objects to psychology on religious grounds. All she could do was to have a talk with me about the boy's compulsion to steal, which was developing into something quite serious; he was stealing in a big way from shops as well as at home. It was not possible for practical reasons to arrange for anything else but for the mother and myself to have a quick meal together in a restaurant, in the course of which she told me about the troubles and asked me for advice. There was nothing for me to do unless I could do it then and there. I therefore explained the meaning of the stealing and suggested that she should find a good moment in her relationship with the boy and make an interpretation to him. It appeared that she and John had a good relationship with each other for a few moments each evening after he had gone to bed; usually at such a time he would discuss the stars and the moon. This moment could be used.

I said: "Why not tell him that you know that when he steals he is not wanting the things that he steals but he is looking for something that he has a right to: that he is making a claim on his mother and father because he feels deprived of their love." I told her to use language which he could understand. I may say that I knew enough of this family, in which both the parents are musicians, to see how it was that this boy had become to some extent a deprived child, although he has a good home.

Some time later I had a letter telling me that she had done what I suggested. She wrote: "I told him that what he really wanted when he stole money and food and things was his mum; and I must say I didn't really expect him to understand, but he did seem to. I asked him if he thought we didn't love him because he was so naughty sometimes, and he said right out that he didn't think we did, much. Poor little scrap! I felt so awful, I can't tell you. So I told him never, never to doubt it again and if he ever did feel doubtful to remind me to tell him again. But of course I shan't need reminding for a long time, it's been such a shock. One seems to need these shocks. So I'm being a lot more demonstrative to try and keep him from being doubtful any more. And up to now there's been absolutely no more stealing."

The mother had had a talk with the form teacher and had explained to her that the boy was in need of love and appreciation, and had gained her co-operation although the boy gives a lot of trouble at school.

Now after eight months it is possible to report that there has been no return of stealing, and the relationship between the boy and his family has very much improved.

In considering this case it must be remembered that I had known the mother very well during her adolescence and to some extent had seen her through an antisocial phase of her own. She was the eldest in a large family. She had a very good home but very strong discipline was exerted by the father, especially at the time when she was a small child. What I did therefore had the effect of a double therapy, enabling this young woman to get insight into her own difficulties through the help that she was able to give to her son. When we are able to help parents to help their children we do in fact help them about themselves.

(In another paper I propose to give clinical examples illustrating the management of children with antisocial tendency; here I do no more than attempt a brief statement of the basis of my personal attitude to the clinical problem.)

This vignette is a lovely illustration of the value of understanding the core of what is wrong in a child, in a family, in an adult. Righting the core of the issues that underlay this child's stealing behavior—getting to his feeling of having been deprived of his parents' love—was in this case wonderfully mutative for the boy and his mother and family. (This case also demonstrates the clinical genius of Winnicott!)

Nature of antisocial tendency

The antisocial tendency *is not a diagnosis.* It does not compare directly with other diagnostic terms such as neurosis and psychosis. The antisocial tendency may be found in a normal individual, or in one that is neurotic or psychotic.

For the sake of simplicity I will refer only to children, but the antisocial tendency may be found at all ages. The various terms in use in Great Britain may be brought together in the following way:

A child becomes a *deprived child* when deprived of certain essential features of home life... Some degree of what might be called the "deprived complex" becomes manifest.

I will pause Winnicott here. "A child ... deprived of certain essential features of home life" (p. 123). Winnicott strongly believed that there were certain essentials of love and care that were absolutely necessary for the proper development of a child. He thought that their absence disadvantages a child to varying degrees, sometimes quite seriously. This theme occurs again and again in his writings. He even coined a term, the "deprived complex" which he suggests might describe the roots of the antisocial tendency in some youth (and might well be a term useful in our current mental health environment). He continues his thought:

Antisocial behaviour will be manifest at home or in a wider sphere. On account of *the antisocial tendency* the child may eventually need to be *deemed maladjusted*, and to receive treatment in *a hostel for maladjusted children*, or may be brought before the courts as beyond control. The child, now a *delinquent*, may then become a *probationer* under a court order, or may be sent to *an approved school*. If the home ceases to function in an important respect the child may be taken over by the Children's Committee (under the Children Act, 1948) and be *given "care and protection"*. If possible a foster home will be found. Should these measures fail the young adult may be said to have become a *psychopath* and may be sent by the courts to a *Borstal* or to prison. There may be an established tendency to repeat crimes for which we use the term *recidivism*.

All this makes no comment on the individual's psychiatric diagnosis.

So Winnicott goes down the trail of the serious consequences that can occur in the life of a child who demonstrates a "deprived complex" that is not adequately addressed at its beginnings.

The antisocial tendency is characterized by an element in it which compels *the environment to be important*. The patient through unconscious drives compels someone to attend to management. It is the task of the therapist to become involved in this patient's unconscious drive, and the work is done by the therapist in terms of management, tolerance, and understanding.

OK. So, the antisocially tending child pulls on his environment to step up and take notice of him. Winnicott uses the word "compels." This represents an active bid for parental attention and intervention. Should the child become involved in a therapy, the therapist has three tasks: management, tolerance, and understanding. He will elaborate each. He continues:

The antisocial tendency implies hope. Lack of hope is the basic feature of the deprived child who, of course, is not all the time being antisocial. In the period of hope the child manifests an antisocial tendency. This may be awkward for society, and for you if it is your bicycle that is stolen, but those who are not personally involved can see the hope that underlies the compulsion to steal. Perhaps one of the reasons why we tend to leave the therapy of the delinquent to others is that we dislike being stolen from?

Winnicott says two important things here: (1) that lack of hope characterizes the deprived child; and (2) that the child's subsequent period of antisocial behavior represents a surge of hope within the child—*hope for that of which he was formerly deprived.* The hope is expressed obliquely, via stealing and other such hard-to-tolerate (and hard-to-understand) behaviors, but the *hope* is at the core of these behaviors.

> The understanding that the antisocial act is an expression of hope is vital in the treatment of children who show the antisocial tendency. Over and over again one sees the moment of hope wasted or withered, because of mismanagement or intolerance. This is another way of saying that the treatment of the antisocial tendency is not psychoanalysis but management, a going to meet and match the moment of hope.

Winnicott observes that such "moment[s] of hope" are often decoded improperly by attending adults, who meet such moments with mismanagement or intolerance.

> There is direct relationship between the antisocial tendency and deprivation. This has long been known by specialists in the field but it is largely due to John Bowlby that there is now a widespread recognition of the relationship that exists between the antisocial tendency in individuals and emotional deprivation, typically in the period of late infancy and the early toddler stage, round about the age of one and two years.

Here Winnicott draws on the research of his colleague, John Bowlby, whose early studies on attachment and loss became the initial theoretical basis of modern attachment theory (Bowlby, 1969). Bowlby's (1944) retrospective study of 44 juvenile thieves posited a direct connection between their delinquency and significantly long separations from their primary caregivers during their first five years of life. Bowlby found that more than half of the group of juvenile thieves he studied had experienced significant separations (more than six months), compared with only two of 44 non-delinquents in the control group. He also found that fourteen of the 44 juvenile thieves displayed a certain "affectionlessness"—an inability to care about or feel affection for others. Of those 14, 12 had spent most of their early years in residential homes or hospitals and were not often visited by their families (Bowlby, 1944).

When there is an antisocial tendency *there has been a true deprivation* (not a simple privation); that is to say, there has been a loss of something good that has been positive in the child's experience up to a certain date,[1] and that has been withdrawn; the withdrawal has extended over a period of time longer than that over which the child can keep the memory of the experience alive. The comprehensive statement of deprivation is one that includes both the early and the late, both the pinpoint trauma and the sustained traumatic condition and also both the near normal and the clearly abnormal.

1 This idea seems to be implied in Bowlby's *Maternal Care and Mental Health*, page 47, where he compares his observations with those of others and suggests that the different results are explained according to the age of a child at the time of deprivation.

Winnicott speaks of deprivation—the loss of good care, connection, and safety—versus privation—the complete absence of such care. He explains that in the development of the antisocial tendency there was initial good care and connection that was, at some point, lost. The loss extended so long that it exceeded the child's capacity to keep the memory of good care and connection alive inside. Winnicott then adds his thoughts on the sources of variability with respect to deprivation: (1) timing—when in the course of a child's development the loss occurred; (2) whether the loss represented a "pinpoint" trauma or sustained conditions of trauma, and (3) whether the deprivation was near normal or clearly abnormal.

Note

In a statement in my own language of Klein's depressive position, I have tried to make clear the intimate relationship that exists between Klein's concept and Bowlby's emphasis on deprivation. Bowlby's three stages of the clinical reaction of a child of two years who goes to hospital can be given a theoretical formulation in terms of the gradual loss of hope because of the death of the internal object or introjected version of the external object that is lost.

Here Winnicott is again referring to Bowlby's work, this time to his 1952 film, "A two-year-old goes to hospital." In this piece, Bowlby observes three progressive stages of a child's distress in response to a short-term separation from her attachment figure: (1) protest; (2) despair; and (3) detachment (Bowlby & Robertson, 1952). Winnicott continues:

What can be further discussed is the relative importance of death of the internal object through anger and contact of "good objects" with hate products within the psyche, and ego maturity or immaturity in so far as this affects the capacity to keep alive a memory.

Bowlby needs Klein's intricate statement that is built round the understanding of melancholia, and that derives from Freud and Abraham; but it is also true that psychoanalysis needs Bowlby's emphasis on deprivation, if psychoanalysis is ever to come to terms with this special subject of the antisocial tendency.

So Winnicott is making a bridge between Klein's concepts of paranoid-schizoid and depressive positions and Bowlby's focus on deprivation. Winnicott is intimating that a child who experiences deprivation must cope with the intense feelings of anger inside, and the collision of good objects—that which has been introjected of the good-enough mother over time—and hate products—the primitive impulse to want to attack and destroy the bad object. Depending upon a child's ego maturity or immaturity at the time of the deprivation, the child may either be able to preserve the good object inside for a time, despite enduring the suffering of separation, or may use paranoid-schizoid defenses to bring about the destruction of the memory of the good object. In this way the internal world and external world are both important and are intertwined in a manner that can sometimes be lost in the psychoanalytic discourse.

There are always two trends in the antisocial tendency although the accent is sometimes more on one than on the other. One trend is represented typically in stealing, and the other in destructiveness. By *one* trend the child is looking for something, somewhere, and failing to find it seeks it elsewhere, when hopeful. By the *other* the child is seeking that amount of environmental stability which will stand the strain resulting from impulsive behaviour. This is a search for an environmental provision that has been lost, a human attitude which, because it can be relied on, gives freedom to the individual to move and to act and to get excited.

Winnicott is identifying two trends: (1) stealing—"I am object-seeking. I want *you* (attachment figure) for myself, but if I can't have *you*, then I will take something else"; and (2) destructiveness—"I want *from you a steady surviving of me*, of my attempts at destruction, so that I can use you, and rely on you in my own development." He returns to this theme in his "The use of an object" paper, wherein he asserts that it is only via surviving a child's attempts at destruction that an external maternal object can truly be discovered and used (Winnicott, 1969).

It is particularly because of the second of these trends that the child provokes total environmental reactions, as if seeking an ever-widening frame, a circle which had as its first example the mother's arms or the mother's body. One can discern a series—the mother's body, the mother's arms, the parental relationship, the home, the family including cousins and near relations, the school, the locality with its police-stations, the country with its laws.

The child looks first to the original environment for the survival of the child's destructiveness. Failing that, he expands the search to an ever-widening circle—the home, followed by the family, the extended family, the school, the community, and finally, the law.

In examining the near-normal and (in terms of individual development) the early roots of the antisocial tendency I wish to keep in mind all the time these two trends: object-seeking and destruction.

These two trends—object-seeking (the affiliative, libidinal trend), and aggression (the trend more related to "destruction" of the object (all the time, hoping that the object survives…)—will be anchor points of Winnicott's thoughts about the antisocial tendency.

Stealing

Stealing is at the centre of the antisocial tendency, with the associated lying. The child who steals an object is not looking for *the object stolen but seeks the mother over whom he or she has rights.* These rights derive from the fact that (from the child's point of view) the mother was created by the child. The mother met the child's primary creativity, and so became the object that the child was ready to find. (The child could not have created the mother; also the mother's meaning for the child depends on the child's creativity.)

Here Winnicott is setting the conceptual table a bit. He is speaking about the early developmental period wherein an infant has no real conception of a world outside of himself. Given that, when he has a need that is met (magic-ally), he feels that he "created" the breast or the need-meeting experience. At the beginning, the child occupies an omnipotent world over which he is the sole proprietor. At its earliest moments, then, the child feels that he created the mother, and therefore has rights to her and over her. So, the child who steals is not really wanting the object he steals, but rather he seeks the mother over whom he has inalienable rights.

Winnicott continues:

> Is it possible to join up the two trends, the stealing and the destruction, the object-seeking and that which provokes, the libidinal and the aggressive compulsions? I suggest that the union of the two trends is in the child and that it represents *a tendency towards self-cure*, cure of a de-fusion of instincts.

OK. This discussion of the two trends of libidinal (object-seeking) and aggressive compulsions requires a bit of background in Winnicott's thoughts on aggression. (These appear throughout his writings, but especially in his paper entitled "Aggression in relation to emotional development" (Winnicott, 1950),

At origin, Winnicott felt that aggression is instinctual activity. Winnicott believes that aggression starts in the womb, initially as motility. As the infant moves out of the womb, he continues to exercise motility, at first through his bodily movements and his oral instincts. A baby thrashes with his arms and chews the nipple with his lips and gums. Winnicott felt that in its initial phases, the baby's primitive love impulse has a "destructive by chance" quality, and that the infant, at first, experiences no intention associated with these activities because of the infant's initial ego immaturity.

Winnicott felt that aggression is a natural part of the primitive expression of love, and that in health, oral eroticism or "mouth love"— also referred to as the libidinal instinct—gathered a large portion of the infant's motility potential/aggression to itself. In other words, a certain percentage of the motility potential became fused with the erotic potential. He felt that the part of the motility potential *not* fused with the erotic potential was left over, and needed to look for and find opposition—something to push against. He felt that each baby should be allowed to pour as much as possible of primitive motility into his primitive love (id) experiences, and that through this motility, two things happened: (1) the environment was constantly discovered and rediscovered; and (2) the experience came to be felt as *real*.

OK, now let's re-capture the question that Winnicott just raised:

> Is it possible to join up the two trends, the stealing and the destruction, the object-seeking and that which provokes, the libidinal and the aggressive compulsions? I suggest that the union of the two trends is in the child and that it represents *a tendency towards self-cure*, cure of a de-fusion of instincts.

So Winnicott is counterpoising love and motility, libidinal and aggressive instincts, object-seeking and "that which provokes." (These are all equivalent dichotomies, and Winnicott will use these various terms interchangeably.) He is wondering if these seemingly opposite trends—the movement toward (stealing) and the movement against (destruction)—might in fact belong somehow developmentally intertwined. He moves on to address this question.

> When there is at the time of the original deprivation some fusion of aggressive (or motility) roots with the libidinal the child claims the mother by a mixture of stealing and hurting and messing, according to the specific details of that child's emotional developmental state.

OK. Let's pause him. He is saying that at the beginning (in health), there is a fusion between the aggressive aspect of the infant and the libidinal (object-seeking) aspect. With these two "roots" intertwined, the child "claims" the mother via his unbridled access to her provisions (aka "stealing"), but also by hurting and messing and being a general nuisance. This is good and necessary. But now, what happens when deprivation in some way disturbs this process? He will get to this, but first he wants to lay out another scenario.

In health, contact with the environment, initiated by/"created by" the infant, is an experience of the individual which builds up the infant from the core of the incipient self outward. This contrasts with the situation where the mother/environment *impinges* on the infant, and contact devolves into a series of reactions to impingements. This leads to less fusion between the object-seeking and aggressive roots in the child. OK. Now Winnicott continues.

> When there is less fusion the child's objectseeking and aggression are more separated off from each other, and there is a greater degree of dissociation in the child.

Pause. If the ultimate developmental agenda for a child is more and more integration, this separation of object-seeking and aggression is problematic in ways that will exhibit themselves as the child grows older. Less fusion means more aggression un-fused with love instincts.

> This leads to the proposition that *the nuisance value of the antisocial child is an essential feature*, and is also, at its best, *a favourable feature* indicating again a potentiality for recovery of lost fusion of the libidinal and motility drives.

Wow. So Winnicott just put a very positive spin on the antisocial child's nuisance activities. He's framing them as a bid for the restoring of the fusion between the libidinal/love and aggressive/motility drives. Let's see where he goes with this.

> In ordinary infant care the mother is constantly dealing with the nuisance value of her infant. For instance, a baby commonly passes water on the mother's lap while feeding at the breast. At a later date this appears as a momentary regression in sleep or at the moment of waking and bed-wetting results. Any exaggeration of the nuisance value of an infant may indicate the existence of a degree of deprivation and antisocial tendency.
>
> The manifestation of the antisocial tendency includes stealing and lying, incontinence and the making of a mess generally. Although each symptom has its specific meaning and value, the common factor for my purpose in my attempt to describe the antisocial tendency is *the nuisance value of the symptoms.* This nuisance value is exploited by the child, and is not a chance affair. Much of the motivation is unconscious, but not necessarily all.

OK. So the common feature in stealing, lying, bedwetting and generally making a mess is their nuisance value. And their nuisance value is their point. OK. So far, so good. But if their nuisance value is the point, then what is the point? Winnicott will take us to the punchline eventually, but he won't get to it right away, so I will tip us off to where he's headed. If the nuisance child is presented with a family environment which endures his aggression via stealing, bedwetting, truancy, messiness, and being generally annoying, *the environment—tested and retested—may be found to be stable and reliable enough to enable the child to use it, and ultimately, to love the enduring parents behind it.* He'll elaborate this more as he continues.

> ### First signs of antisocial tendency
>
> I suggest that the first signs of deprivation are so common that they pass for normal; take for example the imperious behaviour which most parents meet with a mixture of submission and reaction. *This is not infantile omnipotence*, which is a matter of psychic reality, not of behaviour.

Infants are necessarily omnipotent. It's where they start. It's their psychic envelope at first. Imperiousness in an older child is one of the first signs of antisocial behavior.

He will now talk at length between infantile greed, which is an infantile imperative, and greediness in an older child.

> A very common antisocial symptom is greediness, with the closely related inhibition of appetite. If we study greediness we shall find the deprived complex. In other words, if an infant is greedy there is some degree of deprivation and some compulsion towards seeking for a therapy in respect of this deprivation through the environment. The fact that the mother is herself willing to cater for the infant's greediness makes for therapeutic success in the vast majority of cases in which this compulsion can be observed.

Winnicott believed that a symptom and its opposite were expressions of the same thing, so greediness is closely related, in his thinking, to *inhibition* of appetite. He further felt that greediness in a child was inevitably linked to some feeling of deprivation in the child—some feeling that a good-enough provision has been lost or taken away. He felt that a greedy child was seeking "therapy" from the maternal environment with respect to his current deprived state. A mother who is responsive to and gratifying of this greediness, in Winnicott's view, performs effective remedial "therapy."

> Greediness in an infant is not the same as greed. The word greed is used in the theoretical statement of the tremendous instinctual claims that an infant makes on the mother at the beginning, that is to say, at the time when the infant is only starting to allow the mother a separate existence, at the first acceptance of the Reality Principle.

In Winnicott's thinking, greed is different from greediness. Greed is primary to the newborn infant. It aims at extracting all of the goodness that can be had from the object. Greed, to Winnicott, is "the primitive love impulse, the thing which we are frightened to own up to but which is basic to our natures" (1945). He thought greed was infused with life, appetite, and excitement (1936), and that there could be problems for the young child which can result from inhibition of greed, including inhibitions in spontaneity, play, and creativity (1941).

> In parenthesis, it is sometimes said that a mother must fail in her adaptation to her infant's needs. Is this not a mistaken idea based on a consideration of id needs and a neglect of the needs of the ego? A mother must fail in satisfying instinctual demands, but she may completely succeed in not "letting the infant down", *in catering for ego needs*, until such a time as the infant may have an introjected ego-supportive mother, and may be old enough to maintain this introjection in spite of failures of ego support in the actual environment.

Winnicott felt that a mother must at first be perfectly attuned to her infant's needs, only attenuating this attunement as the infant releases her. In parenthesis, he is arguing a bit with Freud, who felt that id preceded ego in the developmental trajectory. Winnicott felt that neither was there at birth, and that the infant's preeminent developmental task was to accrue enough of an integrated ego from introjecting mother's ego support to be able to even experience an id and id demands.

> The (pre-ruth) primitive love impulse is not the same as ruthless greediness. In the process of the development of an infant the primitive love impulse and greediness are separated by the mother's adaptation. The mother necessarily fails to maintain a high degree of adaptation to id needs and to some extent therefore every infant may be deprived, but is able to get the mother to cure this sub-deprived state by her meeting the greediness and messiness, etc., these being symptoms of deprivation. The greediness is part of the infant's compulsion to seek for a cure from the mother who caused the deprivation. This greediness is antisocial; it is the precursor of stealing, and it can be met and cured by the mother's therapeutic adaptation, so easily mistaken for spoiling. It should be said, however, that whatever the mother does, this does not annul the fact that the mother first failed in her adaptation to her infant's ego needs. The mother is usually able to meet the compulsive claims of the infant, and so to do a successful *therapy* of the deprived complex which is near its point of origin. She gets near to a cure because she enables the infant's hate to be expressed while she, the therapist, is in fact the depriving mother.

Winnicott believed that a newborn accessed his mother's provisions without any sense of her actual presence or of the cost to her of her ministrations. The mother provides an environment for the infant outside of the infant's awareness. The mother's job during this initial time is to adapt herself fully to infant need, to willingly allow his illusion of his own omnipotence and his sense that he "created" all that happened to him. Winnicott speaks of this time as the "pre-ruth" era, wherein the infant's primitive love impulses might draw upon the mother ruthlessly—without consciousness of her contribution to him. During this time, the infant would have no need for greediness due to the mother's attuned adaptation.

As the infant developed more capacity and more maturity of his incipient ego, he would signal to the mother his increased capacities to wait just a little bit for her to come to his aid. This developmental step would allow the mother to de-adapt, by degrees, to the infant's cries and gestures. With enough ego development, there is the initiation of an id and id desires in the infant. Winnicott says that "[t]he mother necessarily fails to maintain a high degree of adaptation to id needs" (p. 126). He is talking about this necessary process of de-adaptation to need that must take place so that the infant can develop into a self with an inside separate from his outside. But, Winnicott notes, "to some extent therefore every infant may be deprived" (p. 127). But the infant is able to act on his own behalf—to seek for a cure for this deprivation from his mother via his greediness: "[The infant] is able to get the mother to cure this sub-deprived state by her meeting the greediness and messiness" (p. 127). Winnicott is clear that the infant's sense of deprivation is indeed a failure of the timing of the de-adaptation by the mother, but that "it can be met and cured by the mother's therapeutic adaptation" (p. 127). Winnicott uses the metaphor of the mother becoming a therapist to their child, because she is in the position of a therapist, having to indulge the child's compulsive greediness in order for a cure to be effected. He adds that this therapeutic re-adaptation is "easily mistaken for spoiling" (p. 127), but is necessary for a cure and preventative of further exhibitions of the antisocial tendency.

> It will be noted that whereas the infant is under no obligation to the mother in respect of her meeting the primitive love impulse, there is some feeling of obligation as the result of the mother's therapy, that is to say her willingness to meet the claims arising out of frustration, claims that begin to have a nuisance value. Therapy by the mother may cure, but this is not mother-love.

"Therapy" by the mother in response to the infant's greediness is not mother-love simply because it is only necessary when mother-love has failed to be available to the infant at the time of relative dependence.

> This way of looking at the mother's indulgence of her infant involves a more complex statement of mothering than is usually acceptable. Mother-love is often thought of in terms of this indulgence, which in fact is a *therapy in respect of a failure of mother-love*. It is a therapy, a second chance given to mothers who cannot always be expected to succeed in their initial most delicate task of primary love. If a mother does this therapy as a reaction formation arising out of her own complexes, then what she does is called spoiling. In so far as she is able to do it because she sees the necessity for the child's claims to be met, and for the child's compulsive greediness to be indulged, then it is a therapy that is usually successful. Not only the mother, but the father, and indeed the family, may be involved. She gets near to a cure because she enables the infant's hate to be expressed while she, the therapist, is in fact the depriving mother.

Winnicott continues with his metaphor of the mother, and perhaps the father and the family, as therapist(s). If a mother has failed in the task of primary love—consistent, responsive, timely, attuned care to her early infant—then she has a second chance via indulging the child's compulsive greediness as it comes up. This process will differ from the earlier gratifications of the infant because it will include the infant's expressions of hate. If, however, she does this task of therapeutic indulgence as a reaction formation—as a conscious enacting of the opposite of what she feels toward the child—then this approach will not work to set the infant aright, because then, it will lose some of its true attunement, and more accurately be described as spoiling the infant.

> Clinically, there is an awkward borderline between the mother's therapy which is successful and that which is unsuccessful. Often we watch a mother spoiling an infant and yet this therapy will not be successful, the initial deprivation having been too severe for "mending by first intention" (to borrow a term from the surgery of wounds).

"Mending by first intention" is the complete restoration of the original tissue that occurs in a surgical incision.

Now Winnicott will leave his discussion of greed and greediness and move on to messiness, bedwetting, destructiveness, truancy, and so on.

> Just as greediness may be a manifestation of the reaction to deprivation and of a antisocial tendency, so may messiness and wetting and compulsive destructiveness. All these manifestations are closely interrelated. In bed-wetting, which is so common a complaint, the accent is on regression at the moment of the dream or on the antisocial compulsion to claim the right to wet on mother's body.

Winnicott is bringing us a widened swathe of symptoms that may signal early deprivation: bedwetting, messiness, compulsive destructiveness.

> In a more complete study of stealing I would need to refer to the compulsion to go out and buy something, which is a common manifestation of the antisocial tendency that we meet in our psycho-analytic patients. It is possible to do a long and interesting analysis of a patient without affecting this sort of symptom, which belongs not to the patient's neurotic or psychotic defences but which does belong to the antisocial tendency, that which is a reaction to deprivation of a special kind and that took place at a special time. From this it will be clear that birthday presents and pocket money absorb some of the antisocial tendency that is to be normally expected.

> In the same category as the shopping expedition we find, clinically, a "going out", without aim, *truancy*, a centrifugal tendency that replaces the centripetal gesture which is implicit in thieving.

So, Winnicott is also including compulsive shopping, going out without aim, and truancy in the same category as stealing. They represent a "centrifugal," and, in that way, opposite symptom from thieving, which is centripetal, but Winnicott sees them as coming from the same root—deprivation—an original good experience that was lost.

The original loss

There is one special point that I wish to make. At the basis of the antisocial tendency is a good early experience that has been lost. Surely, *it is an essential feature that the infant has reached to a capacity to perceive that the cause of the disaster lies in an environmental failure.* Correct knowledge that the cause of the depression or disintegration is an external one, and not an internal one, is responsible for the personality distortion and for the urge to seek for a cure by new environmental provision. The state of ego maturity enabling perception of this kind determines the development of an antisocial tendency instead of a psychotic illness. A great number of antisocial compulsions present and become successfully treated in the early stages by the parents. Antisocial children, however, are constantly pressing for this cure by environmental provision (unconsciously, or by unconscious motivation) but are unable to make use of it.

This is worth repeating: "At the basis of the antisocial tendency is a good early experience that has been lost" (p. 129). Winnicott is saying that the antisocial tendency signals that it comes from a time after the ego is organized enough to perceive that the deprivation is coming from a failure of the environment—an environment which he knows *should* be caring for him. This knowledge makes the child seek a cure from the source of the failure: the (parental) environment. If the failure had come before the ego had a certain level of organization, the result would have been a psychotic illness.

> It would appear that the time of the original deprivation is during the period when in the infant or small child the ego is in process of achieving fusion of the libidinal and aggressive (or motility) id roots.

Remember that Winnicott believes that aggression starts in the womb, initially as motility, and that aggression is a natural part of the primitive expression of love. He felt that in health, oral eroticism—the libidinal instinct—gathered a large portion of the infant's aggression to itself, so that a certain part of the aggression potential became fused with the erotic potential. Ok, so—if the original deprivation came at a time when the libidinal and the aggressive instincts were meant to be fusing, then what happens when they don't fuse adequately?

He posits an answer in terms of the child's bid for self-cure:

> In the hopeful moment the child:
>   Perceives a new setting that has some elements of reliability.

This reliability would have been what failed initially.

> Experiences a drive that could be called object-seeking.

Experiencing the de-fused object-seeking part of the double helix.

> Recognizes the fact that ruthlessness is about to become a feature and so stirs up the immediate environment in an effort to make it alert to danger, and organized to tolerate nuisance.

Experiences the de-fused aggressive part of the double helix, and helps the environment arm up for it.

> If the situation holds, the environment must be tested and retested in its capacity to stand the aggression, to prevent or repair the destruction, to tolerate the nuisance, to recognize the positive element in the antisocial tendency, to provide and preserve the object that is to be sought and found.

The environment, so targeted in the hopeful moment by the child, must withstand the aggression in order to provide and preserve the libidinal object that is being sought.

> In a favourable case, when there is not too much madness or unconscious compulsion or paranoid organization, etc., the favourable conditions may

> in the course of time enable the child to find and love a person, instead of continuing the search through laying claims on substitute objects that had lost their symbolic value.

If the child is presented with a family environment which endures his aggression via stealing, bedwetting, truancy, messiness, and being a general nuisance, the environment, tested and retested, may be found to be stable and reliable enough to enable the child to use it, and ultimately, to love the enduring parents behind it.

> In the next stage the child needs to be able to experience despair in a relationship, instead of hope alone. Beyond this is the real possibility of a life for the child. When the wardens and staff of a hostel carry a child through all the processes *they have done a therapy that is surely comparable to analytic work.*

OK. Winnicott throws in the element of despair in relationship here. Every, any relationship has both hopeful and discouraging elements. All real relationships include both love and hate.

> Commonly, parents do this complete job with one of their own children. But many parents who are well able to bring up normal children are not able to succeed with one of their children who happens to manifest an antisocial tendency.
>   In this statement I have deliberately omitted references to the relationship of the antisocial tendency to:
>
> Acting out.
> Masturbation.
> Pathological super-ego, unconscious guilt.
> Stages of libidinal development.
> Repetition compulsion.
> Regression to pre-concern.
> Paranoid defence.
> Sex-linkage in respect of symptomatology.

Winnicott remains enigmatic is this last statement. He may be saying that the antisocial tendency includes many, but not all, elements of psychopathology.

Treatment

Briefly, the treatment of the antisocial tendency is not psychoanalysis. It is the provision of child care which can be rediscovered by the child, and into which the child can experiment again with the id impulses, and which can be tested. It is the stability of the new environmental provision which gives the therapeutics. Id impulses must be experienced, if they are to make sense, in a framework of ego relatedness, and when the patient is a deprived child ego relatedness must derive support from the therapist's side of the relationship. According to the theory put forward in this paper it is the environment that must give new opportunity for ego relatedness since the child has perceived that it was an environmental failure in ego support that originally led to the antisocial tendency.

OK. So, in summary, Winnicott says that the treatment of the antisocial tendency is definitely not psychoanalysis. It is affirmatively the provision of child care. This child care must allow the child to experiment again with id impulses. It must be testably stable and reliable. If the venue in which this is to take place is the therapeutic relationship, then that relationship must be stable, and it must be ego-related, because the adult environment must give to the child what was missing in his early history.

If the child is in analysis, the analyst must either allow the weight of the transference to develop outside the analysis, or else must expect the anti-social tendency to develop full strength in the analytic situation, and must be prepared to bear the brunt.

If the child is in therapy, the therapist must expect the antisocial tendency to emerge in the therapy, and must be prepared to bear the brunt of it.

6   Primary maternal preoccupation

(1956)

Winnicott, D. W. (1956). Primary maternal preoccupation. In *Through paediatrics to psycho-analysis: Collected papers* (pp. 300–305). Levittown, PA: Brunner Mazel, 1992.

In this paper, Winnicott introduces us to the special psychological state that a pregnant mother enters prenatally, and sustains approximately for the first month postnatally. He studies this as both a pediatrician and psychoanalyst, and blends these two vantage points in this paper. Winnicott observes that it takes this state of "primary maternal preoccupation" to allow a mother to feel her way into the infant's place and so to meet his/her needs. As those needs are met and an infant is allowed to be in his/her "going-on-being" place, the infant begins to stretch beyond bodily experiences, and to "imaginatively elaborate" those experiences, ever-so-gradually beginning to become a more integrated "I." He is straightforward about what happens to those who do not experience this good-enough environment. They do not feel real to themselves. They instead feel a deep sense of futility. Throughout the paper, he uses the words "mother" and "maternal," for which we might legitimately substitute the gender-neutral term, "primary caregiver."

He begins:

> This contribution is stimulated by the discussion published in the *Psychoanalytic Study of the Child*, Volume IX, under the heading: "Problems of Infantile Neurosis". The various contributions from Miss Freud in this discussion add up to an important statement of present-day psycho-analytic theory as it relates to the very early stages of infantile life, and of the establishment of personality.

Winnicott writes in the context of the intellectual environment created by Freud and which he currently co-occupies with Anna Freud and Melanie Klein, both child therapists and major contributors to psychoanalytic understandings of child development. He will also draw on the work of Heinz Hartmann in this paper.

> I wish to develop the theme of the very early infant–mother relationship, a theme that is of maximal importance at the beginning, and that only gradually takes second place to that of the infant as an independent being.
>
> It is necessary for me first to support what Miss Freud says under the heading "Current Misconceptions". "Disappointments and frustrations are inseparable from the mother–child relationship … To put the blame for the infantile neurosis on the mother's shortcomings in the oral phase is no more than a facile and misleading generalization. Analysis has to probe further and deeper in its search for the causation of neurosis." In these words Miss Freud expresses a view held by psycho-analysts generally.

So Winnicott begins by naming Anna Freud's position, which is to attempt to limit the blaming of the development of infantile neurosis on the early maternal environment. Infantile neurosis refers to chronic distress in the developing child in the form of symptoms such as depression, anxiety, obsessive behaviors, and so on, during what Freud would refer to as the oral phase.

He continues:

> In spite of this we may gain much by taking the mother's position into account. There is such a thing as an environment that is not good enough, and which distorts infant development, just as there can be a good enough environment, one that enables the infant to reach, at each stage, the appropriate innate satisfactions and anxieties and conflicts.

Heinz Hartmann (1939) had coined the term "average expectable environment" to denote the prevalent view that infants are broadly equipped to adapt to the demands of the environment into which they are born. Hartmann felt that infants are inherently able to fit into a range of physical and psychological environments, and that they could flourish in any environment that was responsive enough to the child's psychological needs (Palombo et al., 2010). Winnicott takes issue with this view in this paper, arguing that there are certain *essentials* that must be there in the very beginning in order for development to proceed normally.

> Miss Freud has reminded us that we may think of pregenital patterning in terms of two people joined to achieve what for brevity's sake one might call "homeostatic equilibrium" (Mahler, 1954). The same thing is referred to under the term "symbiotic relationship". It is often stated that the mother of an infant becomes biologically conditioned for her job of special orientation to the needs of her child. In more ordinary language there is found to be an identification—conscious but also deeply unconscious—which the mother makes with her infant.

OK. Winnicott is positioning his case in the context of what were the current thought currents about mothers and infants. The language of the day suggested that there was a certain automaticity pre-programmed by biology that in some way almost guaranteed an "average expectable environment."

> I think that these various concepts need joining together and the study of the mother needs to be rescued from the purely biological. The term symbiosis takes us no further than to compare the relationship of the mother and the infant with other examples in animal and plant life—physical interdependence. The words homeostatic equilibrium again avoid some of the fine points which appear before our eyes if we look at this relationship with the care it deserves.
>
> We are concerned with the very great psychological differences between, on the one hand, the mother's identification with the infant and, on the other, the infant's dependence on the mother; the latter does not involve identification, identification being a complex state of affairs inapplicable to the early stages of infancy.

OK. So the symbiotic relationship that Anna Freud is addressing requires something more from the mother than mere biology leading to homeostatic equilibrium. According to Winnicott, it requires *identification* with the infant on the part of the mother. He is also clear that the relationship is a psychologically uneven one—that it is not accurately described by the concept of interdependence because it is the infant, not the mother, who is wholly dependent.

> Miss Freud shows that we have gone far beyond that awkward stage in psycho-analytic theory in which we spoke as if life started for the infant with the oral instinctual experience. We are now engaged in the study of early development and of the early self which, if development has gone far enough, can be strengthened instead of disrupted by id experiences.

The ego had been seen by Sigmund Freud as drawing its energy from the instinctual experiences of the id, which Freud believed existed from the very start. He felt that id experiences of frustration and conflict caused the ego to have to grow and develop in order to counter the impulses of the id. Here Winnicott is asserting that instinctual experience—id experience—can be a strengthening instead of a disrupting influence—can be a positive force in the development of the early self.

> Miss Freud says, developing the theme of Freud's term "anaclitic": "the relationship to the mother, although the first to another human being, is not the infant's first relationship to the environment. What precedes it is an earlier phase in which not the object world but the body needs and their satisfaction or frustration play the decisive part."

Let's first define "anaclitic": an adjective describing relationships that are characterized by the strong dependence of one person on another. Winnicott agrees with Anna Freud that there is an early phase of development wherein the infant's bodily needs are the main issue.

> Incidentally I feel that the introduction of the word "need" instead of "desire" has been very important in our theorizing, but I wish Miss Freud had not used the words "satisfaction" and "frustration" here; a need is either met or not met, and the effect is not the same as that of satisfaction and frustration of id impulse.

OK. So Winnicott is re-drawing the playing field. Needs are either met or not met, period. He's suggesting that "satisfaction" and "frustration" are not relevant to the earliest phases of infancy. He does not say this, but it's a ready inference to be made at this point. Needs that are unmet at the earliest phase cause some kind of developmental distortion in the infant, rather than mere momentary frustration.

He continues:

> I can bring Greenacre's reference (1954) to what she names the "lulling" type of rhythmic pleasures. Here we find an example of need that is met or not met, but it would be a distortion to say that the infant who is not lulled reacts as to a frustration. Certainly there is not anger so much as some kind of distortion of development at an early phase.

He's suggesting here that the early phase of infancy cannot be described with full-bodied emotional words like frustration, anger, or satisfaction. It's more simple than that. Ministrations are there or not there. Needs are met or not met. And if not met, some kind of distortion of development takes place. He'll elaborate what he means by distortion of development as he proceeds.

He gathers it up:

Be that as it may, a further study of the function of the mother at the earliest phase seems to me to be overdue, and I wish to gather together the various hints and put forward a proposition for discussion.

Maternal preoccupation

It is my thesis that in the earliest phase we are dealing with a very special state of the mother, a psychological condition which deserves a name, such as *Primary Maternal Preoccupation*. I suggest that sufficient tribute has not yet been paid in our literature, or perhaps *anywhere*, to a very special psychiatric condition of the mother, of which I would say the following things:

It gradually develops and becomes a state of heightened sensitivity during, and especially towards the end of, the pregnancy.
It lasts for a few weeks after the birth of the child.
It is not easily remembered by mothers once they have recovered from it.
I would go further and say that the memory mothers have of this state tends to become repressed.

OK. He's given a name and characteristics to this state of heightened maternal sensitivity toward the end of pregnancy and in the beginning weeks of the life of the infant: primary maternal preoccupation. He continues:

This organized state (that would be an illness were it not for the fact of the pregnancy) could be compared with a withdrawn state, or a dissociated state, or a fugue, or even with a disturbance at a deeper level such as a schizoid episode in which some aspect of the personality takes over temporarily. I would like to find a good name for this condition and to put it forward as something to be taken into account in all references to the earliest phase of infant life. I do not believe that it is possible to understand the functioning of the mother at the very beginning of the infant's life without seeing that she must be able to reach this state of heightened sensitivity, almost an illness, and to recover from it. (I bring in the word "illness" because a woman must be healthy in order both to develop this state and to recover from it as the infant releases her. If the infant should die, the mother's state suddenly shows up as illness. The mother takes this risk.)

He describes this state of heightened maternal sensitivity to her infant as akin to a psychological illness, except that she recovers from it in response to the infant's "releasing" her. Although he is comparing it to an illness, it is not an illness. He believes that this state is crucial to the infant's "undistorted" development.

> I have implied this in the term "devoted" in the words "ordinary devoted mother" (Winnicott, 1949). There are certainly many women who are good mothers in every other way and who are capable of a rich and fruitful life but who are not able to achieve this "normal illness" which enables them to adapt delicately and sensitively to the infant's needs at the very beginning; or they achieve it with one child but not with another. Such women are not able to become preoccupied with their own infant to the exclusion of other interests, in the way that is normal and temporary. It may be supposed that there is a "flight to sanity" in some of these people. Some of them certainly have very big alternative concerns which they do not readily abandon or they may not be able to allow this abandonment until they have had their first babies. When a woman has a strong male identification she finds this part of her mothering function most difficult to achieve, and repressed penis envy leaves but little room for primary maternal preoccupation.

OK, so now Winnicott is defining more specifically what primary maternal preoccupation is: the capacity "to adapt delicately and sensitively to the infant's needs," and "to become preoccupied with their own infant to the exclusion of other interests." He is also saying that not everyone achieves this state, and he enumerates some of the causes that prevent some mothers from achieving this state. (We might think in different terms today about Winnicott's reference to women who have a "strong male identification." He was writing in 1956, and was still influenced by Freud's concept of penis envy. It was, however, part of Winnicott's thinking that the primary issue was attunement to the baby, whether it came from the birth mother, the adoptive mother, the father, the grandparent, etc.). So, he uses the words "mother" and "maternal," for which we might legitimately substitute "primary caregiver."

> In practice the result is that such women, having produced a child, but having missed the boat at the earliest stage, are faced with the task of making up for what has been missed. They have a long period in which they must closely adapt to their growing child's needs, and it is not certain that they can succeed in mending the early distortion. Instead of taking for granted the good effect of an early and temporary preoccupation they

> are caught up in the child's need for therapy, that is to say, for a prolonged period of adaptation to need, or spoiling. They do therapy instead of being parents.

Here Winnicott hints at the consequences that occur when a mother cannot achieve this primary maternal preoccupation: there is "early distortion" and the subsequent need of the child for a prolonged period of adaptation to need. He quips that mothers who have not been able to achieve this state in the first few weeks of an infant's life have to "pay for it" by becoming like the child's "therapist"—meaning, adapting carefully to his every need—for a very long time, instead of simply being his/her parent.

> The same phenomenon is referred to by Kanner (1943), Loretta Bender (1947) and others who have attempted to describe the type of mother who is liable to produce an "autistic child" (Creak, 1951; Mahler, 1954).

Modern research on autism has ruled out parent care as a cause of autism. Research suggests that autism develops from a combination of genetic and non-genetic, or environmental, influences, but researchers have not yet identified causal factors.

Winnicott continues:

> It is possible to make a comparison here between the mother's task in making up for her past incapacity and that of society attempting (sometimes successfully) to bring round a deprived child from an antisocial state towards a social identification. This work of the mother (or of society) proves a great strain because it does not come naturally. The task in hand properly belongs to an earlier date, in this case to the time when the infant was only beginning to exist as an individual.
>
> If this thesis of the normal mother's special state and her recovery from it be acceptable, then we can examine more closely the infant's corresponding state.

Again, Winnicott speaks to consequences that can occur when the initial primary maternal preoccupation is not achieved. Sometimes society has to deal with this lack of sensitive care in the first weeks of life (and perhaps beyond). He speaks of the task of bringing round a "deprived" child from an antisocial or delinquent or acting-out state toward a more pro-social identification. He is straightforward in his language: "The task in hand properly belongs to an earlier date"—to the time when the infant "was only beginning to exist as an individual." Otherwise, it may take much effort to back-fill what should have happened at the very beginning life stage.

He moves on to a description of the postnatal infant:

> The infant has
> A constitution.
> Innate developmental tendencies ("conflict-free area in ego").
> Motility and sensitivity.
> Instincts, themselves involved in the developmental tendency, with changing zone-dominance.

OK. Here he has a list of the starting point for an infant. The first item on his list of what an infant has to begin with is easy to understand. An infant starts with a constitution.

Next on the list is "innate developmental tendencies ('conflict-free area in ego')." This one requires some explanation. "Innate developmental tendencies" include most prominently in Winnicott's thinking the overall tendency toward integration. But here he is less specific. He just says there are developmental tendencies—the tendency to develop over time. But he then qualifies this with: ("conflict-free area in ego"). What does this refer to? Here Winnicott is drawing both on Freud's structural model (id, ego, superego) and Hartmann's revision of Freud's model. Hartmann, the putative father of Ego Psychology, believed, in contrast to Freud, that the ego did not develop *from* the id, but that the id and the ego develop simultaneously from the beginning, and that they function independently, yet in synchrony. Hartmann (1964) also argued that the ego is not limited to its role in conflict resolution (i.e., warding off id impulses and avoiding the guilt and self-punishment meted out by the superego). He thought instead that the healthy ego included an entire sphere of ego functions that were independent of mental conflict. Examples of ego-operations within this conflict-free sphere were capacities like intelligence, cognition, memory, planning, and so on. He felt that the ego could operate to find non-conflictual ways to gratify impulses, and that this was made possible by the opportunities afforded by the person's social/relational context.

OK. So we now know that Winnicott felt that there was an incipient ego from the very start. Not yet developed, but there to develop.

Next on the list is "motility"—an infant moves arms, legs, head, trunk—has muscles that move around. S/he also has "sensitivity"—can feel touch and pressure and pain and warmth and coldness and gravity, and has sensitivities across the other senses of hearing and sight and smell and taste.

Last on his list is "instincts." He reminds us that instincts themselves have a developmental tendency, with changing zone-dominance. All right, so, instincts originate from the somatic organization. They are the source of our bodily needs, wants, desires, and impulses. He does not use the word "id," which has more complex associations, but includes changing zone-dominance, which is an allusion to Freud's psychosexual stages of development: oral, followed by anal, and then by genital and finally by phallic.

OK. So now he moves a bit further:

> The mother who develops this state that I have called "primary maternal preoccupation" provides a setting for the infant's constitution to begin to make itself evident, for the developmental tendencies to start to unfold, and for the infant to experience spontaneous movement and become the owner of the sensations that are appropriate to this early phase of life. The instinctual life need not be referred to here because what I am discussing begins before the establishment of instinct patterns.

In this paragraph he loops backward to the elements of an infant that he has just listed. He says that this state of special sensitivity on the part of the mother "provides a setting" in which three things occur:

1. The infant's constitution begins to make itself evident.
2. The infant's "developmental tendencies" begin to unfold.
3. The infant can begin to experience spontaneous movement (motility) and to "become the owner of" his sensations and sensitivities. He is not right away the owner of his sensations and sensitivities. This takes the provision of this special setting of primary maternal preoccupation.

He leaves instincts off the list because instinct patterns are established later in development—not in these first few weeks.

> I have tried to describe this in my own language, saying that if the mother provides a good enough adaptation to need, the infant's own line of life is disturbed very little by reactions to impingement. (Naturally, it is the reactions to impingement that count, not the impingements themselves.) Maternal failures produce phases of reaction to impingement and these reactions interrupt the "going on being" of the infant. An excess of this reacting produces not frustration but a threat of annihilation. This in my view is a very real primitive anxiety, long antedating any anxiety that includes the word death in its description.

OK. Winnicott is introducing us here to some important Winnicottian concepts and language. First, the "going on being" of the infant. Winnicott will use this evocative phrase in other papers. It means exactly what it says— the uninterrupted being of a little one. This is the state the little newborn needs in order to progress seamlessly to further developmental steps. Second, he introduces "reactions to impingements." Anything that interrupts the going on being of the baby is an impingement to him/her. If a caregiver's care is good enough, there will be very few impingements, but if there is an excess of these impingements, then it causes a *dire* state in the infant. This state is not frustration, which would be beyond the newborn's capacity to feel as frustration. It is instead, in Winnicott's words, the *threat of annihilation*—the threat to cease to exist, to disappear. This is one of the most—if not the most—dreadful anxieties we can experience as humans. It's more profound even than the feeling that one may be imminently facing death; it is the threat of being reduced to nothing, apprehended at a time before one's thinking apparatus has words with which to think about it. It is a state of *sheer terror* that *disrupts the developmental process of the infant*. Winnicott will call this in other works an "unthinkable anxiety."

He continues:

> In other words, the basis for ego establishment is the sufficiency of "going on being", uncut by reactions to impingement. A sufficiency of "going on being" is only possible at the beginning if the mother is in this state that (I suggest) is a very real thing when the healthy mother is near the end of her pregnancy, and over a period of a few weeks following the baby's birth.

"Ego establishment" means the gradually developing sense of being a self, of having an I. This is accomplished over time—not right away—via the sufficiency of "going on being" with few enough reactions to impingement.

> Only if a mother is sensitized in the way I am describing can she feel herself into her infant's place, and so meet the infant's needs. These are at first body-needs, and they gradually becomes ego-needs as a psychology emerges out of the imaginative elaboration of physical experience.

It takes this state of primary maternal preoccupation to allow a mother to feel her way into the infant's place and so to meet his/her needs. Winnicott has already written about this first set of body-needs in his paper "Mind and its relation to the psyche-soma" (1949). As those needs are met and an infant is allowed to be in his/her "going-on-being" place, the infant begins to stretch beyond bodily experiences, and to "imaginatively elaborate" those experiences, ever-so-gradually beginning to become an "I" with, to quote Winnicott, "ego-needs." Thus, a baby's fantasy capacity begins as a developmental achievement.

I'll take the next section thought by thought.

> There comes into existence an ego-relatedness between mother and baby, from which the mother recovers, and out of which the infant may eventually build the idea of a person in the mother.

There is quite a progression that has to take place in the infant before s/he can apprehend that there is a *source* of the things that are happening to him/her, and that the source is a person—the mother. Bodily experiences have to build to the capacity to "imaginatively elaborate" those experiences, which will become the ground for the baby's psyche. Ego-relatedness comes after the psyche begins to stretch into itself in the context of thousands of repetitions of bodily based experiences. It will be weeks to months before there is "ego-relatedness," meaning person-to-person relatedness from the infant's side of things. The infant may eventually build the idea of a person in the mother, but this takes time and development. The mother "recovers" from her primary maternal preoccupation, but from the beginning she can recognize the otherness of the infant. The infant cannot do this from the start.

He continues:

> From this angle the recognition of the mother as a person comes in a positive way, normally, and not out of the experience of the mother as the symbol of frustration.

When a mother is able to achieve this state of primary maternal preoccupation, the infant is able to come to the graceful and gradual recognition of the mother as a person in contrast to what happens when the mother cannot feel her way into the infant's needs, and so is a source of impingement leading to experiences of annihilation in the infant, and thus (gradually) becomes a symbol of frustration.

> The mother's failure to adapt in the earliest phase does not produce anything but an annihilation of the infant's self.

As he has said above, impingements via the mother's failure to adapt in the earliest phase of infancy create the terror of total annihilation in the infant. This is in part because the infant has not yet developed the capacity to feel more sophisticated feelings such as frustration. Needs are either met or not met, leading either to going-on-being or to disruptions in going-on-being (impingements), which can accumulate to unspeakable anxieties, namely, the terror of annihilation of the self—the reduction of the self to nothingness.

What the mother does well is not in any way apprehended by the infant at this stage. This is a fact according to my thesis. Her failures are not felt as maternal failures, but they act as threats to personal self-existence.

Here Winnicott is letting us in on the psychological state of the very first weeks of an infant's life. His observation of the psychic life of infants has led him to posit this as "fact": that an infant is not comprehending the quality of his experience or the source of that experience. The infant does not think, "Ah, this is going well." S/he experiences either going-on-being or impingements to going-on-being which can escalate into unbearable threats to personal self-existence.

In the language of these considerations, the early building up of the ego is therefore silent. The first ego organization comes from the experience of threats of annihilation and from which, repeatedly, there is recovery. Out of such experiences confidence in recovery begins to be something which leads to an ego and to an ego capacity for coping with frustration.

OK. So Winnicott is now using new phrasing: "the first ego organization." The infant at first has only the *potential* for ego organization. Organization of the ego awaits the passing of time, the accruing of experience, and further maturing in order to come into being. He introduces a new thought here: that there are threats of annihilation that can be recovered from. Not at first, but as time passes, impingements that are well timed to the infant's maturing process can actually be growth-producing. Maternal miscues and mis-timings that are not too overwhelming, plus recovery from them (mediated by the attuned mother) can actually precipitate the beginning of the formation of an ego—an evolving sense of I—in the infant. As such experiences—threats of annihilation followed by recovery—occur and recur, the infant begins to build confidence in the process of recovery, which stimulates the growth of the ego, which in turn gradually develops the capacity to identify and cope with frustration.

It will, I hope, be felt that this thesis contributes to the subject of the infant's recognition of the mother as a frustrating mother. This is true later on but not at this very early stage. At the beginning the failing mother is not apprehended as such. Indeed a recognition of absolute dependence on the mother and of her capacity for primary maternal preoccupation, or whatever it is called, is something which belongs to extreme sophistication, and to a stage not always reached by adults. The general failure of recognition of absolute dependence at the start contributes to the fear of *woman* that is the lot of both men and women (Winnicott, 1950, 1957a).

Winnicott here partially restates himself. He is driving home the point that at the earliest stage of absolute dependence the infant does not apprehend that impingements are coming from a failing or frustrating mother. Such a recognition of one's absolute dependence at the beginning of life comes at a much later stage, which Winnicott says actually isn't even reached by some adults. (He will clarify this statement in other papers.) He then offers, parenthetically, that the failure to recognize how absolutely dependent we are in the very beginning of our lives leads to a fear of the life-and-death power of woman, in both men and women. (This may, in fact, be the psychological ground for all expressions of misogyny.)

> We can now say why we think the baby's mother is the most suitable person for the care of that baby; it is she who can reach this special state of primary maternal preoccupation without being ill. But an adoptive mother, or any woman who can be ill in the sense of "primary maternal preoccupation", may be in a position to adapt well enough, on account of having some capacity for identification with the baby.

OK. Here Winnicott asserts some good news: that the baby's biological mother is usually the most suitable person for the care of the baby because she is likely to be able to reach this state of primary maternal preoccupation, but that an adoptive mother can achieve this primary maternal preoccupation also.

> According to this thesis a good enough environmental provision in the earliest phase enables the infant to begin to exist, to have experience, to build a personal ego, to ride instincts, and to meet with all the difficulties inherent in life. All this feels real to the infant who becomes able to have a self that can eventually even afford to sacrifice spontaneity, even to die.

OK. This is a mouthful from Winnicott! He is now shifting his language from maternal care to "environmental provision." With good-enough care/provision for the infant, there is a developmental progression. The infant: (1) begins to exist, and then (2) has experiences, and then (3) (big jump) builds a personal ego, and then is able to (4) "ride instincts," and finally (5) progresses to meet with all the difficulties inherent in life.

Winnicott has touched on the first three on this list, but made only brief mention of instincts in the beginning of his paper. Remember that instincts originate from somatic organization. They are the source of our bodily needs, wants, desires, and impulses, and have shifting zone-dominance over time. An infant at first cannot even apprehend that he has his own needs, wants, desires, and impulses. The awareness of instincts and satisfaction of them requires the slow building up of a personal ego—a self. He ends his paragraph with a complex assertion: that if all these steps that culminate in being able to recognize and seek to satisfy instincts go well enough, "all of this feels real to the infant." He implies the opposite, though, that if these steps do not go well enough, the emerging person will not feel *real*. He will take up this idea of real versus not real in other papers.

Finally, he asserts that those who successfully develop such a self can afford to not "ride" instincts—to sacrifice spontaneity—and even to be real to their own death, a wish that Winnicott is reported to have had concerning himself, "May I be alive when I die" (2016).

He continues:

> On the other hand, without the initial good-enough environmental provision, this self that can afford to die never develops. The feeling of real is absent and if there is not too much chaos the ultimate feeling is of futility. The inherent difficulties of life cannot be reached, let alone the satisfactions. If there is not chaos, there appears a false self that hides the true self, that complies with demands, that reacts to stimuli, that rids itself of instinctual experiences by having them, but that is only playing for time.

So now he is straightforward about what happens to those who do not experience this good-enough environment. They do not feel real to themselves. They feel a sense of futility. They can neither experience the satisfactions of life, nor really show up for the difficulties. They live their lives through the medium of a false self as opposed to a true self. Their false self is compliant with the demands that come from outside itself, and is reactive to stimuli. The false self "rids itself of instinctual experience," meaning that it is not really present to its own bodily needs, wants, desires, and impulses. It enacts them but is not truly present for them. If there is too much chaos, then all there is is the chaos.

> It will be seen that, by this thesis, constitutional factors are more likely to show up in the normal, where the environment in the first phase has been adaptive. By contrast, when there has been failure at this first phase, the infant is caught up in primitive defence mechanisms (false self, etc.) which belong to the threat of annihilation, and constitutional elements tend to become overridden (unless physically manifest).

OK, remember that "constitutional factors" refer to everything that is inherited, genetically encoded, and present at birth. These are more likely to be expressed when the first phase of absolute dependence has been adaptive. When there have been compromises during this phase, constitutional factors do not tend to get expressed unless they are physically manifest, such as hair color, and so on. They tend to be overridden by the emerging child's need to cope with threats of annihilation and the consequent defenses—like the development of the false self.

> It is necessary here to leave undeveloped the theme of the infant's intro-jection of illness patterns of the mother, though this subject is of great importance in consideration of the environmental factor in the next stages, after the first stage of absolute dependence.

OK. He hints at the next phase of development wherein a child can take in the emotional illness patterns of the mother.

> In reconstructing the early development of an infant there is no point at all in talking of instincts, except on a basis of ego development.
>   There is a watershed:
>   Ego maturity—instinctual experiences strengthen ego.
>   Ego immaturity—instinctual experiences disrupt ego.
>   Ego here implies a summation of experience. The individual self starts a summation of resting experience, spontaneous motility, and sensation, return from activity to rest, and the gradual establishment of a capacity to wait for recovery from annihilations; annihilations that result from reactions to environmental impingement. For this reason the individual needs to start in the specialized environment to which I have here referred under the heading: Primary Maternal Preoccupation.

The very early infant does not experience instincts—bodily needs, wants, desires, and impulses—until he has developed enough ego—enough self—to inhabit his own instincts. Then, he can indeed experience his resting self, his spontaneous motility, his sensation, his return to rest. The gradual build-up of confidence in recovery from impingements (timed to the increasing maturity of the infant) builds to an ego that is the summation of an intricate and neces-sary developmental process. Key to this summation is the specialized envir-onment in the very beginning of an infant's life which Winnicott has called primary maternal preoccupation.

References

Bender, L. (1947) 'Childhood schizophrenia'. Am J Orthopsychiatry XVII.
Creak, M. (1951) 'Psychoses in childhood'. J. Ment. Sci. XCVII.
Freud, A. (1954) 'Problems of infantile neurosis – a discussion' Psychoanalytic Study of the Child, 9: 16–71.

Greenacre, P. (1954) 'Problems of infantile neurosis – a discussion'. Psychoanalytic Study of the Child, 9: 16–71.

Kanner, L. (1943) 'Autistic disturbances of affective contact'. The Nervous Child II.

Mahler, M. S. (1954) 'Problems of infantile neurosis-a discussion'. Psychoanalytic Study of the Child, 9: 16–71.

Winnicott, D. W. (1949) 'The ordinary devoted mother and her baby', in The Child and the Family. London: Tavistock, 1957, pp. 3–78.

Winnicott, D. W. (1950) 'Some thoughts on the meaning of the word democracy'. Humsn Relations. III, No. 2, June 1950.

Winnicott, D. W. (1957a) The Child and the Family. London: Tavistock Publications; New York: Basic Books (p. 141).

7 Ego distortion in terms of True and False Self

(1960)

Winnicott, D. W. (1960). Ego distortion in terms of true and false self. In *The maturational processes and the facilitating environment: Studies in the theory of emotional development* (pp. 140–152). London: Karnac, 2007.

In this paper, Winnicott presents the problem of what happens when an infant's primary caregiver (mother) cannot adapt well enough to the infant's needs and gestures. The infant must accept whatever he is getting, however *divergent* from his needs and signals that may be. The infant, then, is in the position of having to comply with the demands of the environment rather than having the environment comply with his needs and demands. As such, he is forced into building up a False Self with a false set of *compliant* needs and *compliant* responses, leading to a false relationship with both the mother and outside world. All of this is a contortion of his True Self, which, by these tactics he manages to hide from the outside world—and in some cases, from himself. The False Self, though it may be "well set up"—and though it may seem to be functioning quite well in life—lacks a certain something which Winnicott identifies as *essential*: the element of creative originality. It can also evidence itself, according to Winnicott, in the feeling that one has not started to exist.

Although Winnicott himself developed the language of True and False Self, he begins his paper with a bit of a disclaimer:

> One recent development in psycho-analysis has been the increasing use of the concept of the False Self. This concept carries with it the idea of a True Self.

Winnicott then moves on to present a bit of history, but as usual, is sparse in terms of direct citations of prior theorists:

History

This concept is not in itself new. It appears in various guises in descriptive psychiatry and notably in certain religions and philosophical systems. Evidently a real clinical state exists which deserves study, and the concept presents psycho-analysis with an aetiological challenge.

He now moves on to the questions of "Psycho-analysis," which are really, in truth, Winnicott's own questions:

Psycho-analysis concerns itself with the questions:

(1) How does the False Self arise?
(2) What is its function?
(3) Why is the False Self exaggerated or emphasized in some cases?
(4) Why do some persons not develop a False Self system?
(5) What are the equivalents to the False Self in normal people?
(6) What is there that could be named a True Self?

He will pursue these, but first, gives some credit to Freud:

It would appear to me that the idea of a False Self, which is an idea which our patients give us, can be discerned in the early formulations of Freud. In particular I link what I divide into a True and a False Self with Freud's division of the self into a part that is central and powered by the instincts (or by what Freud called sexuality, pregenital and genital), and a part that is turned outwards and is related to the world.

Here Winnicott refers to Freud's id, the part that is central and powered by instincts, and the ego, the part that is turned outwards and is related to the world.

Personal contribution

My own contribution to this subject derives from my working at one and the same time

(a) as a paediatrician with mothers and infants and
(b) as a psycho-analyst whose practice includes a small series of borderline cases treated by analysis, but needing to experience in the

> transference a phase (or phases) of serious regression to dependence. My experiences have led me to recognize that dependent or deeply regressed patients can teach the analyst more about early infancy than can be learned from direct observation of infants, and more than can be learned from contact with mothers who are involved with infants. At the same time, clinical contact with the normal and abnormal experiences of the infant–mother relationship influences the analyst's analytic theory since what happens in the transference (in the regressed phases of certain of his patients) is a form of infant–mother relationship.

OK. Winnicott is straightforward here. He's telling us that the sources of his observations include mothers and infants, and "borderline cases." Borderline cases were thought at the time Winnicott wrote this paper to be patients occupying the borderline territory between psychosis and neurosis. The term "borderline" did not designate a fully delineated personality disorder until 1980, when it was included in the third edition of the *Diagnostic and Statistical Manual of Mental Disorders* (DSM III: American Psychiatric Association, 1980). Some of these patients—these "cases"—evinced a periodic need to regress into phases of deep dependence on Winnicott as analyst, dependencies which were similar to and parallel to the dependencies of an infant on its mother. These cases taught him more about the early workings of mother–infant relationships than he could pick up by direct observation of mothers and infants. These various sources in essence cross-pollinated one another in Winnicott's thinking.

> I like to compare my position with that of Greenacre, who has also kept in touch with paediatrics while pursuing her practice of psycho-analysis. With her too it seems to be clear that each of the two experiences has influenced her in her assessment of the other experience. Clinical experience in adult psychiatry can have the effect on a psycho-analyst of placing a gap between his assessment of a clinical state and his understanding of its aetiology. The gap derives from an impossibility of getting a reliable history of early infancy either from a psychotic patient or from the mother, or from more detached observers. Analytic patients who regress to serious dependence in the transference fill in this gap by showing their expectations and their needs in the dependent phases.

This last sentence is the nub of it: patients in serious phases of regression in therapy show their (infantile) expectations and needs quite clearly.

Ego-needs and id-needs

It must be emphasized that in referring to the meeting of infant needs I am not referring to the satisfaction of instincts. In the area that I am examining the instincts are not yet clearly defined as internal to the infant. The instincts can be as much external as can a clap of thunder or a hit. The infant's ego is building up strength and in consequence is getting towards a state in which id demands will be felt as part of the self, and not as environmental. When this development occurs, then id-satisfaction becomes a very important strengthener of the ego, or of the True Self; but id excitements can be traumatic when the ego is not yet able to include them, and not yet able to contain the risks involved and the frustrations experienced up to the point when id-satisfaction becomes a fact.

What's he saying here? In this paragraph, he's talking about infants. He is saying (and now I'll draw from other sources in his writings) that at first, the baby is an immature, non-integrated being, who does not even inhabit his own body. He does not know and cannot make sense of the fact that instinctual tensions are his. They might be said to be external to him, just as an alarm bell or a clap of thunder would be external, but he cannot know this because he has not yet determined that there are things internal and things external. He cannot tell the difference between a discomfort coming from without and one coming from within or even the difference between hunger and cold. He has not yet any capacity to endow bodily sensations with meaning. This will be his psyche's first task: to imaginatively elaborate bodily sensations. So, instinctual demands are not at first frustrations to be relieved or satisfied, they are threats to his going-on-being—to his very psychic existence. A mother in a well-timed, sensitively responsive relationship to her newborn does not confer satisfaction, and does not even stave off frustration. She does something far more basic: she prevents the interruption of his going-on-being, which would be an experience of annihilation to the infant. When the infant matures to the point where he locates himself in his body and where his instinctual (id) demands are felt as a part of the self, then id satisfactions can strengthen the ego, but before then, id excitements can be traumatic.

A patient said to me: "Good management" (ego care) "such as I have experienced during this hour as a feed" (id-satisfaction). He could not have said this the other way round, for if I had fed him he would have complied and this would have played into his False Self defence, or else he would have reacted and rejected my advances, maintaining his integrity by choosing frustration.

Winnicott is saying here that the important part of this is the patient's appropriation of *what he found in the hour of therapy for himself*, on his own terms. It was not served up in such a way as to narcissistically benefit the therapist; it was not forced upon the patient so as to cause him to have to reject it in order to maintain his integrity.

> Other influences have been important for me, as for instance when periodically I have been asked for a note on a patient who is now under psychiatric care as an adult but who was observed by myself when an infant or small child. Often from my notes I have been able to see that the psychiatric state that now exists was already to be discerned in the infant–mother relationship. (I leave out infant–father relationships in this context because I am referring to early phenomena, those that concern the infant's relationship to the mother, or to the father as another mother. The father at this very early stage has not become significant as a male person.)

This paragraph is straightforward. He says that he has been able to see that the psychiatric state that exists in an adult that Winnicott saw initially as an infant or as a small child was already evident to him in the patient's infancy or childhood via observing the infant–mother relationship. It is also significant to note that Winnicott here makes room for a father to be the "mothering" person.

> **Example**
>
> The best example I can give is that of a middle-aged woman who had a very successful False Self but who had the feeling all her life that she had not started to exist, and that she had always been looking for a means of getting to her True Self. She still continues with her analysis, which has lasted many years.

OK. He's saying three quick things in this paragraph: (1) that it's possible to have (or to be) a very successful False Self; (2) that one way a False Self evidences itself is in the feeling that one has not started to exist; and (3) that for some people, there will be a lifelong quest to find their True Self.

> In the first phase of this research analysis (this lasted two or three years), I found I was dealing with what the patient called her "Caretaker Self". This "Caretaker Self":

(1) found psycho-analysis;
(2) came and sampled analysis, as a kind of elaborate test of the analyst's reliability;
(3) brought her to analysis;
(4) gradually after three years or more handed over its function to the analyst (this was the time of the depth of the regression, with a few weeks of a very high degree of dependence on the analyst);
(5) hovered round, resuming caretaking at times when the analyst failed (analyst's illness, analyst's holidays, etc.);
(6) its ultimate fate will be discussed later.

In this case example, the woman's False Self was, to her, the "Caretaker Self." In therapy, she was able, after three years, when deeply regressed, to allow herself to deeply depend on Winnicott and to let go of her caretaking to him. She resumed her self-caretaking when Winnicott was unavailable to her.

From the evolution of this case it was easy for me to see the defensive nature of the False Self. Its defensive function is to hide and protect the True Self, whatever that may be. Immediately it becomes possible to classify False Self organizations:

He observes that the purpose of the False Self is to protect the True Self. Winnicott will now present a five-point spectrum of False Self pathologies, from most severe to least:

(1) At one extreme: the False Self sets up as real and it is this that observers tend to think is the real person. In living relationships, work relationships, and friendships, however, the False Self begins to fail. In situations in which what is expected is a whole person the False Self has some essential lacking. At this extreme the True Self is hidden.

OK, so False Self organization one: the False Self is encountered by observers as the real person. The True Self is hidden. This arrangement does not falter unless the individual is expected to be a whole person (such as in intimate relationships or in response to personal tragedy).

(2) Less extreme: the False Self defends the True Self; the True Self is, however, acknowledged as a potential and is allowed a secret life. Here is the clearest example of clinical illness as an organization with

a positive aim, the preservation of the individual in spite of abnormal environmental conditions. This is an extension of the psycho-analytic concept of the value of symptoms to the sick person.

False Self organization two: the False Self protects an inner True Self, but the True Self is in some ways acknowledged as an internal potential. The True Self may maintain a kind of secret life. Winnicott thinks of the False Self as a set of symptoms—a clinical illness—which functions to preserve and protect a healthier part of an individual whose early environment failed them in some crucial ways.

(3) More towards health: The False Self has as its main concern a search for conditions which will make it possible for the True Self to come into its own. If conditions cannot be found then there must be reorganized a new defence against exploitation of the True Self, and if there be doubt then the clinical result is suicide. Suicide in this context is the destruction of the total self in avoidance of annihilation of the True Self. When suicide is the only defence left against betrayal of the True Self, then it becomes the lot of the False Self to organize the suicide. This, of course, involves its own destruction, but at the same time eliminates the need for its continued existence, since its function is the protection of the True Self from insult.

False Self organization three: the False Self actively seeks out conditions that will allow the safe emergence of the True Self. Although Winnicott classifies this in the middle of the spectrum, he warns that this organization carries a risk of self-destruction (suicide) if its aim to release the imprisoned True Self is thwarted. Better to die early by one's own hand than to risk being annihilated—driven into psychological non-existence by the forces around one, or to languish all of the days of the rest of one's life.

(4) Still further towards health: the False Self is built on identifications (as for example that of the patient mentioned, whose childhood environment and whose actual nannie gave much colour to the False Self organization).

False Self organization four: the False Self is constructed on the basis of positive identifications, a taking in of the characteristics of one whom the growing child emulates and copies. This may seem to confer a sense of aliveness to the affected individual, but since it is not really one's own aliveness, it is ultimately unsatisfying.

> (5) In health: the False Self is represented by the whole organization of the polite and mannered social attitude, a "not wearing the heart on the sleeve", as might be said. Much has gone to the individual's ability to forgo omnipotence and the primary process in general, the gain being the place in society which can never be attained or maintained by the True Self alone.

False Self organization five: "In health." This is a False Self organization whose outward face fits in well with "polite and mannered" society, hiding the true heart essence of the person from public view. This is designed to help the individual achieve gains in society which could never be achieved via the unalloyed True Self. This arrangement represents the exercise of practiced restraint from the individual, allowing neither the brash freshness of childlike omnipotence, nor the spontaneities and vulnerabilities of primary process thinking and expression. Winnicott sees this compromise as a healthy one—perhaps, in Jungian language, a useful persona.

> So far I have kept within the bounds of clinical description. Even in this limited area recognition of the False Self is important, however. For instance, it is important that patients who are essentially False Personalities shall not be referred to students of psycho-analysis for analysis under a training scheme. The diagnosis of False Personality is here more important than the diagnosis of the patient according to accepted psychiatric classifications. Also in social work, where all types of case must be accepted and kept in treatment, this diagnosis of False Personality is important in the avoidance of extreme frustration associated with therapeutic failure in spite of seemingly sound social work based on analytic principles. Especially is this diagnosis important in the selection of students for training in psycho-analysis or in psychiatric social work, that is to say, in the selection of case-work students of all kinds. The organized False Self is associated with a rigidity of defences which prevents growth during the student period.

OK. Winnicott now comments on the clinical diagnosis of the False Self, the treatment of this kind of disorder, and the selection of those who will ultimately be trained to practice psychoanalysis or psychiatric social work. He thinks that this is an important disorder to be recognized on its own merits within psychiatric nosology. He feels that this particular diagnosis is beyond the skills

of students in psychoanalytic training, and that a lack of either diagnostic recognition or treatment sophistication dooms clinicians to therapeutic failures
in working with False Self pathologies. He warns that those who carry this
pathology without their own treatment, and who aspire to become treating
clinicians of others, will port a certain rigidity in their defensive structure that
will effectively block their overall growth as student clinicians.

The mind and the False Self

A particular danger arises out of the not infrequent tie-up between
the intellectual approach and the False Self. When a False Self becomes
organized in an individual who has a high intellectual potential there is
a very strong tendency for the mind to become the location of the False
Self, and in this case there develops a dissociation between intellectual
activity and psychosomatic existence. (In the healthy individual, it must
be assumed, the mind is not something for the individual to exploit in
escape from psycho-somatic being. I have developed this theme at some
length in "Mind and its Relation to the Psyche-Soma", 1949c.) When
there has taken place this double abnormality, (i) the False Self organized
to hide the True Self, and (ii) an attempt on the part of the individual to
solve the personal problem by the use of a fine intellect, a clinical picture
results which is peculiar in that it very easily deceives. The world may
observe academic success of a high degree, and may find it hard to believe
in the very real distress of the individual concerned, who feels "phoney"
the more he or she is successful. When such individuals destroy themselves in one way or another, instead of fulfilling promise, this invariably
produces a sense of shock in those who have developed high hopes of
the individual.

OK. So now Winnicott raises the question of the relationship between the
False Self and what he refers to as the "intellectual approach." He refers to his
own paper on "Mind and its relation to the psyche-soma," (1949) in which he
coins the term "mind-psyche" to refer to this "intellectual approach." He asserts
in that paper that the psyche and soma of an infant are meant to develop along
in a process of mutual interrelation, the product of which forms the core for
the infant's imaginative self. The mind—the thinking apparatus—is then meant
to develop as a natural outgrowth of this psyche-soma. But when there are
significant compromises in the early caretaking environment—when a baby
has to adapt to certain kinds and degrees of maternal failure that *exceed* the
growing baby's psyche-soma's capacities—the mind—the baby's not-yet-ready
thinking process—has to step up and take over prematurely. It has to take over
and organize the care of the baby's own psyche-soma—something that the

maternal environment was meant to do. The mind is, in essence, co-opted into the task of doing what the environment (the mother) should be doing. As a by-product, there can develop an opposition between the mind and bodily based experience, instead of the mind being nested in the psyche-soma as a natural outgrowth of it.

OK. So back to Winnicott's question. What happens when the False Self organization co-occurs with this mind-psyche proclivity/adaptation? His answer is this: "When a False Self becomes organized in an individual who has a high intellectual potential [as still a baby], there is a very strong tendency for the mind to become the location of the False Self." So the False Self sets itself up in a mind which is dissociated from the body.

(And it is this that observers tend to think of as the real person.) But then what? Winnicott's answer is that a clinical picture often emerges in which the individual may become highly academically successful, but may experience a sense of inner distress and vacuity, feeling essentially phony inside—the more successful, the more phony. And, in turn, when this distress leads to self-destruction, as it often does, it is confusing to those on the outside who stood in admiration and harbored great hopes for this seemingly gifted person. He warns clinicians that "a clinical picture results which is peculiar in that it very easily deceives"—meaning that clinicians can easily be seduced by the person's giftedness, and miss the patient's inherent estrangement from themselves.

Aetiology

The main way in which these concepts become of interest to psycho-analysts derives from a study of the way a False Self develops at the beginning, in the infant–mother relationship, and (more important) the way in which a False Self does not become a significant feature in normal development.

OK. So he is about to present a picture of how the False Self develops in the very beginning, and how, in normal development, this does *not* happen.

The theory relative to this important stage in ontogenetic development belongs to the observation of infant-to-mother (regressed patient-to-analyst) living, and it does not belong to the theory of early mechanisms of ego-defence organized against id-impulse, though of course these two subjects overlap.

Here he's differentiating himself from a Freudian perspective which pits ego against id impulses.

> To get to a statement of the relevant developmental process it is essential to take into account the mother's behaviour and attitude, because in this field dependence is real, and near absolute. It is not possible to state what takes place by reference to the infant alone.

Here he is very obliquely also differentiating himself from Klein, who located primitive phantasy—meaning-making—almost exclusively in the psyche of the infant. Winnicott, in contrast, is including the maternal environment as a major contributor.

> In seeking the aetiology of the False Self we are examining the stage of first object-relationships. At this stage the infant is most of the time unintegrated, and never fully integrated; cohesion of the various sensori-motor elements belongs to the fact that the mother holds the infant, sometimes physically, and all the time figuratively. Periodically the infant's gesture gives expression to a spontaneous impulse; the source of the gesture is the True Self, and the gesture indicates the existence of a potential True Self. We need to examine the way the mother meets this infantile omnipotence revealed in a gesture (or a sensori-motor grouping). I have here linked the idea of a True Self with the spontaneous gesture. Fusion of the motility and erotic elements is in process of becoming a fact at this period of development of the individual.

OK. So Winnicott is talking about a very early part of infant development— the stage of first object relationships. The infant is un-integrated. The mother must hold the infant's non-integrated bits and pieces. She is the one who must provide cohesion and continuity of being for the infant. He cannot, at first, provide that for himself. Periodically, the infant has a spontaneous impulse or some kind of sensorimotor expression, which exhibits itself in some kind of gesture—a bodily gesticulation, a grunt, a squirm—something. The gesture itself is an expression of the infant's incipient self—the emergent True Self— trying to come into being. (Winnicott also refers here to the fusion of motility (movement) and erotic (loving) elements, which he will treat head-on in other papers.)

> ## The mother's part
>
> It is necessary to examine the part played by the mother, and in doing so I find it convenient to compare two extremes; by one extreme the mother is a good-enough mother and by the other the mother is not a good-enough mother. The question will be asked: what is meant by the term

> "good enough"? The good-enough mother meets the omnipotence of
> the infant and to some extent makes sense of it. She does this repeatedly.
> A True Self begins to have life, through the strength given to the infant's
> weak ego by the mother's implementation of the infant's omnipotent
> expressions. The mother who is not good enough is not able to imple-
> ment the infant's omnipotence, and so she repeatedly fails to meet the
> infant gesture; instead she substitutes her own gesture which is to be given
> sense by the compliance of the infant. This compliance on the part of the
> infant is the earliest stage of the False Self, and belongs to the mother's
> inability to sense her infant's needs.

Here Winnicott addresses the mother's part of the creation of the True or
False Self. With the mother's adequate holding of the infant's non-integrated
parts, there is enough continuity of being for the baby's true incipient self to
be able to come forth into moments of self-expression, which are met and
responded to by the mother. The good-enough mother, who meets the infant's
omnipotence—(a good thing) by meeting the infant's spontaneous expressions,
repeatedly adds strength to the infant's forming ego. In contrast, the not-good-
enough mother is unable to decode the infant's spontaneous expressions/
gestures accurately. She is unable to sense her infant's needs. She gets it wrong
repeatedly. She substitutes her own misconstructions of the infant's needs and
gestures, forcing the infant to decode *her* well-intentioned, but *off* interventions.
This necessitates effort—and compliance—on the part of the infant—bending
his world to mother's needs—which is the earliest stage of the False Self.

> It is an essential part of my theory that the True Self does not become a
> living reality except as a result of the mother's repeated success in meeting
> the infant's spontaneous gesture or sensory hallucination. (This idea is
> closely linked with Sechehaye's idea contained in the term "symbolic
> realization". This term has played an important part in modern psycho-
> analytic theory, but it is not quite accurate since it is the infant's gesture
> or hallucination that is made real, and the capacity of the infant to use a
> symbol is the result.)

Here Winnicott is referring to Marguerite Sechehaye's work on symbolic
realization.[1]

---

1 Marguerite Sechehaye was a psychoanalyst who wrote about her work with an 18-year-old schizophrenic patient, Renee. Renee later recounted some of her delusions: her hands were cat's paws;
she was alternately nine centuries old and not yet born; she was growing smaller and smaller; her
internal "system" forbade her to eat any food that was not apples picked from a neighboring orchard.

He avers that the road to the True Self goes through the mother's repeated success in accurately decoding and sensitively meeting the infant's (symbolically) expressed needs. This repeated meeting of signaled need makes signal/response seem real to the infant, leading to the infant's eventual use of the signal *and* the symbol of the thing to represent the thing itself.

> There are now two possible lines of development in the scheme of events according to my formulation. In the first case the mother's adaptation is good enough and in consequence the infant begins to believe in external reality which appears and behaves as by magic (because of the mother's relatively successful adaptation to the infant's gestures and needs), and which acts in a way that does not clash with the infant's omnipotence. On this basis the infant can gradually abrogate omnipotence. The True Self has a spontaneity, and this has been joined up with the world's events. The infant can now begin to enjoy the illusion of omnipotent creating and controlling, and then can gradually come to recognize the illusory element, the fact of playing and imagining. Here is the basis for the symbol which at first is both the infant's spontaneity or hallucination, and also the external object created and ultimately cathected.

OK. So now Winnicott continues to depict what happens as a result of good-enough maternal attunement. As the mother meets the infant's expressions, the infant begins to believe in, and have confidence in, external reality. External reality, for a time, behaves as if it were a magical extension of the infant's impulses and not-yet-able-to-be-articulated wishes. Thus, the infant is allowed to have an experience of omnipotence. He can enjoy the illusion of omnipotent creating and controlling, and as a result, over time, can gradually come to recognize the illusory element in all of it, gradually transforming his experience into the fact of playing and imagining. As a further result, the infant comes to be initiated into the use of the symbol—the signal—which is met and responded to by the external world. This leads to his gradual recognition that there *is* an external world, one inhabited by a human object in whom he will ultimately invest emotion and feeling. And, he builds confidence that there is a human who will recognize and respond to expressed needs.

Sechehaye began feeding Renee slices of apple as if she were an infant. Renee experienced the contentment of a tiny baby, and as a result, her perception of things changed radically. Through this process, Renee was able to see reality for the first time: people were no longer automatons; things were just things (Sechehaye, 1951). Sechehaye gave this intervention the name "symbolic realization." Winnicott uses this as a parallel to the process of presenting breast, bottle, milk, etc. to baby. The important thing was that the patient, Renee, was able to "create" an object—to make the apple whatever she needed important thing was that the patient, Renee, was able to "create" an object—to make the apple whatever she needed.

In between the infant and the object is some thing, or some activity or sensation. In so far as this joins the infant to the object (viz. maternal part-object) so far is this the basis of symbol formation. On the other hand, in so far as this something separates instead of joins, so is its function of leading on to symbol formation blocked.

Between the infant and the maternal/outside object there is some thing—some experience. If this joins the two, it is the basis for symbol formation; if it does not, it blocks the process of symbol formation.

In the second case, which belongs more particularly to the subject under discussion, the mother's adaptation to the infant's hallucinations and spontaneous impulses is deficient, not good enough. The process that leads to the capacity for symbol-usage does not get started (or else it becomes broken up, with a corresponding withdrawal on the part of the infant from advantages gained).

In addition to an activity or a sensation happening for the infant, there can be an infant's hallucinations or spontaneous impulses, which a mother needs to decode. If she is able to do this decoding and adapt appropriately, this response leads to the infant's capacity to *use* symbols. If a mother fails at this task, the infant may be impeded in his/her attempts to use symbols, or the infant may withdraw from using signals in part or altogether.

When the mother's adaptation is not good enough at the start the infant might be expected to die physically, because cathexis of external objects is not initiated. The infant remains isolated. But in practice the infant lives, but lives falsely. The protest against being forced into a false existence can be detected from the earliest stages. The clinical picture is one of general irritability, and of feeding and other function disturbances which may, however, disappear clinically, only to reappear in serious form at a later stage.

OK. So, when the mother's adaptation at the start is not good enough, the infant may survive, but, in Winnicott's words, "live falsely." He asserts that this false adaptation by the infant can be observed from the earliest stages via the infant's general irritability or feeding disturbances, and so on. While these initial signs may disappear, they are very likely to reappear "in serious form" in later stages.

In this second case, where the mother cannot adapt well enough, the infant gets seduced into a compliance, and a compliant False Self reacts to environmental demands, and the infant seems to accept them. Through this False Self the infant builds up a false set of relationships, and by means of introjections even attains a show of being real, so that the child may grow to be just like mother, nurse, aunt, brother, or whoever at the time dominates the scene. The False Self has one positive and very important function: to hide the True Self, which it does by compliance with environmental demands.

In the case of a mother who cannot adapt well enough to the infant's needs and gestures, the infant must accept whatever he is getting, however *off* from his needs and signals that may be. He complies with the demands of the environment rather than having the environment comply with his needs and demands. He can appear to truly accept what is offered. He might even unconsciously morph his needs to fit in with what is available—by means of introjection—by replicating within himself aspects of the mother, taking into his developing ego as large as possible a part of the psychic world of the mother. In so doing, he is building up a False Self with a false set of *compliant* needs and *compliant* responses, leading to a false relationship with the mother and outside world. He may not seem to be enacting anything that looks feigned or false, but all of this is a contortion of his True Self, which, by these tactics, he manages to hide from the outside world—and in some cases, from himself.

In the extreme examples of False Self development, the True Self is so well hidden that spontaneity is not a feature in the infant's living experiences. Compliance is then the main feature, with imitation as a speciality. When the degree of the split in the infant's person is not too great there may be some almost personal living through imitation, and it may even be possible for the child to act a special role, that of the True Self as it would be if it had had existence.

In some extreme cases, there is no spontaneity at all in the infant. The infant only knows how to comply, and specializes in imitation rather than living from his own center. In less severe cases, the infant develops into someone who imitates who he might have been had his True Self been allowed to develop along the way.

In this way it is possible to trace the point of origin of the False Self, which can now be seen to be a defence, a defence against that which is unthinkable, the exploitation of the True Self, which would result in its annihilation. (If the True Self ever gets exploited and annihilated this belongs to the life of an infant whose mother was not only "not good enough" in the sense set out above, but was good and bad in a tantalizingly irregular manner. The mother here has as part of her illness a need to cause and to maintain a muddle in those who are in contact with her. This may appear in a transference situation in which the patient tries to make the analyst mad (Bion, 1959; Searles, 1959). There may be a degree of this which can destroy the last vestiges of an infant's capacity to defend the True Self.)

OK. Winnicott here says something alarming. He says that it is possible to destroy the infant's capacity to preserve a hidden True Self within. He says that this dangerous situation pertains in cases where the mother is alternatively good and bad "in a tantalizingly irregular manner." This mother would be expressing a need (as part of her own mental illness) to cause confusion and muddle in those in her world, including her child. This would threaten, and perhaps even cause, the annihilation of the True Self in the child because of the destruction of the infant's capacity to defend it by use of his False Self. As adults in psychotherapy, these are the patients who seem to try to drive their therapists mad.

I have attempted to develop the theme of the part the mother plays in my paper on "Primary Maternal Preoccupation" (1956a). The assumption made by me in this paper is that, in health, the mother who becomes pregnant gradually achieves a high degree of identification with her infant. This develops during the pregnancy, is at its height at the time of lying in, and it gradually ceases in the weeks and months after the confinement.

Winnicott explains in "Primary maternal preoccupation" (1956) that a mother is able to intuit the needs of her newborn via a high degree of identification with her baby, harkening back to her own (unconscious) experience as a baby. The term "lying in" as used here by Winnicott designates a post-partum period of maternal rest and confinement with her baby. Until the 1970s, the standard of care endorsed by the National Health Service in the UK involved ten days in hospital, with the newborns taken to the nursery overnight in order to ensure the mothers would be well-rested by the time they returned home. Beyond that, there was an additional period of relative confinement recommended, ranging from two weeks to two months.

This healthy thing that happens to mothers has both hypochondriacal and secondary narcissistic implications. This special orientation on the part of the mother to her infant not only depends on her own mental health, but also it is affected by the environment. In the simplest case the man, supported by a social attitude which is itself a development from the man's natural function, deals with external reality for the woman, and so makes it safe and sensible for her to be temporarily in-turned, self-centred. A diagram of this resembles the diagram of an ill paranoid person or family. (One is reminded here of Freud's (1920) description of the living vesicle with its receptive cortical layer....)

OK. This is straightforward. If the woman is to be free to focus on her new-born with what Winnicott calls a "special orientation," and elsewhere, "primary maternal preoccupation," there must be socially and economically sanctioned structures in place to deal with the other aspects of external reality for the mother–infant couple. He suggests that the father is the likely candidate to make it safe and sensible for the mother to be so temporarily "in-turned" and "self-centred." He links this to hypochondriacal and narcissist patterns, only in the sense that the mother's focus is so exclusively on the physical and emotional entity of the mother/mother–infant couple.

The development of this theme does not belong here, but it is important that the function of the mother should be understood. This function is by no means a recent development, belonging to civilization or to sophistication or to intellectual understanding. No theory is acceptable that does not allow for the fact that mothers have always performed this essential function well enough. This essential maternal function enables the mother to know about her infant's earliest expectations and needs, and makes her personally satisfied in so far as the infant is at ease. It is because of this identification with her infant that she knows how to hold her infant, so that the infant starts by existing and not by reacting. Here is the origin of the True Self which cannot become a reality without the mother's specialized relationship, one which might be described by a common word: devotion.[1]

1   On account of this I called my series of talks to mothers, 'The Ordinary Devoted Mother and Her Baby' (Winnicott, 1949a).

This paragraph is also straightforward. Winnicott asserts that this making room for the special relationship between mother and newborn is not a practice limited to the insights of modern man or sophisticated cultures, but a practice long held across time and cultures. The end of his paragraph is significant in its own right, so I will just re-quote two parts:

This essential maternal function enables the mother to know about her infant's earliest expectations and needs…It is because of this identification with her infant that she knows how to hold her infant, so that the infant starts by existing and not by reacting.

Given these accommodations to the mother and her own primary maternal preoccupation, the infant is allowed to start by existing (nurturing of his True Self) and not by reacting (necessitating the development of a False Self).

The True Self

The concept of "A False Self" needs to be balanced by a formulation of that which could properly be called the True Self. At the earliest stage the True Self is the theoretical position from which come the spontaneous gesture and the personal idea. The spontaneous gesture is the True Self in action.

So, we start with a nascent True Self, which awaits experience in order to develop. The spontaneous gesture is a direct expression of the True Self.

Only the True Self can be creative and only the True Self can feel real. Whereas a True Self feels real, the existence of a False Self results in a feeling unreal or a sense of futility. The False Self, if successful in its function, hides the True Self, or else finds a way of enabling the True Self to start to live. Such an outcome may be achieved by all manner of means, but we observe most closely those instances in which the sense of things being real or worth while arrives during a treatment. My patient to whose case I have referred has come near the end of a long analysis to the beginning of her life. She contains no true experience, she has no past. She starts with fifty years of wasted life, but at last she feels real, and therefore she now wants to live.

Winnicott is again quite straightforward here: the True Self is the basis of true creativity and confers the feeling of being real. In contrast, the False Self imparts a feeling that one is not quite real, or that one's existence is futile. The False Self's job is to hide, protect, and defend the True Self; to look for ways for the True Self to come into its own so as to enable real life. He says that this outcome can be achieved in many ways, but he will speak to how it can occur via the process of therapy.

> The True Self comes from the aliveness of the body tissues and the working of body-functions, including the heart's action and breathing.

OK. Let's stop here and take this in. The body is the basis of the True Self. (The mind is designed to be just a specialized function of the body, and not a separate entity unto itself.)

> It is closely linked with the idea of the Primary Process, and is, at the beginning, essentially not reactive to external stimuli, but primary. There is but little point in formulating a True Self idea except for the purpose of trying to understand the False Self, because it does no more than collect together the details of the experience of aliveness.

OK. Let's stop again. At the beginning the True Self's essence—its only job—is to experience aliveness, and to collect the details of the experience of aliveness, including bodily parts, feelings, and functions, the heart's action, breathing, skin sensations, movement, and so on. Winnicott goes on to say (next paragraph) that the True Self appears as soon as there is any mental organization of the individual at all, and it means little more than the summation of sensori-motor aliveness.

> Gradually the degree of sophistication of the infant becomes such that it is more true to say that the False Self hides the infant's inner reality than to say that it hides the True Self.

OK. There's a lot of development before the infant has an inner reality. There are the achievements of spatialization and temporalization (the location of the infant in space and time), and of personalization (the inhabiting of the body and the repeated imaginative elaboration of sensory experience). There are the repeated experiences of the infant's omnipotence—his "creating" what was presented to him, leading to a sense of primary creativity, a feeling of being real, and a sense of belief in the reliability of the world he inhabits. With the passage of time and further maturation of the ego, there then comes, around eight to ten months, a small break in the infant's omnipotence. Some characteristics of external reality begin to enter the infant's world. He enters the stage of transitionality, signaled by the infant's adoption of a "transitional object," which he imbues with maternal characteristics, but which does not adapt to him as completely as the mother did. From *being* the object, the baby experiments with *possessing* the object. Objects (and reality in general) formerly subjectively perceived begin to move toward being objectively perceived. Further, there comes the gradual emergence of a sense that the world he inhabits has always been there, independent of him; that it pre-existed him, but the feeling still remains that the world is personally created. This coincides with the process of de-adaptation initiated by the mother because of the infant's increasing capacities and maturity. All of these things make it possible for the infant to recognize an external reality, and to begin differentiating what is internal from what is external.

> By this time the infant has an established limiting membrane, has an inside and an outside, and has become to a considerable extent disentangled from maternal care. It is important to note that according to the theory being formulated here the concept of an individual inner reality of objects applies to a stage later than does the concept of what is being termed the True Self. The True Self appears as soon as there is any mental organization of the individual at all, and it means little more than the summation of sensori-motor aliveness. The True Self quickly develops complexity, and relates to external reality by natural processes, by such processes as develop in the individual infant in the course of time. The infant then comes to be able to react to a stimulus without trauma because the stimulus has a counterpart in the individual's inner, psychic reality.

OK. So the True Self of the infant acquires the capacity to relate to external reality. The infant, because of such ego-maturational processes as the development of memory, is gradually able to respond to stimuli from the outside without experiencing them as impingements or as traumatic disruptions of his going-on-being.

> The infant then accounts for all stimuli as projections, but this is a stage that is not necessarily achieved, or that is only partially achieved, or it may be reached and lost. This stage having been achieved, the infant is now able to retain the sense of omnipotence even when reacting to environmental factors that the observer can discern as truly external to the infant. All this precedes by years the infant's capacity to allow in intellectual reasoning for the operation of pure chance.

When referring to the initial stages, Winnicott often uses this term, "projection" to designate the baby's imagined creation of the object or world. So with increasing ego maturity, the infant feels that he has created what is happening to him, and no longer is as exquisitely sensitive to impingements.

Every new period of living in which the True Self has not been seriously interrupted results in a strengthening of the sense of being real, and with this goes a growing capacity on the part of the infant to tolerate two sets of phenomena: These are:

(1) Breaks in continuity of True Self living. (Here can be seen a way in which the birth process might be traumatic, as for instance when there is delay without unconsciousness.)
(2) Reactive or False Self experiences, related to the environment on a basis of compliance. This becomes the part of the infant which can be (before the first birthday) taught to say "Ta", or, in other words, can be taught to acknowledge the existence of an environment that is becoming intellectually accepted. Feelings of gratitude may or may not follow.

OK, so if the True Self is allowed to develop unimpeded, every new developmental period represents a strengthening of the True Self and of the feeling of being real.

The infant becomes more and more able to tolerate breaks in the continuity of True Self living. He mentions here how a prolonged birthing process might be an example of a break in the continuity of True Self living. He cites also as an example of False Self "experiences" the situation of an infant's being trained into using proto-speech sounds not of his own initiation.

The normal equivalent of the False Self

In this way, by natural processes, the infant develops an ego organization that is adapted to the environment; but this does not happen automatically and indeed it can only happen if first the True Self (as I call it) has become a living reality, because of the mother's good-enough adaptation to the infant's living needs. There is a compliant aspect to the True Self in healthy living, an ability of the infant to comply and not to be exposed. The ability to compromise is an achievement. The equivalent of the False Self in normal development is that which can develop in the child into a social manner, something which is adaptable. In health this social manner represents a compromise. At the same time, in health, the compromise ceases to become allowable when the issues become crucial. When this happens the True Self is able to override the compliant self. Clinically this constitutes a recurring problem of adolescence.

OK. If the True Self is well established via good-enough parental adaptation to infant need, it is not inherently destructive of the True Self for parents to require some compliance to family rules as the child becomes mature enough. The infant can comply without being "exposed"—without being compromised away from his True Self. There is virtue in adaptability. But if the compliance would truly compromise something crucial about the individual, a healthy True Self stands up for itself—does not compromise. This, he mentions, is a recurring theme in the clinical treatment of adolescents.

Degrees of False Self

If the description of these two extremes and their aetiology is accepted it is not difficult for us to allow in our clinical work for the existence of a low or a high degree of the False Self defence, ranging from the healthy polite aspect of the self to the truly split-off compliant False Self which is mistaken for the whole child. It can easily be seen that sometimes this False Self defence can form the basis for a kind of sublimation, as when a child grows up to be an actor. In regard to actors, there are those who can be themselves and who also can act, whereas there are others who can only act, and who are completely at a loss when not in a role, and when not being appreciated or applauded (acknowledged as existing). In the healthy individual who has a compliant aspect of the self but who exists and who is a creative and spontaneous being, there is at the same time a capacity for the use of symbols. In other words health here is closely bound up with the capacity of the individual to live in an area that is intermediate between the dream and the reality, that which is called the cultural life. (See "Transitional Objects and Transitional Phenomena", 1951.)

In speaking of the possible degrees of a False Self adaptation, Winnicott again references a spectrum that ranges from healthy to unhealthy uses of a False Self. He says that sometimes a child is forced by his environment to sublimate aspects of himself—to morph an aspect of himself into something that pleases parents or others in one's life more than would a more natural, true, real expression of one's True essence. Winnicott uses the example of actors, contrasting on the one hand those whose acting is not a replacement for their real selves with those who can only act and cannot be or feel real, whose act has replaced all semblance of the True Self that would come from within.

He goes on to say that it's entirely possible to have a socially adaptive compliant-to-external-demands aspect of the self, but to maintain primary creativity and spontaneity. He links this creativity and spontaneity to the capacity to use symbols. The capacity for creativity allows a baby to "create" what is there to be found in the external world, and gradually to progress to the area of transitionality, where he experiences the omnipotence of creating the "dream" while simultaneously allowing objective reality to be real. Symbols stand as an intermediary between the "dream" of the thing and the thing itself; their use calls upon this creative capacity to access an intermediate area of experience.

By contrast, where there is a high degree of split between the True Self and the False Self which hides the True Self, there is found a poor capacity for using symbols, and a poverty of cultural living. Instead of cultural pursuits one observes in such persons extreme restlessness, an inability to concentrate, and a need to collect impingements from external reality so that the living-time of the individual can be filled by reactions to these impingements.

In contrast to those who can use symbols to represent their experience, those with a high degree of "False-Selfness" are often unable to operate in the intermediate zone between external and internal reality because of the compromise of their primary creativity. They default in the direction of external reality and are unable to enjoy the expansive experience of "cultural living," by which Winnicott means the whole spectrum of the arts, music, fantasy, and so on. Such impoverished individuals are marked by symptoms of extreme restlessness, inability to concentrate, and the seeming need to fill their lives with impingements from external reality which pull them away from their true experiential center. Such impingements and pursuits come in to fill the space where a True Self might otherwise live within them.

Clinical application

Here Winnicott is going to give some valuable guidance to clinicians who treat patients on the False Self spectrum.

Reference has already been made to the importance of a recognition of the False Self personality when a diagnosis is being made for the purposes of the assessment of a case for treatment, or the assessment of a candidate for psychiatric or social psychiatric work.

Consequences for the psycho-analyst

If these considerations prove to have value, then the practising psycho-analyst must be affected in the following ways:

(a)   In analysis of a False Personality the fact must be recognized that the analyst can only talk to the False Self of the patient about the patient's True Self. It is as if a nurse brings a child, and at first the analyst

> discusses the child's problem, and the child is not directly contacted. Analysis does not start until the nurse has left the child with the analyst, and the child has become able to remain alone with the analyst and has started to play.

OK. Winnicott is now talking to us as clinicians, and giving some valuable clinical insights. First, the analyst/therapist cannot contact the True Self directly. S/he must start with a contact with and recognition of the False Self. The True Self is at first inaccessible; the False Self is charged with the task of hiding/ protecting it. Winnicott will explain shortly that there must be a truthful recognition by the therapist of the poverty of the False Self, and of how it has felt to the patient to have to live from this impoverished part of himself.

> (b) At the point of transition, when the analyst begins to get into contact with the patient's True Self, there must be a period of extreme dependence. Often this is missed in analytic practice. The patient has an illness, or in some other way gives the analyst a chance to take over the False Self (nursemaid) function, but the analyst at that point fails to see what is happening, and in consequence it is others who care for the patient and on whom the patient becomes dependent in a period of disguised regression to dependence, and the opportunity is missed.

Winnicott predicts that when the analyst/therapist makes contact with the hidden True Self, there will arise a period of extreme dependence in the patient. This gives the therapist the task of stepping into a fulsome (psychological) caretaking function for the patient. Winnicott does not describe what this caretaking function would look like, but the situation of extreme psychological dependence must be taken seriously by the therapist, and met by the therapist. Otherwise, the opportunity to allow the True Self to come forward safely is missed. (Such caretaking might entail more frequent appointments and more accessibility to the patient, as well as a special degree of care, attunement, and patience.)

> (c) Analysts who are not prepared to go and meet the heavy needs of patients who become dependent in this way must be careful so to choose their cases that they do not include False Self types.

He's straightforward about this requirement. One must be prepared, willing, and able to meet the deep dependencies involved in doing this kind of work.

In psycho-analytic work it is possible to see analyses going on indefinitely because they are done on the basis of work with the False Self. In one case, a man patient who had had a considerable amount of analysis before coming to me, my work really started with him when I made it clear to him that I recognized his non-existence.

Here Winnicott has done the necessary task of truthfully recognizing the poverty of his patient's life as lived through the False Self, and of naming how it has felt to the patient to have to live from this impoverished part of himself.

He made the remark that over the years all the good work done with him had been futile because it had been done on the basis that he existed, whereas he had only existed falsely. When I had said that I recognized his non-existence he felt that he had been communicated with for the first time. What he meant was that his True Self that had been hidden away from infancy had now been in communication with his analyst in the only way which was not dangerous. This is typical of the way in which this concept affects psycho-analytic work.

Here Winnicott has illustrated how one must talk to the False Self about the False Self. He has said above that the analyst can only talk to the False Self of the patient about the patient's True Self. He follows this with his metaphor of a nurse bringing a child to an analyst for treatment, and at first the analyst discussing the child's problem with the nurse, but not directly contacting the child. Here the child is the patient's True Self and the nurse is the False Self. There must be an initial discussion of the problem with the nurse/False Self, but the therapy does not truly begin until the child (the True Self) has become able to remain alone with the analyst (no longer protected by the False Self way of being) and has started to play.

I have referred to some other aspects of this clinical problem. For instance, in 'Withdrawal and Regression' (1954a) I traced in the treatment of a man the evolution in the transference of my contact with (his version of) a False Self, through my first contact with his True Self, to an analysis of a straightforward kind. In this case withdrawal had to be converted into regression as described in the paper.

He now cites a case example in another paper, for further elucidation.

A principle might be enunciated, that in the False Self area of our analytic practice we find we make more headway by recognition of the patient's non-existence than by a long-continued working with the patient on the basis of ego-defence mechanisms. The patient's False Self can collaborate indefinitely with the analyst in the analysis of defences, being so to speak on the analyst's side in the game. This unrewarding work is only cut short profitably when the analyst can point to and specify an absence of some essential feature: "You have no mouth", "You have not started to exist yet", "Physically you are a man, but you do not know from experience anything about masculinity", and so on.

Here he has given us direct samples from his analytic practice of the moment when he speaks to the False Self about its impoverishment.

These recognitions of important fact, made clear at the right moments, pave the way for communication with the True Self. A patient who had had much futile analysis on the basis of a False Self, co-operating vigorously with an analyst who thought this was his whole self, said to me: "The only time I felt hope was when you told me that you could see no hope, and you continued with the analysis."

Here he provides another example of such a moment of truth in the therapy. But notice that he adds that such truth-telling must be done "at the right moments." This clear recognition of the False Self requires clinical sensitivity from the therapist.

On the basis of this one could say that the False Self (like the multiple projections at later stages of development) deceives the analyst if the latter fails to notice that, regarded as a whole functioning person, the False Self, however well set up, lacks something, and that something is the essential central element of creative originality.

The therapist must be on the alert to notice that the False Self, though it may be "well set up"—and that it may seem to be functioning quite well in life—lacks a certain something which Winnicott identifies as essential: the central element of creative originality. Here, he's given us the vital piece to help us identify what is missing or "off" with some patients who seem otherwise "well set up."

> Many other aspects of the application of this concept will be described in the course of time, and it may be that in some ways the concept itself will need to be modified. My object in giving an account of this part of my work (which links with the work of other analysts) is that I hold the view that this modern concept of the False Self hiding the True Self along with the theory of its aetiology is able to have an important effect on psycho-analytic work. As far as I can see it involves no important change in basic theory.

He ends his paper as he began it: with a deferential nod to the tradition of psychoanalysis, without directly citing such precursors to his thoughts on the true/false self, such precursors as Helene Deutsch's "as if" personality, or Joan Riviere's narcissist's masquerade, or Michael Balint's "basic fault," or Ronald Fairbairn's "compromised ego." His last sentence, that "it involves no important change in basic theory," is likewise deferential, and may not be entirely correct, given the overall impact of Winnicott's revisions of psychoanalysis over time.

8 The aims of psycho-analytical treatment

(1962)[1]

Winnicott, D. W. (1962). The aims of psycho-analytical treatment. In *The maturational processes and the facilitating environment: Studies in the theory of emotional development* (pp. 166–170). London: Karnac, 2007.

In this short but important paper, Winncott gives us, after more than 30 years of practice, some of his most seasoned conclusions regarding what he has come to see as the aims of psychodynamic therapy. He writes in almost tongue-in-cheek fashion in this paper, describing how he does therapy, and even telling on himself regarding the ways he lapses into relative ineffectiveness at times. Some of the points of emphasis include that Winnicott is patient-centered and non-directive. He follows the patient; it is not the other way around. Another is his understanding that the patient will make the therapist into whatever he imagines the therapist to be, irrespective of the therapist's real characteristics. Winnicott recognizes that this openness to being painted in whatever colors the patient chooses occurs at the same time as the therapist stays rooted in external reality. In this way, given that the therapist is both a subjective object and a purveyor of reality, he becomes, in Winnicott's words, a "transitional phenomenon"—representing both fantasy and reality at one and the same time.

He sees that it is at first the therapist's job to provide ego support to the patient in the measure in which it is needed. This includes the careful listening, the consistencies of the frame, the making initial sense of the patient's needs, gestures, and unconscious transferences. As the (successful) therapy proceeds, the patient gathers his/her personal history into the area of personal omnipotence—even including genuine traumata—meaning that s/he owns what has happened to him/her, and s/he assigns his/her own meaning to those events. The final result is a sense of no longer being trapped, no longer being held up in one's own growth process. One finally feels free to take possession of who s/he is, and who s/he was meant to be.

---

1 Presented to the British Psycho-Analytical Society, March 7, 1962.

In doing psycho-analysis I aim at:

Keeping alive
Keeping well
Keeping awake

I aim at being myself and behaving myself.

This delightful introduction gives us a sense of Winnicott's almost whimsical, certainly tongue-in-cheek rendering of his mature and well-developed experience as a practicing analyst.

Having begun an analysis I expect to continue with it, to survive it, and to end it.

I enjoy myself doing analysis and I always look forward to the end of each analysis. Analysis for analysis' sake has no meaning for me. I do analysis because that is what the patient needs to have done and to have done with. If the patient does not need analysis then I do something else. In analysis one asks: how much can one be allowed to do? And, by contrast, in my clinic the motto is: how little need be done?

He continues in his whimsical tone: "I do analysis because that is what the patient needs to have done and to have done with." But one thing that surfaces quite quickly is Winnicott's commitment to *survive* in order to see an analysis to its natural end. I actually knew one of his patients. And he did die unexpectedly while she was in analysis with him. As she progressed into her older years of being an analyst, she changed her practice exclusively to consultative work. She was explicit about not wanting to die while a patient was in treatment with her, so great was the strain of her loss of Winnicott.

But these are surface matters. What are the deeper aims? What does one do in the professional setting that is so carefully prepared and maintained? I do adapt quite a little to individual expectations at the very beginning. It is unhuman not to do so.

Yet I am all the time manoeuvring into the position for standard analysis. What I must try to state is the meaning for me of the term standard analysis. For me this means communicating with the patient from the position in which the transference neurosis (or psychosis) puts me. In this position I have some of the characteristics of a transitional phenomenon, since although I represent the reality principle, and it is I who must keep an eye on the clock, I am nevertheless a subjective object for the patient.

OK, now what is Winnicott saying? He recounts that as he begins with a patient, he attempts to adapt himself "quite a little" to the patient's needs and expectations. But at the same time, he attempts to nudge the patient in the direction of "standard analysis." By standard analysis he means a therapy characterized by attention to and a focus on the transference–countertransference matrix. This means that his focus is on the therapeutic relationship *as the patient experiences it* (because this is a window into the patient's internal and external relational worlds). Standard analysis also includes a recognition of the unconscious. These two elements, along with free association and the acceptance of infantile sexuality (according to Freud), differentiate psychoanalysis from other genres of therapy. Winncott describes such analysis succinctly at the end of this paper: "[If our aim is] to verbalize the nascent conscious in terms of the transference, then we are practising analysis." Winnicott further understands that he will be a subjective object for the patient, meaning that the patient will make the therapist into whatever he imagines the therapist to be, irrespective of the therapist's real characteristics. He recognizes that this openness to being painted in whatever colors the patient chooses occurs at the same time as the therapist stays rooted in external reality, e.g., "it is I who must keep an eye on the clock." In this way, given that the therapist is both a subjective object and a purveyor of reality, he becomes, in Winnicott's words, a "transitional phenomenon"— representing both fantasy and reality at one and the same time.

Most of what I do is of the nature of a verbalization of that which the patient brings for me to use today. I make interpretations for two reasons:

(1) If I make none the patient gets the impression that I understand everything. In other words, I retain some outside quality by not being quite on the mark—or even by being wrong.
(2) Verbalization at exactly the right moment mobilizes intellectual forces. It is only a bad thing to mobilize the intellectual processes when these have become seriously dissociated from psychosomatic being.

He now comments on the rationale and the art of interpretation. Interpretation is most basically the offering of an alternative perspective to what the patient is perceiving. The rationale for Winnicott's offering of interpretations in session is first to limit the patient's fantasy of his (the therapist's) omniscience. The second rationale for interpretation is that, made in exactly the right moment, it engages the patient's sense-making cognitive capacities. He then observes that moving a patient into cognitive processing is the wrong strategy for those who are estranged from inhabiting their own bodies. Then, the task is to move them away from cognition and into their psycho-somatic being, e.g., "As you're talking to me right now, how do you experience what you're saying in your body?"

My interpretations are economical, I hope. One interpretation per session satisfies me if it has referred to the material produced by the patient's unconscious co-operation. I say one thing, or say one thing in two or three parts. I never use long sentences unless I am very tired. If I am near exhaustion point I begin teaching. Moreover, in my view an interpretation containing the word "moreover" is a teaching session. The stuff of the secondary process is applied to the stuff of the primary process, as a contribution to growth and integration.

Here Winnicott continues in his tongue-in-cheek fashion to present the nuts and bolts of how he does therapy, and to tell on himself regarding the ways he lapses into relative ineffectiveness. In Winnicott's case, this is by being long-winded or by becoming a teacher rather than being a therapist. He then continues to describe his mindset in session.

What does the patient bring to me today? This depends on unconscious co-operation which is set up at the time of the first mutative interpretation, or earlier. It is axiomatic that the work of the analysis is done by the patient, and that this is called unconscious co-operation. It includes such things as dreaming, the remembering of dreams and the reporting of them in a useful way.

Let's pause here. Winnicott is telling us who does the work of therapy: the *patient*. Winnicott asks, "What does the patient bring to me today?" Winnicott follows the patient; it is not the other way around. The patient, without knowing consciously that he is doing so, determines the course of the therapy: where it will go, session by session. This, Winnicott calls "unconscious co-operation." He says that this process of unconscious cooperation starts at the point at which the therapist can offer something "mutative"—something that facilitates change in the patient, on whatever level. But sometimes this cooperation comes about even before that point. He then continues to explain what the patient contributes to the therapy.

Unconscious co-operation is the same as resistance, but the latter belongs to a negative transference element. The analysis of resistance releases the co-operation which belongs to positive transference elements.

What's he saying now? He uses the terms "resistance," "negative transference," "analysis of resistance," and "positive transference." Let's visit each first, and then make sense of what Winnicott is saying.

First, "resistance." Resistance is thought to be a defense whereby the individual seeks to avoid memories, perceptions, or insights which would arouse anxiety. It is thought by Freud to indicate a deep-seated (often unconscious) opposition to the bringing up of repressed (unconscious) material to awareness. More generally, it refers to a patient's unwillingness to cooperate with some aspect of the therapy. But it may also indicate a patient's distrust of or resistance to the *therapist*, which can be the product of a negative transference, but can also sometimes be attributable to the therapist, and to the fact that the therapist is not being able to position him/herself in a manner to be used by the patient.

"Negative transference" is the directing of feelings such as anger, sadness, disappointment, distrust, and so on, toward the therapist and the therapy, either explicitly or implicitly. These are thought to be feelings which originally existed in the matrix of the patient's primary relationships with his caregivers which are being brought forward and transferred on to the therapist. In many cases, such negative thoughts, attitudes, and feelings could not be voiced in the patient's original familial matrix without significant repercussions.

"Positive transference" is the directing of positive feelings and attitudes toward the therapist which originally existed in the patient's primary relationships with his caregivers.

"Analysis of resistance": when the negative feelings are transferred forward on to the therapist and the therapy, and the therapist facilitates conversation about this resistance and invites the patient to put these feelings into words, there is the potential to experience the therapist's acceptance despite the patient's negativity. In other words, the therapist engages with the patient in a manner that enables a certain fluidity in how the therapist is experienced by the patient, so the work can move forward. If this is the case, the patient's negative transference may yield a positive result.

And so, to loop back to Winnicott's narrative above, "[t]he analysis of resistance releases the co-operation which belongs to positive transference elements." He now continues:

> Although psycho-analysis may be infinitely complex, a few simple things may be said about the work I do, and one is that I expect to find a tendency towards ambivalence in the transference and away from more primitive mechanisms of splitting, introjection and projection, object retaliation, disintegration, etc. I know that these primitive mechanisms are universal and that they have positive value, but they are defences in so far as they weaken the direct tie to the object through instinct, and through love and hate.

OK, What's this? In this first sentence, Winnicott says he expects to find a tendency toward ambivalence in the relationship of the patient toward the therapist. Or at least, he's always alert to this possibility.

In his former paper, "Hate in the counter-transference" (1949), Winnicott explains that ambivalence, in contrast to "coincident love and hate," is the capacity to hold and integrate opposing feelings of love and hate toward the same object. It is a developmental achievement to be able to be ambivalent in a relationship. The patient who tends toward ambivalence is able to tolerate the coexistence of these two opposite feelings, and sees the therapist as having both in potential toward himself, but expects to receive the love side of this ambivalence from the therapist.

This means a move away from more primitive ego defenses such as splitting, introjection, projection, object retaliation, and disintegration. These are defenses used by pre-depressive position infants and toddlers (and some adults) to keep their developing ego from being crushed under the weight of too much emotional complexity, too little simplicity. Winnicott comments further that these more primitive defenses have positive value (in normal development) but beyond a certain maturity point, they weaken the tie to the object, in this case, to the therapist—a tie that is impelled by instinct and that transacts both loving and hateful feelings in the therapy. So the therapist is aiming toward a maturity point beyond these primitive defenses.

> At the end of endless ramifications in terms of hypochondriacal fantasy and persecutory delusion a patient has a dream which says: I eat you. Here is stark simplicity like that of the Oedipus complex. Stark simplicity is only possible as a bonus on top of the ego-strengthening that analysis brings about.

OK. He's making an observation here that he will explain more fully as he continues the paper, so we'll leave it for now. He continues:

> I would like to make special reference to this but first I must refer to the fact that in many cases the analyst displaces environmental influences that are pathological, and we gain insight of the kind that enables us to know when we have become modern representatives of the parent figures of the patient's childhood and infancy, and when by contrast we are displacing such figures.

Here Winnicott says that the therapist in many cases "displaces environmental influences that are pathological." He's talking about the myriad ways in which a therapist should purposely set up an interpersonal environment that is different from what the patient may have experienced in his infancy and childhood. These include:

all the samenesses and consistencies of the frame;
the tolerance of the patient's needs;

the enduring of the patient's resistances and negative transferences;

the bearing of the patient's transferences in general, even when they are positive;

the bearing of the burden of loving and hating the patient;

the non-retaliation, the seeing and responding to the patient at both conscious and unconscious levels;

the following and not leading the patient;

the waiting for the right times to intervene;

the waiting and waiting for the patient's ego to strengthen so that they can emerge to live their lives more fully and freely.

In so far as we come through this, we see ourselves affecting the patient's ego in three phases:

(a) We expect a kind of ego-strength in the early stages of an analysis, because of the ego-support that we give simply by doing standard analysis and by doing it well. This corresponds to the ego support of the mother which (in my theorizing) makes the infant ego strong if and only if the mother is able to play her special part at this time. This is temporary and belongs to a special phase.

OK. Winnicott has written extensively on the special attunement that a mother needs to have toward the emerging infant. Without the mother's ministrations (entirely invisible to the baby at first), the infant's nascent ego would collapse in on itself and suffer annihilation. So too the therapist must at first provide ego support to the patient in the measure in which it is needed. Standard analysis—including the careful listening, the consistency, the making initial sense of the patient's needs, gestures, and unconscious transferences— these are the elements that must be provided at first to support the ego of the patient in the early stages of therapy.

(b) Then follows a long phase in which the patient's confidence in the analytic process brings about all kinds of experimenting (on the part of the patient) in terms of ego independence.

Similar to the stage of relative dependence that Winnicott has written about, there follows a long phase in which the patient settles into the process of therapy, and, given a certain confidence in the therapy itself, begins to experiment with new ways of seeing the self, the world, one's history, other people, and new ways of acting in response to all of these. This includes new ways of acting toward the therapist.

(c) In the third phase the now independent ego of the patient begins to show and to assert its own individual characteristics, and the patient begins to take for granted a feeling of existing in his or her own right.

In this third phase, the patient's ego begins to be able to stand on its own, without the direct support of the therapist. The patient occupies the center of himself.

It is this ego-integration that particularly concerns me, and gives me pleasure (though it must not be for my pleasure that it takes place). It is very satisfactory to watch the patient's growing ability to gather all things into the area of personal omnipotence, even including the genuine traumata. Ego-strength results in a clinical change in the direction of a loosening up of the defenses which become more economically employed and deployed, with the result that the individual feels no longer trapped in an illness, but feels free, even if not free from symptoms. In short, we see growth and emotional development that had become held up in the original situation.

This is a lovely summary from Winnicott. It needs a little explanation. He says that it is this ego-integration that concerns him, or, more directly, that is his goal as a therapist. He references the gathering of all things into the area of personal omnipotence. To Winnicott, this is the place from which we start as infants—within the area of personal omnipotence. In that area, we "create" everything that comes into our lives. We take ownership of it. We sign it with our personal signature. Gathering one's personal history into the area of personal omnipotence—even including genuine traumata—means that we own what has happened to us, and we assign our own meaning to those events. The net result, as Winnicott says, is a sense of no longer being trapped, no longer being held up in our own growth process. We finally feel free to take possession of who we are, and who we were meant to be.

What about modified analysis? I find myself working as a psycho-analyst rather than doing standard analysis when I meet certain conditions that I have learned to recognize.

In modified analysis, the analytic setting is used as a potential space in which the meeting of the patient's needs takes priority over the interpretation of the transference. In addition, for Winnicott, the process of internalization of the empathic ministrations of the therapist—displacing the original environmental misattunements—was seen as more important than the analysis of internalized phenomena. Winnicott lists the diagnoses that led him to modify his technique:

(a) Where fear of madness dominates the scene.

(b) Where a false self has become successful, and a facade of success and even brilliance will be destroyed at some phase if analysis is to succeed.

(c) Where in a patient an antisocial tendency, either in the form of aggression or of stealing or of both, is the legacy of a deprivation.

(d) Where there is no cultural life—only an inner psychic reality and a relationship to external reality—the two being relatively un-linked.

(e) Where an ill parental figure dominates the scene.

These and many other illness-patterns make me sit up. The essential thing is that I do base my work on diagnosis. I continue to make a diagnosis of the individual and a social diagnosis as I go along, and I do definitely work according to diagnosis. In this sense I do psycho-analysis when the diagnosis is that this individual, in his or her environment, wants psycho-analysis. I might even try to set going an unconscious co-operation, when conscious wish for analysis is absent. But by and large, analysis is for those who want it, need it, and can take it. When I am faced with the wrong kind of case I change over into being a psycho-analyst who is meeting the needs, or trying to meet the needs, of that special case. I believe this non-analytic work can usually be best done by an analyst who is well versed in the standard psycho-analytic technique.

Winnicott leaves room here for a wide swathe of cases wherein he as a psycho-analyst seeks to meet the needs of the patient rather than observing the more standard techniques of psychoanalysis. In other words, he made it his goal to meet people where they are.

Finally, I would like to say this: I have based my statement on the assumption that all analysts are alike in so far as they are analysts. But analysts are not alike. I am not like what I was twenty or thirty years ago. Some analysts undoubtedly work best in the simplest and most dynamic area where the conflict between love and hate, with all its ramifications in conscious and unconscious fantasy, constitutes the main problem. Other analysts work as well or better when they are able to deal with more primitive mental mechanisms in the transference neurosis or transference psychosis. In this way by interpreting part object retaliations, projections and introjections, hypochondriacal and paranoid anxieties, attacks on linkages, thinking disturbances, etc., etc., they extend the field of operation and the range of the cases they can tackle. This is research analysis, and the danger is only that the patient's needs in terms of infantile dependence may be lost in the course of the analyst's performance. Naturally as we come to gain confidence in the standard technique through our use of it in suitable cases we like to feel that we can tackle the borderline case without deviating, and I see no reason why the attempt should not be made, especially as the diagnosis may alter in our favour as the result of our work. In my opinion our aims in the practice of the standard technique are not altered if it happens that we interpret mental mechanisms which belong to the psychotic types of disorder and to primitive stages in the emotional stages of the individual. If our aim continues to be to verbalize the nascent conscious in terms of the transference, then we are practising analysis; if not, then we are analysts practising something else that we deem to be appropriate to the occasion. And why not?

In this final paragraph, Winnicott, at age 66 and having been in practice for three decades, softly challenges the aim of standard analytic practice: "to verbalize the nascent conscious in terms of the transference." Instead, he suggests that psychodynamic therapists who are treating a diagnosis not envisioned by Freud's focus on neurosis may have to modify their techniques in the direction of meeting the primitive needs of their patients. This, then, would be, to Winnicott, a therapist at work as is appropriate to the circumstances s/he finds.

9 Notes on ego integration in child development

(1962)

Winnicott, D. W. (1962). Notes on ego integration in child development. In *The maturational processes and the facilitating environment: Studies in the theory of emotional development* (pp. 56–63). London: Karnac, 2007.

This is a wide-ranging paper from Winnicott in which he covers many crucially important topics. His major focus is to examine the development of the ego—and the caregiving that supports its integration, personalization, and capacities for object relating. The newborn is part of an infant–mother couple. The "ego-coverage" given by the mother means that, because the infant cannot supply anything for himself, she is reading, anticipating, and responding to need before it registers as need and before it escalates into what would be overwhelming and psychologically annihilating for the infant. The mother is the "I" for the infant before the infant has an "I" from which to cover himself. Winnicott explicitly links compromises of very early infant care (in the first hours and days of life) to later-expressed serious pathologies of nervous system, attentional, and psychological processes.

I have rearranged some of Winnicott's paragraphs, without excluding any of his writing, because his sometimes elliptical style in so dense a paper makes following it a bit difficult for the reader. For further clarity, I offer outline elements along the way to orient the reader to the topics Winnicott covers in this paper.

Ego defined

The term ego can be used to describe that part of the growing human personality that tends, under suitable conditions, to become integrated into a unit.

Right away in this paper, Winnicott puts out his major theme and his definition of "ego"—the part of the personality that tends toward integration.

> It will be seen that the ego offers itself for study long before the word self
> has relevance. The word self arrives after the child has begun to use the
> intellect to look at what others see or feel or hear and what they conceive
> of when they meet this infant body. (The concept of the self will not be
> studied in this chapter.)

Here Winnicott considers the semantic difference between "ego" and "self."
"Self" connotes that stage of development wherein the child can perceive
others and conceive of what those others might be experiencing.

Winnicott is actually using a term—"ego"—that was generated and owned
by Freud, and is giving it a different definition from Freud's. So let's first square
up what Freud means by "id" and "ego," because Winnicott will put out his
contrasting notions and timings of id and ego development in this paper.

The "id" (Latin for "it"), is, according to Freud, the disorganized part of the
personality structure that contains humans' basic, instinctual drives. Freud felt
that the id is the only component of human personality that is present from
birth. (Winnicott disagreed with him here, seeing id as coming into play only
after there is enough ego development to experience the id.) Freud felt that the
id is the source of our bodily needs, wants, desires, and impulses (Freud, 1923).

The "ego" (Latin for "I"), according to Freud, is developed in response to the
id, and "is that part of the id which has been modified by the direct influence of
the external world" (Freud, 1923, p. 25). The ego represents what may be called
reason and common sense, in contrast to the id, which contains the passions.
The ego is charged with reining in id passions (Freud, 1923).

OK. So at this point in this paper Winnicott is going to begin with an argument about the inception of id and ego by using a pediatrician's consideration of
children born with anencephaly—the absence of a major portion of the brain,
skull, and scalp that occurs during embryonic development. But here, I'm going
to exercise my prerogative as Winnicott's translator, and insert this part of his paper
at the end because it will make the rest of it much more understandable. So here
we go, moving some paragraphs around, and cutting and pasting as we go along.

Now he moves on to more direct considerations about the nature of
the ego.

The nature of the ego

Winnicott will now address the following questions and topics:

  Is there an ego from the start?
  Is the ego strong or weak?
  The infant has a brief experience of omnipotence
  The baby eventually has subjective object and objective object mixed
    experiences

Winnicott:

> *The first question* that is asked about that which is labelled ego is this: is
> there an ego from the start? The answer is that the start is when the ego
> starts.[1]
>
> 1   It is well to remember that the beginning is a summation of beginnings.

Here he footnotes himself as follows:

"It is well to remember that the beginning is a summation of beginnings."

His cryptic footnote means that the ego, as he sees it, is the result of a
process in the newborn—it is not there from the beginning, but represents a
summation of a series of beginnings.

He continues:

> Then *the second question* arises: is the ego strong or weak? The answer to
> this second question depends on the actual mother and her ability to
> meet the absolute dependence of the actual infant at the beginning, at the
> stage before the infant has separated out the mother from the self.

He has already written a paper about the special state of sensitivity that a
good-enough mother needs to experience at the very beginning. He has called
this state "Primary Maternal Preoccupation" (1956).

> In my terminology the good enough mother is able to meet the needs
> of her infant at the beginning, and to meet these needs so well that the
> infant, as emergence from the matrix of the infant–mother relationship
> takes place, is able to have a brief *experience of omnipotence*. (This has to be
> distinguished from *omnipotence*, which is the name given to a quality of
> feeling.)

OK. What is an experience of omnipotence? Winnicott believes that at first,
in the first few weeks of an infant's life, the infant does not perceive that *any-*
thing is happening from outside of him/herself. S/he is gradually building the
capacity to experience—to have bodily experience—and for a time is imper-
vious to intervention from the outside. So, as needs are met, it comes to feel
to the infant that there is a rather direct link between the (pre-)emergence of
need and the meeting of that need, and thus, that the infant has created the
experience. As such, for a while, the infant has the experience of omnipotence.

S/he does not have the *feeling* of omnipotence, because *feeling it* would be too developmentally advanced. But the *experience* of omnipotence is important for the future development of many essential elements of personality. Included here is the psychic sense in the baby that s/he has arrived and lives in a benign place that enables providing for one's self—not that the baby has any of these thoughts as such—but this is a basic thread in the weaving of the ego, and ultimately of the self.

Winnicott continues:

> The mother can do this because of her having temporarily given herself over, to the one task, that of the care of this one infant. Her task is made possible by the fact that the baby has a capacity, when this matter of the mother's supportive egofunction is operative, to relate to *subjective objects*. In this respect the baby can meet the reality principle here and there, now and then, but not everywhere all at once; that is, the baby retains areas of subjective objects along with other areas in which there is some relating to objectively perceived objects, or "not-me" ("non-I") objects.

OK. Winnicott moves ahead in time here a bit. Mother has given herself over to the care of this one infant. Good. The infant, *eventually*, because of mother's support of his/her emerging ego, can intermittently relate to objects outside himself to which s/he, the infant him/herself, assigns the meaning. Winnicott calls these "subjective objects"—objects whose meaning is assigned by the infant, and thus, are not yet objectively perceived, and not yet repudiated as "not me." This precedes but eventually intermixes with the infant's capacity to conceptualize and relate to entities as they really are, which Winnicott calls "objectively perceived objects."

Winnicott's next section:

Ego development

Ego development is characterized by the following trends:

1. Integration in space
   Integration in time

2. Personalization

3. Object relating

Winnicott explains:

> Ego development is characterized by various trends:
>
> (1) The main trend in the maturational process can be gathered into the various meanings of the word *integration*. Integration in time becomes added to (what might be called) integration in space.

OK. This word "integration" is very important in the thinking and writing of Winnicott. He felt that our whole developmental program was about integration—taking various parts and pieces and blending them into a growing and meaningful whole as a person. He then mentions a very early piece of the integration process for an infant: *integration in space*. An infant has to find himself outside the womb, breathing air, feeling gravity, encountering the visual world, darkness, and light—all of these things; locating him/herself in space.

In addition, an *infant begins to integrate the element of time*. The consciousness of the passing of time is perhaps a new element to be encountered and, in some nascent way, to be made sense of by the newborn.

Winnicott next explains the next part of ego development: personalization:

> (2) The ego is based on a body ego, but it is only when all goes well that the person of the baby starts to be linked with the body and the body-functions, with the skin as the limiting membrane. In favourable circumstances the skin becomes the boundary between the me and the not-me. In other words, the psyche has come to live in the soma and an individual psycho-somatic life has been initiated.

OK. *Personalization*. This is another important element in Winnicott's thinking: that the ego is at first bodily sensations that over time become "imaginatively elaborated." This process, according to Winnicott, is the basis for the development of the psyche, which has emerged from and come to live in the soma (the body). The person of the baby begins to become aware of and become linked to his own body, and to get that his/her body stops where the skin stops. The skin comes to mean the boundary between the me and the not-me, so skin functions both literally and metaphorically.

Winnicott goes on:

> I have used the term *personalization* to describe this process, because the term depersonalization seems at basis to mean a loss of firm union between ego and body, including id-drives and id-satisfactions. (The term depersonalization has gathered to itself a more sophisticated meaning in psychiatric writings.)

So he here refers to *personalization—the process of inhabiting the body*—and depersonalization—losing a sense of inhabiting one's own body. The body includes id-drives (bodily needs, wants, desires, and motoric impulses) and id-satisfactions (the exercise and satisfaction of bodily needs, wants, desires, and motoric impulses), but the perception of these and the integration of these do not happen right away. The ego, in Winnicott's thinking, has processes to accomplish before the id can be experienced.

He now continues to explain the third aspect of ego development: object relating.

> (3) The ego initiates *object-relating*. With good-enough mothering at the beginning the baby is not subjected to instinctual gratifications except in so far as there is ego-participation. In this respect it is not so much a question of giving the baby satisfaction as of letting the baby find and come to terms with the object (breast, bottle, milk, etc.).

Ok, so this third element of ego development, object relating—which ultimately builds to include human relating—is a complex process which follows upon the infant's becoming oriented in space and time, inhabiting his own body and using his incipient imagination to elaborate the feelings of inhabiting his body. He at the same time encounters objects—breast, bottle, milk, etc.—which are supplied to him, but he does not at first understand that they are coming from the outside. His not-yet-developed capacities encounter objects simultaneously with his own (pre-)need states, and so he at first imagines that he *did* them; he made them happen; he made them exist. And from the mother's side, this is the task at first: her maternal ministrations have to be *synced-up* with his needs quite closely, such that he is not presented with instinctual gratifications that are dissociated from his own need states and disconnected from his incipient ego-participation. It does not at first make sense to talk about gratifying his instincts because there is not yet in the newborn the capacity to understand that there are forces from the inside and ministrations that are from outside. Nothing is sought. It has to be there at the right time and to be found by him.

OK. Now he makes a somewhat parenthetical reference to the work of another analyst who wrote a few years before he published this paper.

> When we attempt to assess what Sechehaye (1951) did when she gave her patient an apple at the right moment ("symbolic realization") it is of but little moment whether the patient ate the apple, or just looked at it, or took it and kept it. The important thing was that the patient was able to create an object, and Sechehaye did no more than enable the object

to take appleshape, so that the girl had created a part of the actual world, an apple.

Winnicott is referring here to the work of Marguerite Sechehaye (1951), a psychoanalyst writing about her work with an 18-year-old schizophrenic patient, Renee. Renee later recounted some of her delusions: her hands were cat's paws; she was alternately nine centuries old and not yet born; she was growing smaller and smaller; her internal "system" forbade her to eat any food that was not apples picked from a neighboring orchard. Sechehaye began feeding Renee slices of apple as if she were an infant. Renee experienced the contentment of a tiny baby, and as a result, her perception of things changed radically. Through this process, Renee was able to see reality for the first time: people were no longer automatons; things were just things. Sechehaye gave this intervention the name "symbolic realization." Winnicott uses this as a parallel to the process of presenting breast, bottle, milk, etc., to baby. The important thing was that the patient, Renee, was able to "create" an object—to make the apple whatever she needed it to be—just as the important thing is that the baby is allowed to create the object—to make the breast or the milk whatever he needs, what he has created.

OK. So now pulling it together, Winnicott has named three elements— integration in space and time, personalization, and object relating—as elements in the process of ego development. He then goes another step:

Elements of ego development corresponding to aspects of maternal care:

He writes:

> It would seem to be possible to match these three phenomena of ego-growth with three aspects of infant and child-care:
>
> Integration matches with holding
> Personalization matches with handling
> Object-relating matches with object-presenting.

These are three functions provided by the good-enough mother: holding (physical and emotional), which promotes integration in space and time; handling (handling which is sensitive to the baby's fragility), which promotes personalization; and object presenting, which promotes object relating. He'll discuss integration (matched with holding) first.

Integration/holding

a. Integration from motor/sensory elements.
b. Integration with the goal of becoming a unit self.

Back to Winnicott:

> This leads to a consideration of two problems associated with the idea of integration:

> It is useful to think of the material out of which integration emerges in terms of motor and sensory elements, the stuff of primary narcissism.

(According to Freud, "primary narcissism" is the desire and energy that drive one's instinct to survive.)

He's talked above about integration in space and time. Now he adds something: that integration first emerges in the context of the infant's sensory experiences and via the exercise of motor movements of his body.

He then continues:

> This would acquire a tendency towards a sense of existing.

These motor and sensory elements would "acquire a tendency towards a sense of existing." He's using the most delicate and tentative language possible to describe the initial parts of the process of ego development. He continues:

> Other language can be used to describe this obscure part of the maturational process, but the rudiments of an imaginative elaboration of pure body-functioning must be postulated if it is to be claimed that this new human being has started to be, and has started to gather experience that can be called personal.

OK, so integration emerges out of motor and sensory elements, which would then "acquire a tendency towards a sense of existing." This new human starts to gather experience (beyond mere integration in space and time), and to imaginatively elaborate that experience. This is integration in its very initial stage. Winnicott recognizes that he is describing an obscure, hard-to-describe part of the process of ego development. Then he raises the next question:

Integration with what?

> All this tends towards the establishment of a unit self, but it cannot be over-emphasized that what happens at this very early stage depends on the ego-coverage given by the mother of the infant–mother coupling.

The infant is not an independent entity yet; he has not yet achieved "unit status"; he is part of an infant–mother couple. The "ego-coverage" given by the mother means that, because the infant cannot supply anything for himself, she is reading need, anticipating need, responding to need before it registers as need and before it escalates into what would be overwhelming for the infant. She is the "I" for the infant before the infant has an "I" from which to cover himself.

> It can be said that good-enough ego-coverage by the mother (in respect of the unthinkable anxieties) enables the new human person to build up a personality on the pattern of a continuity of going-on-being. All failures (that could produce unthinkable anxiety) bring about a reaction of the infant, and this reaction cuts across the going-on-being. If reacting that is disruptive of going-on-being recurs persistently it sets going a pattern of fragmentation of being.

OK. Now this is crucial. Winnicott now introduces the term "unthinkable anxieties" in this context of integration. This is a pivotal Winnicottian construct. Winnicott observes that lack of closely attuned maternal coverage can create moments of anxiety in the infant (who has no sense of his own agency yet, no language with which to think about an attunement failure, and no sense that the distress will ever stop). Winnicott will detail these anxieties later in this paper, but the result of the infant's being catapulted into such anxiety is that the infant experiences a disruption of his going-on-being. If these unthinkable anxieties occur persistently, the infant's attempts to integrate and to build eventually to an "I" are *severely* compromised, and s/he instead experiences *fragmentation*. This is so very important to take in! When an infant's attempts to integrate and to build an "I" are not supported, or, even worse, are subverted by abuse or chaos or disconnection or distraction or disaffection or depression or parental neglect or even by circumstance, the "I" that s/he builds will be a fundamentally compromised structure, with gaping vulnerabilities—which will exhibit themselves physically, mentally, socially, emotionally, spiritually—in his/her subsequent life over time. Winnicott says exactly this in the next paragraph.

> The infant whose pattern is one of fragmentation of the line of continuity of being has a developmental task that is, almost from the beginning, loaded in the direction of psychopathology. Thus there may be a very early factor (dating from the first days or hours of life) in the aetiology of restlessness, hyperkinesis, and inattentiveness (later called inability to concentrate).

Here Winnicott explicitly links compromises of very early infant care (in the first hours and days of life) to later-expressed pathologies of both nervous system and attentional processes. In other places he links these compromises to quite severe psychopathologies.

> It is pertinent here to state that, whatever the external factors, it is the individual's view (fantasy) of the external factor that counts. Alongside this it is necessary to remember, however, that there is a stage before the individual has repudiated the not-me. So that there is, at this very early stage, no external factor; the mother is part of the child. At this stage the infant's pattern includes the infant's experience of the mother, as she is in her personal actuality.

It is the particular infant's experience of these caregiving factors that matters. Two infants may experience disruptions differently. So it is the infant's subjective experience that counts. (Some infants will be disrupted more easily than others by failures of maternal care.) Also, he notes again that in the earliest hours and days, mother and child are not differentiated, from the child's point of view. The infant experiences himself linked to all of what the mother does and to her whole way of being—her "personal actuality."

He goes on:

> The opposite of integration would seem to be disintegration. This is only partly true. The opposite, initially, requires a word like unintegration. Relaxation for an infant means not feeling a need to integrate, the mother's ego-supportive function being taken for granted. The understanding of unexcited states requires further consideration in terms of this theory.

OK, so unintegration is an OK state, a state of relaxation for the infant when the task of being integrated is on temporary pause. This is made possible by his/her being held in the ego support of the mother.

> The term disintegration is used to describe a sophisticated *defence*, a defence that is an active production of chaos in defence against unintegration in the absence of maternal ego-support, that is, against the unthinkable or archaic anxiety that results from failure of holding in the stage of absolute dependence.

So disintegration is a dreadful state for the infant. It is like unintegration, but it is unintegration in the absence of maternal support, in the absence of physical/psychological holding during this initial stage of absolute dependence. And here we have the ever observant pediatrician in Winnicott: he observes an infant actively produce the chaos of disintegrating inside himself so as not to experience the full brunt of the unthinkable anxieties inherent in not being held when holding/maternal ego-support is so acutely necessary to his going-on-being.

> The chaos of disintegration may be as "bad" as the unreliability of the environment, but it has the advantage of being produced by the baby and therefore of being non-environmental. It is within the area of the baby's omnipotence. In terms of psycho-analysis, it is analysable, whereas the unthinkable anxieties are not.

OK. So this "chaos of disintegration" in the infant is a defense against the experience of sensing that he is not being held psychically by his (maternal) environment. Internal chaos that the infant falls into of his own accord is preferable to his not being held by the maternal environment because it is not caused by the forces external to her/him. It is, in Winnicott's language, "non-environmental." It is, therefore, in some small measure, in the infant's control, which is better than living in a (failing) environment/relationship in which he is both utterly dependent and utterly out of control.

Now Winnicott links integration with holding, and describes the trajectory of the integration process in the infant:

> Integration is closely linked with the environmental function of holding. The achievement of integration is the unit. First comes "I" which includes "everything else is not me". Then comes "I am, I exist, I gather experiences and enrich myself and have an introjective and projective

interaction with the not-me, the actual world of shared reality". Add to this: "I am seen or understood to exist by someone"; and, further, add to this: "I get back (as a face seen in a mirror) the evidence I need that I have been recognized as a being."

OK. So, somewhere farther along the developmental path (well beyond the first hours and days), as the integration task continues, the infant figures out the distinction between "me" and "everything else [that] is not me." This is a huge developmental achievement! Then there comes the realization that "I am"! I take in from the environment; I give out to the environment. I exist in inter-action with the actual world of reality, not just the world I create via my imagin-ation. And finally, I am mirrored; I am understood to exist by someone else.

But, in Winnicott's observation,

The establishment of a state of I am, along with the achievement of psycho-somatic indwelling or cohesion constitutes a state of affairs which is accompanied by a specific anxiety affect that has an expectation of per-secution. This persecutory reaction is inherent in the idea of the repudi-ation of the "not-me", which goes with the limitation of the unit self in the body, with the skin as the limiting membrane.

OK, so the downside of reaching the status of "I am" and with figuring out the distinction between "me" and "not-me" is that if I repudiate or in some way differentiate from or reject the not-me, it has the power to repudiate me back. The not-me can attack the me. Hmm. I therefore have anxiety about being persecuted by the not-me.

So, all of the above has addressed integration which is "matched with" (or related to) maternal holding in Winnicott's mind. Remember he's describing the process of ego integration, and matching three phenomena of ego-growth with three aspects of infant and child care. The second of his list of three aspects of ego-growth is personalization, which he associates with the aspect of *handling* in infant and child care. He'll now discuss:

Personalization/handling

a. Establishing a psycho-somatic partnership
b. Psycho somatic illness

Handling describes the environmental provision that corresponds loosely with the establishment of a psycho-somatic partnership. Without

> good-enough active and adaptive handling the task from within may well prove heavy, indeed it may actually prove impossible for this development of a psychosomatic inter-relationship to become properly established.

OK—he's talking here about the process of the infant's inhabiting his body, personalization, or the establishing of a psycho-somatic partnership. He's saying that good-enough, sensitive-enough physical handling by the mother promotes the knitting together of the baby's psyche with his soma (his body). He's asserting also that the absence of such holding may in fact disturb or even prevent this inter-relationship from developing.

> In psycho-somatic illness of one kind there is in the symptomatology an insistence on the interaction of psyche and soma, this being maintained as a defence against threat of a loss of psycho-somatic union or against a form of depersonalization.

He asserts that some kinds of psychosomatic illnesses are the attempt to knit the psyche and the soma together such that the psyche and soma do not come apart from one another.

The third of his list of three aspects involved in ego integration is object relating, which he links with maternal object presenting. He'll now discuss:

Object relating/process of object presenting

a.   Baby has as the origin of the process an unformulated need with a vague expectation
b.   Mother presents an object or manipulation that meets the need
c.   Baby begins to need what mother presents
d.   Baby feels confident in being able to create objects, world.

Winnicott explains:

> The initiation of object-relating is complex. It cannot take place except by the environmental provision of object-presenting, done in such a way that the baby creates the object. The pattern is thus: the baby develops a vague expectation that has origin in an unformulated need. The adaptive mother presents an object or a manipulation that meets the baby's needs, and so the baby begins to need just that which the mother presents. In this way the baby comes to feel confident in being able to create objects and to create the actual world. The mother gives the baby a brief period in which omnipotence is a matter of experience.

OK. Such a clear explanation of this part of the process from Winnicott! It needs no elaboration. (But read it again!) He continues.

> It must be emphasized that in referring to the initiating of object relating I am not referring to id-satisfactions and id-frustrations. I am referring to the preconditions, internal to the child as well as external, conditions "Which make an ego-experience" out of a satisfactory breast feed (or a reaction to frustration).

The maturing psyche-soma eventually includes enough ego to experience id-satisfactions (the exercise and satisfaction of bodily needs, wants, desires, and motoric impulses) and id-frustrations (the non-satisfaction of these bodily needs, etc.), but in the earliest stage, these are not able to be conceptualized by the baby. What is relevant is the meeting of the "unformulated need" by the mother so that the baby makes an ego-experience—an ego building block—out of him/herself "creating" the solution to his/her as yet unformulated need.

He then continues,

> But id-functioning is normally not lost; it is collected together in all its aspects and becomes ego-experience. There is thus no sense in making use of the word "id" for phenomena that are not covered and catalogued and experienced and eventually interpreted by ego-functioning.

He's saying that the ego is necessary for experiencing id phenomena, so it makes no sense to posit an id in the absence of an ego. (He's again expressing a theoretical difference from Freud here.)

> In the very early stages of the development of a human child, therefore, ego-functioning needs to be taken as a concept that is inseparable from that of the existence of the infant as a person. What instinctual life there may be apart from ego-functioning can be ignored, because the infant is not yet an entity having experiences. There is no id before ego. Only from this premise can a study of the ego be justified.

Here he's staked out a position that is consistent in his writings over time; that is, that the infant begins as an entity not yet even capable of having conscious experiences. Here he's at odds with Freud, who believed that the id pre-exists the ego. (Perhaps Freud just did not yet know how to describe the somatic experiencing that Winnicott elaborates!)

Now as he moves to this final section, Winnicott speaks of the consequences to ego development that happen when good-enough mothering is absent at the very beginning. Here I present the rest of his outline for continuity's sake.

Good-enough mothering vs. not: such a difference

a. Infant is not able to get started with ego maturation, or else with ego-development

Infant anxieties

a. Infant should be thought of as being on edge of unthinkable anxieties
b. Four anxieties:

    i. Going to pieces
    ii. Falling in space
    iii. Depersonalization
    iv. Loss of orientation in time, space.

Fate of baby missing good-enough care

a. Distortions of the ego-organization—schizoid
b. Defense of self-holding
c. Infantile schizophrenia or autism
d. Latent schizophrenia
e. False Self-defence
f. Schizoid personality

Anencephalia

> So much difference exists between the beginning of a baby whose mother can perform this function well enough and that of a baby whose mother cannot do this well enough that there is no value whatever in describing babies in the earliest stages except in relation to the mother's functioning. When there is not-good enough mothering the infant is not able to get started with ego maturation, or else ego-development is necessarily distorted in certain vitally important respects.

Here he's been clear. Not-good-enough mothering—mothers who have not been able to achieve primary maternal preoccupation from the very beginning—leads to a stunting of ego maturation in the infant or distortion in certain vitally important respects.

He next elaborates some of the characteristics of this good-enough versus not-good-enough caregiving, and he is crystal-clear about why caretaking needs to be so well-matched to infant need:

> It must be understood that when reference is made to the mother's adaptive capacity this has only a little to do with her ability to satisfy the infant's oral drives, as by giving a satisfactory feed. What is being discussed here runs parallel with such a consideration as this. It is indeed possible to gratify an oral drive and by so doing to violate the infant's ego-function, or that which will later on be jealously guarded as the self, the core of the personality. A feeding satisfaction can be a seduction and can be traumatic if it comes to a baby without coverage by ego-functioning. At the stage which is being discussed it is necessary not to think of the baby as a person who gets hungry, and whose instinctual drives may be met or frustrated, but to think of the baby as an immature being who is all the time on the brink of unthinkable anxiety. Unthinkable anxiety is kept away by this vitally important function of the mother at this stage, her capacity to put herself in the baby's place and to know what the baby needs in the general management of the body, and therefore of the person. Love, at this stage, can only be shown in terms of body-care, as in the last stage before full-term birth.

So, Winnicott is saying that the newborn must be thought of not just as a hungry or wet being, but as a being who is all the time on the brink of unthinkable anxiety, which is averted by mother's capacity to put herself empathically into the baby's place and to care sensitively for his bodily self. He has mentioned unthinkable anxieties before in the text of this paper. He will now go on to explain the nature of an infant's unthinkable anxiety. (This may be one of Winnicott's most important ideas and contributions to grasping the deep pathological adaptions that humans make to these unthinkable anxieties.)

> Unthinkable anxiety has only a few varieties, each being the clue to one aspect of normal growth.
>
> (1) Going to pieces.
> (2) Falling for ever.
> (3) Having no relationship to the body.
> (4) Having no orientation.
>
> It will be recognized that these are specifically the stuff of the psych-otic anxieties, and these belong, clinically, to schizophrenia, or to the emergence of a schizoid element hidden in an otherwise non-psychotic personality.

OK. Now he's just said something that's crucial for clinicians to understand. Some people we see in practice may have experienced one or all of these unthinkable anxieties as babies, and may hold the experience in a part of their psyche that they have hidden from themselves and others. The fear of going to pieces, of falling forever, of disinhabiting their own body, of having no orientation whatsoever in time and space—these are unthinkable and unimaginable experiences, but are in fact the real experience of some infants of misattuned care. He links the experience of these anxieties to psychotic processes, to a schizoid element in the personality, or to the development of a false self.

> From here it is necessary to interrupt the sequence of ideas in order to examine the fate of the baby who misses good-enough care in the early stage before the baby has separated off the "not me" from the "me".

Let's consider this distinction he has just made: the early stage before the baby has separated off the "not-me" from the "me." At first the baby has only bodily experiences, which, with progress, s/he elaborates with his/her growing capacity to imagine. But during that initial time, there is no "not-me" for the baby. There is only the incipient awareness of the "me."

He then continues:

> This is a complex subject because of all the degrees and varieties of maternal failure. It is profitable, first, to refer to:
>
> (1) distortions of the ego-organization that lay down the basis for schizoid characteristics, and
> (2) the specific defence of self-holding, or the development of a caretaker self and the organization of an aspect of the personality that is false (false in that what is showing is a derivative not of the individual but of the mothering aspect of the infant–mother coupling). This is a defence whose success may provide a new threat to the core of the self though it is designed to hide and protect this core of the self.

OK. So now Winnicott is laying out two categories of consequences that occur in babies who are the receivers of not-good-enough maternal care in the very earliest stages:

(1) distortions of the organization of the ego can cause a schizoid element to be hidden in an otherwise non-psychotic personality;
(2) the emergence of the false self whose task is to hold itself instead of being held by the mother, leading to a false self which is prematurely and

compulsively attuned to the needs of the other, and who easily disattends to his own needs. He'll elaborate these further below.

The consequences of defective ego support by the mother can be very severely crippling, and include the following:

Infantile schizophrenia or autism

This well-known clinical grouping contains disorders secondary to physical brain lesions or deficiency, and also includes some degree of every kind of failure of the earliest maturational details. In a proportion of cases there is no evidence of neurological defect or disease.

It is a common experience in child psychiatry for the clinician to be unable to decide between a diagnosis of primary defect, mild Little's disease, pure psychological failure of early maturation in a child with brain intact, or a mixture of two or all of these. In some cases there is good evidence of a reaction to failure of ego-support of the kind I am describing in this chapter.

(Little's disease is a chronic neuromuscular condition of hypertonia and spasticity in the muscles of the lower extremities of the human body.)

So Winnicott is asserting that some diseases in children can be the result of failures of ego support. He continues to list conditions A through D.

Latent schizophrenia

There are many clinical varieties of latent schizophrenia in children who pass for normal, or who may even show special brilliance of intellect or precocious performance. The illness shows in the brittleness of the "success". Strain and stress at later stages of development may trigger off an illness.

False Self-defence

The use of defences, especially that of a successful false self, enables many children to seem to give good promise, but eventually a breakdown reveals the fact of the true self's absence from the scene.

The false self is a concept that Winnicott elaborates in other papers. It is characterized by the infant's development of caregiving elements toward the self and ultimately toward others, which leaves the person with a core feeling of futility, and can, in some cases, eventuate in psychological breakdown.

Schizoid personality

> Commonly there develops personality disorder which depends on the fact that a schizoid element is hidden in a personality that is otherwise sane. Serious schizoid elements become socialized in so far as they can hide in a pattern of schizoid disorder that is accepted in a person's local culture.

Students of personality diagnosis recognize schizoid personality disorders to be evident in people uninterested in and unable to make relationships with other humans. They live their lives psychically protected from the risks and rewards of human relationship.

> These degrees and kinds of personality defects can be related, in investigations of individual cases, to various kinds and degrees of failure of holding, handling and object-presenting at the earliest stage. This is not to deny the existence of hereditary factors, but rather: to supplement them in important respects.

Winnicott's thesis linking early environmental failure to serious subsequent psychological disease states is quite straightforward. He does not rule out hereditary factors, but suggests compromises of the earliest stage of maternal care to be another causal factor to be considered.

Now I move to an argument which Winnicott placed first in this paper. I moved it to the last position.

> In the body of an anencephalic infant functional events, including instinctual localizations, may be taking place, events that would be called experiences of id-function if there were a brain. It could be said that if there had been a normal brain there would have been an organization of these functions, and to this organization could have been given the label ego. But with no electronic apparatus there can be no experience, and therefore no ego.

OK, so no ego can exist without a functioning brain. But then Winnicott takes the argument a step further in this brief quasi-philosophical consideration of the existence versus non-existence of id and ego in an anencephalic infant.

He says in essence that, if there is no ego there to interpret experience, it's of no use to hypothesize the existence of an id. In this way, he quietly differentiates himself from Freud once again.

Summary

My object is to make a bare-bone statement of my conception of the beginnings of the ego. I use the concept of ego-integration, and the place of ego-integration in the initiation of emotional development in the human child in the child who is all the time moving from absolute dependence to relative dependence, and towards independence. I also trace the beginnings of objectrelating within the framework of a baby's experience and growth.

Further, I attempt to assess the importance of the actual environment at the earliest stage, that is, before the baby has separated out the not-me from the me. I contrast the ego-strength of the baby who gets ego-support from the mother's actual adaptive behaviour, or love, with the ego-weakness of the baby for whom environmental provision is defective at this very early stage.

Winnicott's major focus in this paper has been to examine the development of the ego—and the caregiving that supports its integration, personalization, and capacities for object relating. He has also explored what happens when an infant does not receive necessary maternal support during the time when the incipient ego is developing.

10 Mirror-role of mother and family in child development

(1967)[1]

Winnicott, D. W. (1971). Mirror-role of mother and family in child development. In *Playing and reality* (Ch. 9, pp. 1–6). London: Tavistock Publications.

In this paper, Winnicott presents thoughts and case material on the role of the mother's face in the development of a child. He discusses the ways in which a mother's face functions as an emotional mirror for an infant. When a baby looks at a mother's face, the baby sees a reflection of what the mother sees in the baby. What a baby sees in the eyes and face of the mother becomes the basis for what the baby begins to infer about him- or herself. Also, if a baby does not sense attunement in the face of the mother, that child is forced to use his mind prematurely to begin to take care of his own needs. And when a baby has to fast-forward developmentally, the natural progression that allows a little one the full freedom to create and be spontaneous in the world he inhabits may be co-opted, siphoned off, or may begin to atrophy. Winnicott ends by making the comparison to psychotherapy—that psychotherapy is a complex derivative of the mother's face that reflects what is there to be seen in the patient.

> In individual emotional development the precursor of the mirror is the mother's face. I wish to refer to the normal aspect of this and also to its psychopathology.
>
> Jacques Lacan's paper 'Le Stade du Miroir' (1949) has certainly influenced me. He refers to the use of the mirror in each individual's ego development. However, Lacan does not think of the mirror in terms of the mother's face in the way that I wish to do here.
>
> I refer only to infants who have sight. The wider application of the idea to cover infants with poor sight or no sight must be left over till the main theme is stated. The bare statement is this: in the early stages of the emotional development of the human infant a vital part is played by the environment

1 Published in P. Lomas (ed.), *The Predicament of the Family: A Psycho-analytical Symposium* (1967). London: Hogarth Press and the Institute of Psycho-Analysis.

which is in fact not yet separated off from the infant by the infant. Gradually the separating-off of the not-me from the me takes place, and the pace varies according to the infant and according to the environment. The major changes take place in the separating-out of the mother as an objectively perceived environmental feature. If no one person is there to be mother the infant's developmental task is infinitely complicated.

Winnicott begins with a simple statement: "the precursor of the mirror is the mother's face." He will spend his time in this paper discussing the ways in which a mother's face functions as an emotional mirror for an infant, telling him/her something of what s/he is experiencing. Winnicott quickly refers to his observation that, for a while in infancy, the environment around a baby, which is controlled and mediated by the mother, is not encountered as "external" by the baby, nor is the mother encountered as "external" by the baby because there is no "external" or "internal" for the newborn. Rather, all is encountered by the newborn infant as experience. The baby is, at first, an experiencing being, who only later, with time and development, will perceive his mother and the environment she creates as external to him. Here Winnicott characterizes the fast-forwarding that some infants have to do. They must be vigilant, studying the mother's visage for signs of safety or unsafety. When it's safe, the infant can relax and be an infant. When something clouds the mother's countenance, the baby has to become alert to the situation.

He continues:

Let me simplify the environmental function and briefly state that it involves:

1. Holding
2. Handling
3. Object-presenting.

The infant may respond to these environmental provisions, but the result in the baby is maximal personal maturation. By the word maturation I intend to include the various meanings of the word integration, as well as psychosomatic interrelating and object relating.

OK. Winnicott is beginning to use *his* language to speak of the baby's experience. Winnicott posits that personal maturation entails the progressive march of more and more integration in a baby via being held, handled, and presented with things that he requires. Personal maturation/integration means, at first, the knitting together of the psychosomatic—the soma (bodily experience) with the psyche (the imaginative elaboration of bodily experience). He will elaborate this more specifically in another paper entitled "Mind and its relation to the psyche-soma" (1949). This integration of the psyche-soma is ultimately followed by the infant's capacity to encounter the maternal presence who provides for the infant's needs, but each of these is a developmental step.

Back to Winnicott:

> A baby is held, and handled satisfactorily, and with this taken for granted is presented with an object in such a way that the baby's legitimate experience of omnipotence is not violated.

Winnicott is talking here about the physicality of being held as an infant, and the physical sensations of being handled in all the ways an infant is and must be handled. With the holding and handling in place, the infant is presented with objects such as the breast or the bottle or the bath water or the diaper. But Winnicott felt that it was of ultimate importance that the baby's experience of not having to be aware of the sources of these things—of instead "owning" what was happening to him—and he felt that the baby's "omnipotence" should not be violated. This is where the infant is developmentally at first, and it must not be abridged. In other words, this time and this set of experiences set a foundation within the infant. It should convey the following message: the world into which you have been born is purposed to facilitate your growth, as your needs, wants, and capacities emerge.

Winnicott continues:

> The result can be that the baby is able to use the object, and to feel as if this object is a subjective object, and created by the baby.

Winnicott here coins the phrase, "subjective object," which means the mother's ministrations which are "created" by the infant—which have no relation to the real external reality of a separate mother, and are in the baby's (developing) mind created by the baby her/himself. This is the first, entirely necessary step of development in a baby's life.

Winnicott continues:

> All this belongs to the beginning, and out of all this comes the immense complexities that comprise the emotional and mental development of the infant and child.[1]
>
> 1   For further and detailed discussion of these ideas the reader can consult my paper 'The Theory of the Parent–Infant Relationship' (1960b).

He then proceeds:

> Now, at some point the baby takes a look round. Perhaps a baby at the breast does not look at the breast. Looking at the face is more likely to be a feature (Gough, 1962). What does the baby see there? To get to the answer we must draw on our experience with psycho analytic patients who reach back to very early phenomena and yet who can verbalize (when they feel they can do so) without insulting the delicacy of what is preverbal, unverbalized, and unverbalizable except perhaps in poetry.
>
> What does the baby see when he or she looks at the mother's face? I am suggesting that, ordinarily, what the baby sees is himself or herself. In other words the mother is looking at the baby and *what she looks like is related to what she sees there.*

OK. What did Winnicott just say? What does a baby see when he or she looks at the mother's face? The baby sees a reflection of what the mother sees in the baby. If she sees a good child, the baby sees her attitude toward and love for the child in her arms. If she sees a perplexing, worrisome child, that's what the baby sees reflected in her face. What the mother sees in the baby is what the baby sees in the eyes and face of the mother, and this is the basis for what the baby begins to infer about him- or herself. Good or bad, welcome or unwelcome. A blessing or a bother. Likewise, if a baby is feeling distress but sees no sense of concern reflected in a mother's face, s/he sees a face disconnected from him/her.

He continues:

> All this is too easily taken for granted. I am asking that this which is naturally done well by mothers who are caring for their babies shall not be taken for granted. I can make my point by going straight over to the case of the baby whose mother reflects her own mood or, worse still, the rigidity of her own defences.

A baby looks but does not see himself/herself reflected. S/he sees something other than the mother reflecting back to her what she may be feeling or experiencing in the moment. She may see a mother's mood state, e.g., depression or anxiety, which is unreflective of what the baby is experiencing. Or she may see someone caught up in the rigidity of her own defenses—meaning someone who is chronically caught up in a way of seeing and being in the world that is inflexible and not adapted to the baby's cues.

Then Winnicott explains:

> In such a case what does the baby see? Of course nothing can be said
> about the single occasions on which a mother could not respond. Many
> babies, however, do have to have a long experience of not getting back
> what they are giving. They look and they do not see themselves. There are
> consequences. First, their own creative capacity begins to atrophy, and in
> some way or other they look around for other ways of getting something
> of themselves back from the environment.

OK. This is a theme to which Winnicott will refer in other writings. If a baby
does not sense attunement from the mother—in the face of the mother—if
he looks and does not see himself, that child is forced to use his mind prematurely to begin to take care of his own needs—or, in Winnicott's language, to
become "prematurely and compulsively attuned" to his/her caretaker or to the
caretaking environment. When this happens, the natural progression that allows
a little one the full freedom to create the world he inhabits, and to be spontaneous in that world—the natural progression that builds to the capacity to be
creative as an individual—that progression may be co-opted, may be siphoned
off, may begin to atrophy. He will address this topic of the development of creativity in later papers.

He continues:

> They may succeed by some other method, and blind infants need to get
> themselves reflected through other senses than that of sight. Indeed, a
> mother whose face is fixed may be able to respond in some other way.
> Most mothers can respond when the baby is in trouble or is aggressive,
> and especially when the baby is ill.
>
> Second, the baby gets settled in to the idea that when he or she looks,
> what is seen is the mother's face. The mother's face is not then a mirror.
> So perception takes the place of apperception, perception takes the place
> of that which might have been the beginning of a significant exchange
> with the world, a two-way process in which self-enrichment alternates
> with the discovery of meaning in the world of seen things.

OK. So what is he saying here? Why would it be bad if, when he or she
looks, what is seen is the mother's face? It's bad because it is not yet what a
baby is equipped to see—not yet. The baby at first needs to see only his/her
own world and experience reflected back to him/her. Winnicott explains this
by using the terms perception and apperception. We ordinarily think of perception—the taking in of something from the world around us—as preceding

apperception—our interpretation of what we've taken in. But in the initial world of an infant there is no division between external and internal. There is only what the baby makes of his own experiencing. There is only, for a while, apperception without a consciousness of perception. Winnicott goes on to say that if mother's face is not a mirror of what the infant is experiencing, but instead is unrelated to what the infant is experiencing, the baby has to fast-forward developmentally, skipping over the first steps in which there is infinite room for the baby's sense of omnipotence—of his having sole ownership and authorship of his/her experience without having to pay attention to or try to make sense of things outside himself. Skipping over this step compromises the beginning of a significant exchange with the world which will gradually, with time and development, move from the baby's sense of omnipotence to the taking in of things seen in the external world, whose ultimate end product is self-enrichment.

He continues:

> Naturally, there are half-way stages in this scheme of things. Some babies do not quite give up hope and they study the object and do all that is possible to see in the object some meaning that ought to be there if only it could be felt. Some babies, tantalized by this type of relative maternal failure, study the variable maternal visage in an attempt to predict the mother's mood, just exactly as we all study the weather. The baby quickly learns to make a forecast: "Just now it is safe to forget the mother's mood and to be spontaneous, but any minute the mother's face will become fixed or her mood will dominate, and my own personal needs must then be withdrawn otherwise my central self may suffer insult."

Here Winnicott characterizes the fast-forwarding that some infants have to do. They must be vigilant, studying the mother's visage for signs of safety or unsafety. When it's safe, the infant can relax and be an infant. When something clouds the mother's countenance, the baby has to become alert to the situation, stealing from him his own experience of spontaneity—which should be his birthright and his only concern as a newborn.

> Immediately beyond this in the direction of pathology is predictability, which is precarious, and which strains the baby to the limits of his or her capacity to allow for events. This brings a threat of chaos, and the baby will organize withdrawal, or will not look except to perceive, as a defence. A baby so treated will grow up puzzled about mirrors and what the mirror has to offer. If the mother's face is unresponsive, then a mirror is a thing to be looked at but not to be looked into.

OK. Winnicott is saying that those babies who have mothers farther out on the spectrum of pathology must anticipate chaos in a way that they are certainly not equipped to do. This leaves only two pathways: either (1) withdrawal or (2) only looking to "perceive"—meaning, to read the signals from the external interpersonal world. He then (parenthetically) predicts that these children will have a different experience of actual mirrors when they grow up.

He then continues:

> To return to the normal progress of events, when the average girl studies her face in the mirror she is reassuring herself that the mother-image is there and that the mother can see her and that the mother is *en rapport* with her.

Winnicott in speaking of the "average girl" is here referring to children of good-enough parenting. Such a girl will infuse the mirror experience with experience of being seen and valued by, and being in harmony with her own mother, even if unconsciously.

> When girls and boys in their secondary narcissism look in order to see beauty and to fall in love, there is already evidence that doubt has crept in about their mother's continued love and care. So the man who falls in love with beauty is quite different from the man who loves a girl and feels she is beautiful and can see what is beautiful about her.

If, in terms of this mirror function, girls and boys of *not*-good-enough care look in the mirror in later life, they hope to behold their own beauty, but are beset with doubt about their internal value. He suggests, even if just by hinting, that falling in love with external beauty is secondary in value to falling in love with the internal person of the other, and imbuing them with beauty as an expression of that love.

> I will not try to press home my idea, but instead I will give some examples so that the idea I am presenting can be worked over by the reader.

What will follow now will be a series of illustrations from Winnicott's practice and/or experience. They are more like paintings that are left to the interpretation of the observer, so I will not attempt to render them as tightly as I have rendered Winnicott's narrative to this point.

Illustration I

I refer first to a woman of my acquaintance who married and brought up three fine male children. She was also a good support to her husband who had a creative and important job. Behind the scenes this woman was always near to depression. She seriously disturbed her marital life by waking every morning in a state of despair. She could do nothing about it. The resolution of the paralysing depression came each day when at last it was time to get up and, at the end of her ablutions and dressing, she could "put on her face". Now she felt rehabilitated and could meet the world and take up her family responsibilities. This exceptionally intelligent and responsible person did eventually react to a misfortune by developing a chronic depressive state which in the end became transformed into a chronic and crippling physical disorder.

Here is a recurring pattern, easily matched in the social or clinical experience of everyone. What is illustrated by this case only exaggerates that which is normal. The exaggeration is of the task of getting the mirror to notice and approve. The woman had to be her own mother. If she had had a daughter she would surely have found great relief, but perhaps a daughter would have suffered because of having too much importance in correcting her mother's uncertainty about her own mother's sight of her.

Here Winnicott expresses it straightforwardly: "getting the mirror to notice and approve," and that "the woman had to be her own mother."

He then brings up the example of Francis Bacon's art:

The reader will already be thinking of Francis Bacon. I refer here not to the Bacon who said: "A beautiful face is a silent commendation" and "That is the best part of beauty, which a picture cannot express", but to the exasperating and skilful and challenging artist of our time who goes on and on painting the human face distorted significantly. From the standpoint of this chapter this Francis Bacon of today's date is seeing himself in his mother's face, but with some twist in him or her that maddens both him and us. I know nothing of this artist's private life, and I bring him in only because he forces his way into any present day discussion of the face and the self. Bacon's faces seem to me to be far removed from perception of the actual; in looking at faces he seems to me to be painfully striving towards being seen, which is at the basis of creative looking.

I see that I am linking apperception with perception by postulating a historical process (in the individual) which depends on being seen:

> When I look I am seen, so I exist. I can now afford to look and see. I now look creatively and what I apperceive I also perceive. In fact I take care not to see what is not there to be seen (unless I am tired).

He posits that the function of the mother's mirror role is to give the assurance that "When I look, I am seen …I exist." And so, I now have the freedom to perceive—to look, to see, to perceive, to create.

Illustration II

A patient reports: "I went to a coffee bar last night and I was fascinated to see the various characters there", and she describes some of these characters. Now this patient has a striking appearance, and if she were able to use herself she could be the central figure in any group. I asked: "Did anyone look at you?" She was able to go over to the idea that she did in fact draw some of the fire, but she had taken along with her a man friend, and she could feel that it was at him that people were looking.

From here the patient and I were together able to make a preliminary survey of the patient's early history and childhood in terms of being seen in a way that would make her feel she existed. Actually the patient had had a deplorable experience in this respect.

This subject then got lost for the time being in other types of material, but in a way this patient's whole analysis revolves round this "being seen for what she in fact is", at any one moment; and at times the being actually seen in a subtle way is for her the main thing in her treatment. This patient is particularly sensitive as a judge of painting and indeed of the visual arts, and lack of beauty disintegrates her personality so that she recognizes lack of beauty by herself feeling awful (disintegrated or depersonalized).

Here he is observing the centrality, for this patient, of being seen for what she in fact is because her experience of being seen in early childhood was "deplorable."

Illustration III

I have a research case, a woman who has had a very long analysis. This patient has come through, late in life, to feeling real, and a cynic might say: to what end? But she feels it has been worth while, and I myself have learned a great deal of what I know of early phenomena through her.

This analysis involved a serious and deep regression to infantile depend-ence. The environmental history was severely disturbing in many respects, but here I am dealing with the effect on her of her mother's depression. This has been worked over repeatedly and as analyst I have had to displace this mother in a big way in order to enable the patient to get started as a person.[2]

Just now, near the end of my work with her, the patient has sent me a portrait of her nurse. I had already had her mother's portrait and I have got to know the rigidity of the mother's defences very intimately. It became obvious that the mother (as the patient said) had chosen a depressed nurse to act for her so that she might avoid losing touch with the children altogether. A lively nurse would automatically have "stolen" the children from the depressed mother. This patient has a marked absence of just that which characterizes so many women, an interest in the face. She certainly had no adolescent phase of self examination in the mirror, and now she looks in the mirror only to remind herself that she "looks like an old hag" (patient's own words).

This same week this patient found a picture of my face on a book-cover. She wrote to say she needed a bigger version so that she could see the lines and all the features of this "ancient landscape". I sent the pic-ture (she lives away and I see her only occasionally now) and at the same time I gave her an interpretation based on what I am trying to say in this chapter.

This patient thought that she was quite simply acquiring the portrait of this man who had done so much for her (and I have). But what she needed to be told was that my lined face had some features that link for her with the rigidity of the faces of her mother and her nurse.

I feel sure that it was important that I knew this about the face, and that I could interpret the patient's search for a face that could reflect herself, and at the same time see that, because of the lines, my face in the picture reproduced some of her mother's rigidity.

Actually this patient has a thoroughly good face, and she is an excep-tionally sympathetic person when she feels like it. She can let herself be concerned with other people's affairs and with their troubles for a limited period of time. How often this characteristic has seduced people into thinking of her as someone to be leaned on! The fact is, however, that the moment my patient feels herself being involved, especially in someone's depression, she automatically withdraws and curls up in bed with a hot water bottle, nursing her soul. Just here she is vulnerable.

2 An aspect of this case was reported by me in my paper 'Metapsychological and Clinical Aspects of Regression within the Psycho-Analytical Set-Up' (1954).

A few observations:

He says of this patient that she has "come through … to feeling real." He feels that feeling real is a consummate developmental achievement and a quite worth-while outcome of her (and really, anyone's) long-term psychotherapy. He discusses the effects of her mother's depression. He mentions that she has a marked absence of interest in the face, and is denigrating of her own mirror image (looks like an old hag). She needed to discern in the picture of Winnicott the link between Winnicott's lined face (because of age) and her mother's and nurse's face (due to their depression). She also needed Winnicott to understand her search for a face that could reflect herself (her need as a small child), but a face that could also reproduce some of the familiarity of her mother's face's quality of rigidity.

Illustration IV

After all this had been written a patient brought material in an analytic hour which might have been based on this that I am writing. This woman is very much concerned with the stage of the establishment of herself as an individual. In the course of this particular hour she brought in a refer-ence to "Mirror mirror on the wall, etc." and then she said: "Wouldn't it be awful if the child looked into the mirror and saw nothing!"

The rest of the material concerned the environment provided by her mother when she was a baby, the picture being of a mother talking to someone else unless actively engaged in a positive relating to the baby. The implication here was that the baby would look at the mother and see her talking to someone else. The patient then went on to describe her great interest in the paintings of Francis Bacon and she wondered whether to lend me a book about the artist. She referred to a detail in the book. Francis Bacon says that he likes to have glass over his pictures because "then when people look at the picture what they see is not just a picture; they might in fact see themselves."[3]

After this the patient went on to speak of "Le Stade du Miroir" because she knows of Lacan's work, but she was not able to make the link that I feel I am able to make between the mirror and the mother's face. It was not my job to give this link to my patient in this session because the patient is essentially at a stage of discovering things for herself, and pre-mature interpretation in such circumstances annihilates the creativity of the patient and is traumatic in the sense of being against the maturational process. This theme continues to be important in this patient's analysis, but it also appears in other guises.

This glimpse of the baby's and child's seeing the self in the mother's face, and afterwards in a mirror, gives a way of looking at analysis and at the psychotherapeutic task. Psychotherapy is not making clever and apt interpretations; by and large it is a long-term giving the patient back what the patient brings. It is a complex derivative of the face that reflects what is there to be seen.

I like to think of my work this way, and to think that if I do this well enough the patient will find his or her own self, and will be able to exist and to feel real. Feeling real is more than existing; it is finding a way to exist as oneself, and to relate to objects as oneself, and to have a self into which to retreat for relaxation. But I would not like to give the impression that I think this task of reflecting what the patient brings is easy. It is not easy, and it is emotionally exhausting. But we get our rewards. Even when our patients do not get cured they are grateful to us for seeing them as they are, and this gives us a satisfaction of a deep kind.

This to which I have referred in terms of the mother's role of giving back to the baby the baby's own self continues to have importance in terms of the child and the family. Naturally, as the child develops and the maturational processes become sophisticated, and identifications multiply, the child becomes less and less dependent on getting back the self from the mother's and the father's face and from the faces of others who are in parental or sibling relationships (Winnicott, 1960a). Nevertheless, when a family is intact and is a going concern over a period of time each child derives benefit from being able to see himself or herself in the attitude of the individual members or in the attitudes of the family as a whole. We can include in all this the actual mirrors that exist in the house and the opportunities the child gets for seeing the parents and others looking at themselves. It should be understood, however, that the actual mirror has significance mainly in its figurative sense.

This could be one way of stating the contribution that a family can make to the personality growth and enrichment of each one of its individual members.

3 See Francis Bacon: Catalogue raisonné and documentation (Alley, 1964). In his Introduction to this book, John Rothenstein writes: "... to look at a painting by Bacon is to look into a mirror, and tosee there our own afflictions and our fears of solitude, failure, humiliation, old age, death and of nameless threatened catastrophe. His avowed preference for having his paintings glazed is also related to his sense of dependence on chance. The preference is due to the fact that glass sets paintings somewhat apart from the environment (just as his daisies and railings set his subjects apart from their pictorial environment), and that glass protects but what counts more in this case is his belief that the fortuitous play of reflections will enhance his pictures. His dark blue pictures in particular, I heard him observe gain by enabling the spectator to see his own face in the glass."

Several observations:

One is that Winnicott slips in his perspective on the process of therapy almost parenthetically:

> It was not my job to give this link [the relation of the mirror to the
> mother's face] to my patient in this session because the patient is essen-
> tially at a stage of discovering things for herself, and premature interpret-
> ation in such circumstances annihilates the creativity of the patient and is
> traumatic in the sense of being against the maturational process.

Then he provides a stunningly clear meta-statement of what he thinks of as
the goal of therapy:

> Psychotherapy is not making clever and apt interpretations; by and large
> it is a long-term giving the patient back what the patient brings. It is a
> complex derivative of the face that reflects what is there to be seen.
>   I like to think of my work this way, and to think that if I do this well
> enough the patient will find his or her own self, and will be able to exist
> and to feel real. Feeling real is more than existing; it is finding a way to
> exist as oneself, and to relate to objects as oneself, and to have a self into
> which to retreat for relaxation.

He follows this with a statement about the wear and tear of being a therapist:

> But I would not like to give the impression that I think this task of
> reflecting what the patient brings is easy. It is not easy, and it is emotion-
> ally exhausting. But we get our rewards. Even when our patients do not
> get cured they are grateful to us for seeing them as they are, and this gives
> us a satisfaction of a deep kind.

He finishes with an observation that falls backward over the entire paper: "It
should be understood, however, that the actual mirror has significance mainly
in its figurative sense."

11 The use of an object

(1969)

Winnicott, D. W. (1969). The use of an object. *International Journal of Psycho-Analysis* 50, 711–716.

This paper was read by Winnicott to the New York Psychoanalytic Society, on November 12, 1968 and published in the *International Journal of Psycho-Analysis* in 1969, two years before he died. In this paper, Winnicott presents the process whereby an infant begins to discover an inside and an outside to himself, and to the other who occupies the outside. Winnicott distinguishes between object relating—relating to objects created by the infant's fantasy, and within his omnipotence—and object usage—relating to objects that have a real existence external to him. He highlights the cruciality of the mother's survival of the infant/subject's attempts at destruction of the object external to him, and the importance of this process in the work of psychotherapy.

> In this paper I propose to put forward for discussion the idea of the use of an object. The allied subject of relating to objects seems to me to have had our full attention. The idea of the use of an object has not, however, been so much examined, and it may not even have been specifically studied.

Winnicott starts this paper by acknowledging that he has written extensively on the idea of object relating, which is a reference to the child's developmental discovery of a relational world from within his omnipotently created world, but he is now turning to the use of an object, a further developmental progression.

> This work on the use of an object arises out of my clinical experience and is in the direct line of development that is peculiarly mine. I cannot assume, of course, that the way my ideas have developed has been followed by others, but I would like to point out that there has been a sequence, and the order that there may be in the sequence belongs to the evolution of my work.

Here Winnicott is claiming authorship of the idea of the "use" of an object, and is communicating that the ideas he is about to present are "peculiarly [his]," and proceed from his clinical experience.

> My work on transitional objects and phenomena which followed on naturally after 'The Observation of Infants in a Set Situation' (Winnicott, 1941) is fairly well known. Obviously the idea of the use of an object is related to the capacity to play. I have recently given attention to the subject of creative playing (Winnicott, 1968a). This is near to my present subject. Then also there is a natural development from my point of view along the line of the concepts of the holding environment, this facilitating the individual's discovery of the self. Arising out of failure in this area of the facilitating environment can be seen the whole subject of the development of character disorders associated with the setting up of various kinds of false self, these representing failures of self-establishment and self-discovery. All this makes sense, for me, of the special focus that there is in my work on what I have called transitional phenomena and the study of the minute details that are available to the clinician that illustrate the gradual build-up of the individual's capacity to play and the capacity to find and then to use the "external" world with its own independence and autonomy.

Winnicott is giving us historical context for his ideas regarding the use of an object in terms of his own thinking and writing over time. He says that obviously, "the use of an object is related to the capacity to play." This is "obvious" to him, but to us, his audience, it is not yet so obvious. He is relating to his own paper on creative playing in children (1968). He is also making reference to his former work on transitional objects (1953), wherein the infant begins to discover both an inside and an outside to himself, and to the other who occupies the outside. He does this discovery initially through the vehicle of transitional objects—objects that occupy both the territory created by the infant's fantasy, within his omnipotence, and the territory of external reality, outside of his omnipotence. The infant begins to relate to an object outside of his omnipotence; to recognize that there *is* an object beyond his own needs and wants. Winnicott focuses in his last sentence on the meat of the matter at hand: the gradual build-up of the individual's capacity to play, and the capacity to first find and then "use" the external world.

> What I have to say in this present paper is extremely simple. Although it comes out of my psychoanalytical experience I would not say that it could have come out of my psychoanalytical experience of two decades ago, because I would not then have had the technique to make possible

the transference movements that I wish to describe. For instance, it is only in recent years that I have become able to wait and wait for the natural evolution of the transference arising out of the patient's growing trust in the psychoanalytic technique and setting, and to avoid breaking up this natural process by making interpretations. It will be noticed that I am talking about the making of interpretations and not about interpretations as such. It appalls me to think how much deep change I have prevented or delayed in patients *in a certain classification category* by my personal need to interpret. If only we can wait, the patient arrives at understanding creatively and with immense joy, and I now enjoy this joy more than I used to enjoy the sense of having been clever. I think I interpret mainly to let the patient know the limits of my understanding. The principle is that it is the patient and only the patient who has the answers. We may or may not enable him or her to be able to encompass what is known or become aware of it with acceptance.

OK. This is a block-busting paragraph from Winnicott! He is saying that (after more than four decades of functioning as an analyst in the footsteps of Freud) he has come to a modification of technique that is indeed significant: that the therapist's interpretations may in some, perhaps many, cases need to be subordinated to the *patient's* interpretations. His words are direct and impactful. He extols the virtue of waiting for the patient to speak interpretive truth for himself:

> It appalls me to think how much deep change I have prevented or delayed in patients of a certain classification category by my personal need to interpret. If only we can wait, the patient arrives at understanding creatively and with immense joy….The principle is that it is the patient and only the patient who has the answers.

Here Winnicott is offering a quietly radical revision of psychoanalytic technique. He contextualizes his perspective on the patient's interpretations with a focus on the evolution of the therapeutic relationship: "the natural evolution of the transference arising out of the patient's growing trust in the psychoanalytic technique and setting."

By contrast with this comes the interpretative work which the analyst must do and which distinguishes analysis from self-analysis. This interpreting by the analyst, if it is to have effect, must be related to the patient's ability *to place the analyst outside the area of subjective phenomena.* What is then involved is the patient's ability to use the analyst, which is the subject of this paper. In teaching, as in the feeding of a child, the capacity to use objects is taken for granted, but in our work it is necessary for us to be concerned with the development and the establishment of the capacity to use objects and to recognize a patient's inability to use objects, where this is a fact.

OK. So now he's developing his argument. He definitely feels that there's a role for interpretations by the therapist, and that there's a difference between his allowing the patient to come to his own interpretive insights in the therapy and a "self-analysis." But, he says, if the therapist's interpretations are to have any effect, they must come when the patient is able to place the analyst "outside the area of subjective phenomena." Here he is harvesting concepts he has developed over the decades: that an infant (and, in parallel, many patients) start out with a world that is defined by their own subjectivity—their own experience, their own thoughts, their own narratives, their own perspectives; their own reality. In this subjective world, the infant (and in parallel, the patient) rejects or refracts all interpretive offerings by the therapist to make them comport with his subjectively conceived views of self, others, and the world. Before a patient can benefit from the interpretations offered by a therapist, he must be able to place the therapist outside of this subjectively created world. The patient has to "experience" the therapist as not only outside but separate from himself. He will explain further what this entails.

It is in the analysis of the borderline type of case that one has the chance to observe the delicate phenomena that give pointers to an understanding of truly schizophrenic states. By the term "a borderline case" I mean the kind of case in which the core of the patient's disturbance is psychotic, but the patient has enough psychoneurotic organization always to be able to present psychoneurosis or psychosomatic disorder when the central psychotic anxiety threatens to break through in crude form. In such cases the psychoanalyst may collude for years with the patient's need to be psychoneurotic (as opposed to mad) and to be treated as psychoneurotic.

Winnicott is writing at a time when the term "borderline" was used by early psychiatrists (starting in the 1930s) to describe people who were thought to be on the "border" between the diagnoses of neurosis and psychosis. (It was not until 1980 that borderline personality disorder became an official personality disorder in the third edition of Diagnostic and *Statistical Manual of Mental Disorders* (DSM-III: American Psychiatric Association, 1980.) At the time, people with neurosis were believed by many to be treatable, whereas people with psychoses were deemed by many to be untreatable. Winnicott observed a set of underlying "psychotic" anxieties that distinguished psychotic and borderline patients from neurotic patients: (1) disintegration of the individual's personality; (2) a sense of falling forever; (3) depersonalization (disinhabiting one's body); (4) derealization (loss of the sense of things seeming real); and (5) loss of the capacity to relate to objects. These were the underlying anxieties that Winnicott saw some patients to have but to be able to mask, and therefore to present as neurotic "as opposed to mad," (meaning more seriously disturbed).

Winnicott continues:

> The analysis goes well, and everyone is pleased. The only drawback is that the analysis never ends. It can be terminated, and the patient may even mobilize a psychoneurotic false self for the purpose of finishing and expressing gratitude. But, in fact, the patient knows that there has been no change in the underlying (psychotic) state and that the analyst and the patient have succeeded in colluding to bring about a failure. Even this failure may have value if both analyst and patient acknowledge the failure. The patient is older and the opportunities for death by accident or disease have increased, so that actual suicide *may* be avoided. Moreover, it has been fun while it lasted. If psychoanalysis could be a way of life, then such a treatment might be said to have done what it was supposed to do. But psychoanalysis is no way of life. We all hope our patients will finish with us and forget us, and that they will find living itself to be the therapy that makes sense. Although we write papers about these borderline cases we are inwardly troubled when the madness that is there remains undiscovered and unmet. I have tried to state this in a broader way in a paper on classification (Winnicott, 1959–64).

Winnicott is serious about this piece: we need as therapists to get to the bottom of things and not to engage in window-dressing when the real damage is to the foundation.

> It is perhaps necessary to prevaricate a little longer to give my own view on the difference between object-relating and object-usage. In object-relating the subject allows certain alterations in the self to take place, of a kind that has caused us to invent the term cathexis. The object has become meaningful. Projection mechanisms and identifications have been operating, and the subject is depleted to the extent that something of the subject is found in the object, though enriched by feeling.

OK. What's he saying here? Object relating. When he speaks of object relating, he is speaking of a specific window of development. In this process, at first, the baby (the subject) maintains a narcissistic attitude toward the external object; the object is an extension of or a projection of the baby's self. At this point, says Winnicott, the *subject* (the baby) allows certain alterations to take place; he allows "cathexis"—the investment of emotional and psychic energy in the other, which is an alteration in the (developmentally appropriate) absorption with the self. The baby/subject is depleted by this process to some extent, to the degree that he has allowed parts of his energy to be invested in the object, and parts of himself to be found outside himself—in the other—via projection.

> Accompanying these changes is some degree of physical involvement (however slight) towards excitement, in the direction of the functional climax of an orgasm. (In this context I deliberately omit reference to the very important aspect of relating that is an exercise in cross-identifications. This must be omitted here because it belongs to a phase of development that is subsequent to and not prior to the phase of development with which I am concerned in this paper, that is to say, the move from self-containment and relating to subjective objects into the realm of object-usage.) (Winnicott, 1968b.)

Winnicott's reference to cross-identifications refers to the ability to stand in another's shoes, to take another's perspective, to feel another's feelings—the realization and awareness of someone who is entirely "not me." He will not discuss this because it comes *after* the phases of object relating and object usage which Winnicott discusses in this paper. He continues:

> "Object-relating" is an experience of the subject that can be described in terms of the subject as an isolate (Winnicott, 1958), (1963). When I speak of the use of an object, however, I take object-relating for granted, and add new features that involve the nature and the behaviour of the object. For instance, the object, if it is to be used, must necessarily be real in the sense of being part of shared reality, not a bundle of projections. It is this, I think, that makes for the world of difference that exists between relating and usage.

OK. So Winnicott is making the distinction here between object relating— the baby's narcissistic way of seeing objects as extensions or projections of the self—and the shift to a more advanced mode, object usage, in which the baby recognizes the object as separate and distinct from the self. Winnicott will address the process whereby the subject comes to place the object "outside the area of the subject's omnipotent control."

> If I am right in this, then it follows that discussion of the subject of relating is a much easier exercise for analysts than is the discussion of usage, since relating may be examined as a phenomenon of the subject, and psychoanalysis always likes to be able to eliminate all factors that are

> environmental, except in so far as the environment can be thought of
> in terms of projective mechanisms. But in examining usage there is no
> escape; the analyst must take into account the nature of the object, not as
> a projection, but as a thing in itself.

Here Winnicott is asserting that it's easier for analysts and therapists to think
in terms of their patient's engaging in object relating than object usage. The
former allows the therapist to construe all that happens in the therapy as a
product of the inner world of the patient. The latter requires the therapist to
factor himself and his unique impacts on the patient into the equation.

> For the time being may I leave it at that, that relating can be described in
> terms of the individual subject, and that usage cannot be described except
> in terms of acceptance of the object's independent existence, its property
> of having been there all the time? You will see that it is just these problems
> that concern us when we look at the area which I have tried to draw
> attention to in my work on what I have called transitional phenomena.

So here Winnicott is catching his breath, about to launch into his treatise
on object usage. His reference to the object's "independent existence" and to
the object's "having been there all the time" is taken directly from his work on
transitional objects, treated in his 1953 paper, "Transitional objects and transitional phenomena."

> But this change does not come about automatically, by maturational pro-
> cess alone. It is this detail that I am concerned with.
>   In clinical terms: two babies are feeding at the breast; one is feeding on the
> self in the form of projections, and the other is feeding on (using) milk from
> a woman's breast. Mothers, like analysts, can be good or not good enough;
> some can and some cannot carry the baby over from relating to usage.

Here Winnicott is making the point that a baby (and a patient) must be
carried over by the mother/therapist from object relating (feeding via omnipotent projection of the self) to object usage (feeding from the actual external
source).

> I would like to put in a reminder here that the essential feature in the
> concept of transitional objects and phenomena (according to my pres-
> entation of the subject) is *the paradox, and the acceptance of the paradox:* the

baby creates the object but the object was there waiting to be created and to become a cathected object. I tried to draw attention to this aspect of transitional phenomena by claiming that in the rules of the game we all know that we will never challenge the baby to elicit an answer to the question: did you create that or did you find it?

Here Winnicott is again making brief reference to his 1953 paper on "Transitional objects and transitional phenomena"—that the baby, in his initial omnipotence, "creates" the object magically, but that the object pre-existed the baby's "creation" of her, and was there the whole time, waiting to be "created."

I am now ready to go straight to the statement of my thesis. It seems I am afraid to get there, as if I fear that once the thesis is stated the purpose of my communication is at an end, because it is so very simple.

To use an object the subject must have developed a *capacity* to use objects. This is part of the change to the reality principle.

This capacity cannot be said to be inborn, nor can its development in an individual be taken for granted. The development of a capacity to use an object is another example of the maturational process as something that depends on a facilitating environment.[1]

In the sequence one can say that first there is object-relating, then in the end there is object-use; in between, however, is the most difficult thing, perhaps, in human development; or, the most irksome of all the early failures that come for mending.

This thing that there is in between relating and use is the subject's placing of the object outside the area of the subject's omnipotent control, that is, the subject's perception of the object as an external phenomenon, not as a projective entity, in fact recognition of it as an entity in its own right.[2]

1   In choosing the title for my Hogarth book I was showing how much I was influenced by Dr Phyllis Greenacre at the Edinburgh Congress. Unfortunately, I failed to put into the book an acknowledgement of this fact.

2   I was influenced in my understanding of this point by W. Clifford M. Scott (personal communication, *c.* 1940).

OK. What did he just say there? Several things: (1) that the capacity to "use" objects is not inborn; it depends upon a facilitating environment (meaning attuned, responsive maternal holding and care); (2) that object relating must precede object usage; (3) that the transition between these two ways of being is a most difficult process; and (4) that the transition between these two states entails the baby/subject's placing of the object outside of the subject's omnipotent control. He will now take us through this process.

> This change (from relating to use) means that the subject destroys the object. From here it could be argued by an armchair philosopher that there is therefore no such thing in practice as the use of an object; if the object be external, then the object is destroyed by the subject. Should the philosopher come out of his chair and sit on the floor with his patient, however, he will find that there is an intermediate position. In other words, he will find that after "subject relates to object" comes "subject destroys object" (as it becomes external); and then may come "*object survives* destruction by the subject". But there may or may not be survival. A new feature thus arrives in the theory of object-relating. The subject says to the object: "I destroyed you", and the object is there to receive the communication. From now on the subject says: "Hullo object!" "I destroyed you." "I love you." "You have value for me because of your survival of my destruction of you." "While I am loving you I am all the time destroying you in (unconscious) *fantasy*." Here fantasy begins for the individual. The subject can now *use* the object that has survived. It is important to note that it is not only that the subject destroys the object because the object is placed outside the area of omnipotent control. It is equally significant to state this the other way round and to say that it is the destruction of the object that places the object outside the area of the subject's omnipotent control. In these ways the object develops its own autonomy and life, and (if it survives) contributes in to the subject, according to its own properties.

OK. We'll take this slowly because it is the heart of the matter. The baby/subject starts out in the position of having complete omnipotent control of all aspects of the (mother)/object. The baby "creates" and, at some level, takes ownership over everything that happens to him. The object is a functionary in the baby's world. This is the realm of omnipotence that allows the baby the protection from reality he needs in order initially to go-on-being and to develop.

But as time and development move on, the baby develops a new capacity: that is, the capacity to encounter the object as external to himself, and along with this, the capacity to encounter external reality. This changeover from subjective to objective interpersonal worlds is mediated by the baby's active *destruction* of the object.

It is the baby who initiates this process. It is as though destruction is the birth canal through which a new way of being emerges. The baby must destroy the object over which he was formerly omnipotent in order to make room for a post-omnipotent object. This battle for the destruction of the object occurs both in real time (baby versus object) and in fantasy (baby, in fantasy versus fantasied object).

There are two elements at play here: (1) the baby destroys the object because it is outside of the area of his omnipotent control; and (2) the destruction *itself* places the object outside the area of omnipotent control. One way or the other, the baby forcibly contends against the object with the goal of its destruction (and of its survival).

And then, there is one more crucial element to this "birthing" process: that the (mother)/object being destroyed must *survive* the baby's attempts at destruction. In fact, the object has value for the baby if and only if s/he survives the baby's attempts at destruction—only if s/he can be found to be the real external object that the baby encounters on the other side of the process of destruction.

So, what are the net results of this "difficult" process of destruction? If the mother/object survives it, the baby finds a real person on the other side, one with its own autonomy and life, one that can contribute to the baby in unique ways, according to her own personality and attributes. In addition, the baby gains entrée into the world of objective reality.

OK, back to Winnicott:

> In other words, because of the survival of the object, the subject may now have started to live a life in the world of objects, and so the subject stands to gain immeasurably; but the price has to be paid in acceptance of the ongoing destruction in unconscious fantasy relative to object-relating.

Winnicott contends that this forcible overthrow of the "subjective" object continues to go on in unconscious fantasy, even after all the weapons of war have been put down and the peace treaties have been signed.

He continues:

> Let me repeat. This is a position that can only be arrived at by the individual in early stages of emotional growth through the actual survival of cathected objects that are at the time in process of becoming destroyed because real, becoming real because destroyed (being destructible and expendable).

OK. So Winnicott is reaffirming the necessity of the survival of the objects of destruction. But this elliptical sentence suggests something more. The object is destroyed because real—OK. But "becoming real because destroyed." What does this mean? And why would the object *have* to be destroyed? The answer may be that the object needs to survive; that the destruction is a form of testing the mettle of the object. If the object can maintain itself through this testing/

destruction process, then it is more real, more external, more separate, more reliable, more able to be used by the infant/subject/patient.

> From now on, this stage having been reached, projective mechanisms assist in the act of *noticing what is there*, but are not *the reason why the object is there*. In my opinion this is a departure from orthodox psychoanalytic theory, which tends to think of external reality only in terms of the individual's projective mechanisms.

Winnicott here is saying that those practicing orthodox psychoanalysis tend to think that all perception of external reality is based upon a patient's projective mechanisms. Winnicott disagrees. He feels that if an individual is able to successfully wage the above-referenced battle, his grasp of external reality may in some measure be aided by projection, but it is not entirely comprised of projection. It includes the *real* offerings of the objectively perceived external object/therapist. (And in this way he departs from Klein and her traditional followers.)

> I have now nearly made my whole statement. Not quite, however, because it is not possible for me to take for granted an acceptance of the fact that the first impulse in the subject's relation to the object (objectively perceived, not subjective) is destructive.
>
> The central postulate in this thesis is that whereas the subject does not destroy the subjective object (projection material), destruction turns up and becomes a central feature in so far as the object is objectively perceived, has autonomy, and belongs to "shared" reality. This is the difficult part of my thesis, at least for me.

OK. The first impulse in the subject's relation to the objectively perceived (external) object/mother is destruction. The baby/subject in his initial stages of development does not intentionally try to destroy its subjective object—the one comprised of the baby/subject's omnipotent projections—although his demands may in fact exact a heavy toll from the mother. But at the point where the object is beginning to be objectively perceived, there is the impulse to destroy it—to make it retreat back into the world of the baby's omnipotence.

> It is generally understood that the reality principle involves the individual in anger and reactive destruction, but my thesis is that the destruction plays its part in making the reality, placing the object outside the self. For this to happen, favourable conditions are necessary.

This paragraph is parenthetical. Winnicott is disagreeing with those who feel that our general orientation toward reality and toward the reality principle is anger and reactive destruction. Winnicott instead sees the destructive impulse more specifically as inherent to the baby's struggle to make external reality real. He then continues:

> This is simply a matter of examining the reality principle under high power. As I see it, we are familiar with the change whereby projection mechanisms enable the subject to take cognizance of the object, without projection mechanisms being the reason for the object's existence. At the point of development that is under survey the subject is creating the object in the sense of finding externality itself, and it has to be added that this experience depends on the object's capacity to survive.

The subject/baby is in the process of finding externality itself—the world beyond the baby's projections/omnipotence. The success of this very important process depends directly on the object's/mother's capacity to survive the subject's/baby's attempts at destruction.

> (It is important that this means "not retaliate".) If it is in an analysis that these matters are taking place, then the analyst, the analytic technique, and the analytic setting all come in as surviving or not surviving the patient's destructive attacks. This destructive activity is the patient's attempt to place the analyst outside the area of omnipotent control, that is, out in the world. Without the experience of maximum destructiveness (object not protected) the subject never places the analyst outside and therefore can never do more than experience a kind of self-analysis, using the analyst as a projection of a part of the self. In terms of feeding, the patient, then, can only feed on the self and cannot use the breast for getting fat. The patient may even enjoy the analytic experience but will not fundamentally change.

Winnicott adds this very important point: survival of the maternal/therapist object does *not* include retaliation. Winnicott then comments specifically about what "survival" consists of *in the process of therapy*: such things as consistencies in the person of the therapist, consistencies in the rules that govern his/her therapeutic technique, and consistencies in the setting of the therapy—meaning regularities of time, place, session length, and so on. Winnicott explains that attacks by the patient on the therapy or on the therapist or resistances such as coming late to the therapy or skipping sessions may be thought of as parallel to an infant's destructive activity (depending upon when they occur in the course of therapy). Winnicott asserts that this activity is done in the service of an attempt to place the therapist outside of the patient's area of projections/ omnipotence. Without such activity, the patient never places the therapist into the world of external reality, and therefore cannot take in difference from himself in terms of the therapist's offerings. Without this, the patient is confined to his own limited thoughts and perspectives, which Winnicott characterizes as "self-analysis." The patient, in the language of the nursing couple, cannot use the milk that the therapist provides, but instead can only feed on himself—his own thoughts, perspectives, insights.

And if the analyst is a subjective phenomenon, what about waste-disposal? A further statement is needed in terms of output.

In psychoanalytic practice the positive changes that come about in this area can be profound. They do not depend on interpretative work. They do depend on the analyst's survival of the attacks, which includes the idea of absence of a change to retaliation. These attacks may be very difficult for the analyst to stand, especially when they are expressed in terms of delusion or through manipulation which makes the analyst actually do things that are technically bad. (I refer to such a thing as unreliability at moments when reliability is all that matters, as well as to survival in terms of keeping alive and the absence of the quality of retaliation.)

OK. Winnicott gets more specific about what surviving the patient's attacks and being non-retaliatory might mean in a therapy. The patient may harbor and express delusional thoughts about the therapist. He may manipulate the therapist into doing things that are technically not normal and not advised. Winnicott reasserts that at certain moments, certainly in the pique of such attacks, the therapist's *reliability* is all that matters.

The analyst feels like interpreting, but this can spoil the process and for the patient can seem like a kind of self-defence, the analyst parrying the patient's attack. Better to wait till after the phase is over, and then discuss with the patient what has been happening. This is surely legitimate, for as analyst one has one's own needs; but verbal interpretation at this point is not the essential feature and brings its own dangers. The essential feature is the analyst's survival and the intactness of the psychoanalytic technique.

Here Winnicott is even more specific in his guidance to therapists. In the midst of patient attacks on the therapy and therapist, the therapist may well feel like defending himself by the use of interpretation. Winnicott says that interpretation in these moments is not the point, is not essential, and brings its own dangers. The point is the therapist's/the therapy's survival.

> Imagine how traumatic can be the actual death of the analyst when this kind of work is in process, although even the actual death of the analyst is not as bad as the development in the analyst of a change towards retaliation. These risks simply must be taken by the patient. Usually the analyst lives through these phases of movement in the transference, and after each phase there comes reward in terms of love, reinforced by the fact of the backcloth of unconscious destruction.

If a therapist happens to die in the midst of such a struggle, there will be psychological trauma to be worked through by the patient. But a therapist's death would be less traumatizing to his patient than a therapist's retaliatory behavior, no matter how cleverly disguised.

> It appears to me that the idea of a developmental phase involving survival of object does affect the theory of the roots of aggression. It is no good saying that a baby of a few days old envies the breast. It is legitimate, however, to say that at whatever age a baby begins to allow the breast an external position (outside the area of projection) then this means that destruction of the breast has become a feature. I mean the actual impulse to destroy. It is an important part of what a mother does, to be the first person to take the baby through this first version of the many that will be encountered, of attack that is survived. This is the right moment in the child's development, because of the child's relative feebleness, so that destruction can fairly easily be survived. Even so it is a very tricky matter; it is only too easy for a mother to react moralistically when her baby bites and hurts.[3] But this language involving the breast is jargon. The whole area of development and of management is involved in which adaptation is related to dependence, apart, that is, from the important detail of relating to the breast.
>
> 3 It will be seen that, although destruction is the word I am using, this actual destruction belongs to the object's failure to survive. Without this failure, destruction remains potential. The word "destruction" is needed, not because of the baby's impulse to destroy, but because of the object's liability not to survive.

Winnicott is simultaneously arguing with Kleinian and Freudian advocates here. Winnicott does not believe that a baby starts out with envious impulses toward the mother's breast. But he thinks that at whatever point the baby begins to conceptualize the breast as external to him—not his own omnipotent creation—at that point his impulse is toward destruction. Survival of the infant's initial attempts at destruction of the breast is a relatively low-amplitude destructive event, given the infant's feebleness. A mother must survive this attempt rather than react to it with offense—or retaliation.

Destruction only happens if the object cannot, does not survive it.

> The way of looking at things that belongs to my presentation of this paper makes possible a new approach to the whole subject of the roots of aggression. For instance, it is not necessary to give inborn aggression more than that which is its due in company with everything else that is inborn. Undoubtedly inborn aggression must be variable in a quantitative sense in the same way that everything else that is inherited is variable as between individuals. The variations in inborn aggression are slight as compared with the total inheritance of that which can lead to aggressiveness. By contrast, the variations are great that arise out of the differences in the experiences of various newborn babies according to whether they are or are not seen through this very difficult phase. Such variations in the field of experience are indeed immense. Moreover, the babies that have been seen through this phase well are likely to be more aggressive *clinically* than the ones who have not been seen through the phase well, and for whom aggression is not something that can be encompassed (become ego-syntonic), or can be retained only in the form of a liability to be the object of attack.

Here Winnicott gives more generally his thoughts on aggression. He feels that aggression is both a genetically endowed trait and one potentially exacerbated by negative experience. He feels that the experience component is a far more significant contributor to variation than the genetic part. He also observes that those babies whose micro-expressions of aggression are recognized and met appropriately are more likely to have the positive aspects of aggression at their disposal as they mature than those whose aggression was not dealt with appropriately. For this latter group, he observes that their aggression does not become ego-syntonic and therefore useful to them. Alternatively, they so suppress their aggression that they are likely in later life to become victims.

> This involves a rewriting of the theory of the roots of aggression since most of that which has already been written by analysts has been formulated without reference to that which is being discussed in this paper. The assumption is always there, in orthodox theory, that aggression is reactive to the encounter with the reality principle, whereas here it is the destructive drive that creates the quality of externality.

Here he simply restates a thesis he has developed well in this paper. But he also moves us forward. He has maintained in other writings that a baby has a certain "instinctual aggressiveness" that is originally a part of appetite, or some other form of instinctual love. This is followed, developmentally, by a time when the baby's aggression is *meant*. And finally, this is followed by a stage wherein the baby feels a sense of responsibility for the damage wrought upon the object. Aggression, according to Winnicott, is an inborn property in all babies, a sense in which they both press in on the world and also seek the resistance of that which they kick into. He is reaffirming that it is that aggressive drive that seeks out and finds the quality of externality.

> Let me look for a moment at the exact place of this attack and survival in the hierarchy of relationships. More primitive and quite different is annihilation. Annihilation means "no hope"; cathexis withers up because no result completes the reflex to produce conditioning. Attack in anger relative to the encounter with the reality principle is a more sophisticated concept, postdating the destruction that I postulate here. In the destruction of the object to which I am referring *there is no anger*.

OK, here at the end Winnicott is making a few other observations. He wants to calibrate the magnitude of this attack-and-survival that he has discussed, compared to two other developmental constructs. The first is annihilation, which he notes is more primitive, different in nature, and by inference, more damaging because it results in the withering of cathexis—or primitive love—and results in a state of hopelessness in an infant. Its effects are devastating. The second is anger at the reality principle—or frustration at the limitations on immediate gratification—which he says comes *after* the battle against the existence of external reality. The attempt at destruction of the external object is not a battle waged in anger; it is waged instinctually. He then elaborates:

> There could be said to be joy at the object's survival. From this moment, or arising out of this phase, the object is *in fantasy* always being destroyed. This quality of "always being destroyed" makes the reality of the surviving object felt as such, strengthens the feeling tone, and contributes to object constancy. The object can now be used.

He contends that the child actually *wants* the object to survive the struggle. There is joy at its survival, just as when a baby throws a spatula on to the ground, and hopes that it survives his attack and is there to be played with further. The internalized object of fantasy continues to be destroyed—is always being destroyed in fantasy—which makes the external object of reality more real, more sturdy, more constant, and ready to be used.

I wish to conclude with a note on using and usage. By "use" I do not mean "exploitation". As analysts, we know what it is like to be used, which means that we can see the end of the treatment, be it several years away. Many of our patients come with this problem already solved—they can use objects and they can use us and can use analysis, just as they have used their parents and their siblings and their homes. However, there are many patients who need us to be able to give them a capacity to use us. In meeting the needs of such patients, we shall need to know what I am saying here about our survival of their destructiveness. A backcloth of unconscious destruction of the analyst is set up and we survive it or, alternatively, we shall become involved in yet another analysis interminable.

"Use" versus "exploitation." "Use" in Winnicott's world is a positive process with a positive endpoint. Our job as therapists is to be able to give patients the capacity to use us. This means that we must endure, survive, be resilient to the moments of destruction they bring to us, because these are brought in the service of a higher goal: that of being able to encounter and use us as reliable, sturdy external objects.

Summary

Object-relating can be described in terms of the experience of the subject. Description of object-usage involves consideration of the nature of the object. I am offering for discussion the reasons why, in my opinion, a capacity to use an object is more sophisticated than a capacity to relate to objects; and relating may be to a subjective object, but usage implies that the object is part of external reality.

This sequence can be observed: (1) Subject *relates* to object. (2) Object is in process of being found instead of placed by the subject in the world. (3) Subject *destroys* object. (4) Object survives destruction. (5) Subject can *use* object.

The object is always being destroyed. This destruction becomes the unconscious backcloth for love of a real object; that is, an object outside the area of the subject's omnipotent control.

Study of this problem involves a statement of the positive value of destructiveness. The destructiveness plus the object's survival of the destruction places the object outside the area in which projective mental mechanisms operate, so that a world of shared reality is created which the subject can use and which can feed back into the subject.

Finally, Winnicott reaffirms the positive value of the process of object destruction and survival—that the point is the destruction *plus* the survival, which, in combination, place the object and the subject into the world of external, shared reality, where the object can indeed be used by the subject in ways that are unique to that object, and that can feed back into and enhance the world of the subject.

References

Winnicott, D. W. (1941). The observation of infants in a set situation. In *Collected papers*. London: Tavistock Publications, 1958.

Winnicott, D. W. (1958). The capacity to be alone. In Winnicott (1965).

Winnicott, D. W. (1959–64). Classification: Is there a psycho-analytic contribution to psychiatric classification? In Winnicott (1965).

Winnicott, D. W. (1963). Communicating and not communicating leading to a study of certain opposites. In Winnicott (1965).

Winnicott, D.W. (1964). Roots of aggression. In *The child, the family, and the outside world*. Harmondsworth: Penguin Books.

Winnicott, D. W. (1965). *The maturational processes and the facilitating environment*. London: Hogarth Press.

Winnicott, D. W. (1967). The location of cultural experience. *Int. J. Psychoanal.* 48:368–372.

Winnicott, D. W. (1968a). Playing: its theoretical status in the clinical situation. *Int. J. Psychoanal.* 49:591–599.

Winnicott, D. W. (1968b). La interrelación en términos de identificaciones cruzadas. *Rev. Psicoanál.* 25.

12 Fear of breakdown

(1974)

Winnicott, D. W. (1974). Fear of breakdown. *International Review of Psycho-Analysis*, 1, 103–107.

In this clinically *extremely important* paper, Winnicott attempts to show that patients' fear of breakdown can be a fear of events that have already occurred, but that were never fully experienced—and so, have yet to be experienced. The word "breakdown" refers to a breakdown of one's defensive structures—a coming apart at the very core of one's own ego—what Winnicott refers to as the breakdown of the "unit self." The patient with a fear of breakdown carries within a deep need to remember in the present these events and the unthinkable anxieties that they induced, so as to be able to place the events into the past, instead of fearing their emergence in the future. The therapist must provide a safe-enough holding environment in order for this process to occur.

> ### Preliminary statement
>
> My clinical experiences have brought me recently to a new understanding, as I believe, of the meaning of a fear of breakdown.

This paper, written by Winnicott shortly before his death, and published posthumously by his wife, Clare Winnicott, represents a lifetime of clinical experience. The fact that Winnicott would write about a "new" understanding he had achieved after more than 40 years of clinical experience should pique our interest from the get-go.

> It is my purpose here to state as simply as possible this understanding, which is new for me and which perhaps is new for others who work in psychotherapy. Naturally, if what I say has truth in it, this will already have been dealt with by the world's poets, but the flashes of insight that come in poetry cannot absolve us from our painful task of getting step by step

away from ignorance towards our goal. It is my opinion that a study of this limited area leads to a restatement of several other problems that puzzle us as we fail to do as well clinically as we would wish to do, and I shall indicate at the end what extensions of the theory I propose for discussion.

Winnicott is stating at the outset that what he will share with us in this paper has implications for places in our clinical practice where "we fail to do as well clinically as we would wish to do," and implications for the broader corpus of psychological and clinical theory upon which our work rests.

Individual variations

Fear of breakdown is a feature of significance in some of our patients, but not in others. From this observation, if it be a correct one, the conclusion can be drawn that fear of breakdown is related to the individual's past experience, and to environmental vagaries. At the same time there must be expected a common denominator of the same fear, indicating the existence of universal phenomena; these indeed make it possible for everyone to know empathetically what it feels like when one of our patients shows this fear in a big way. (The same can be said, indeed, of every detail of the insane person's insanity. We all know about it, although this particular detail may not be bothering us.)

OK. So fear of breakdown may be a salient feature of some, but not all, of our patients. And Winnicott is asserting that this fear must be related to an individual's past experience and what he refers to as "environmental vagaries." In other papers he has used the term "environment" to indicate the whole of the emotional and caregiving environment into which each baby is born. "Environmental vagaries," then, appears to refer to compromises in this early caregiving environment. OK. So, now, no sooner has he indicated that some, but not others, will have this fear of breakdown, than he refers to this fear as a "universal phenomen[on]" and a "common denominator." What he is suggesting is that we all have something of this fear of breakdown within us, and that this *something* equips us to be able to empathize with those who have this fear "in a big way." He extends this by saying that the same is true of the experience of being insane—that we all have within our psyches the experience of being crazy. Now, this is a radical thought, and it makes us have to decide if we think Winnicott is speaking something that is true of us or not. And if we have no sense of this within ourselves, why is it that Winnicott is able to be in touch with something that we are perhaps excluding from our own consciousness? With this de-centering prelude, he heads into his main discussion.

Emergence of the symptom

Not all our patients who have this fear complain of it at the outset of a treatment. Some do; but others have their defences so well organized that it is only after a treatment has made considerable progress that the fear of breakdown comes to the fore as a dominating factor.

For instance, a patient may have various phobias and a complex organization for dealing with these phobias, so that dependence does not come quickly into the transference. At length, dependence becomes a main feature, and then the analyst's mistakes and failures become direct causes of localized phobias and so of the outbreak of fear of breakdown.

OK. So for some, this fear of breakdown is explicit and is there from the beginning of treatment. For others whose defenses are perhaps better or more tightly organized, this fear may emerge later in the treatment. The medium in which the fear emerges in this latter group is the development of dependence on the therapist in the transference. As this dependence deepens, the patient is more deeply affected by the therapist's mistakes and failures, which, in Winnicott's example of a phobic patient, may give rise to an exacerbation of his phobic symptoms. The patient may come to fear deeply what is happening to him and may in fact fear that he is breaking down (or that he is going crazy).

Meaning of "breakdown"

I have purposely used the term "breakdown" because it is rather vague and because it could mean various things. On the whole, the word can be taken in this context to mean a failure of a defence organization. But immediately we ask: a defence against what? And this leads us to the deeper meaning of the term, since we need to use the word "breakdown" to describe the unthinkable state of affairs that underlies the defence organization.

OK. So "breakdown" refers to a breakdown of one's defensive structures. So then, Winnicott poses the next logical question: defense against or from what? What is being defended? He makes a first pass at it by saying that were the defenses to break down, the patient would experience an "unthinkable state of affairs." Winnicott will proceed to clarify this for us.

It will be noted that whereas there is value in thinking that in the area of psychoneurosis it is castration anxiety that lies behind the defences, in the more psychotic phenomena that we are examining it is a breakdown of the establishment of the unit self that is indicated. The ego organizes defences against breakdown of the ego organization, and it is the ego organization that is threatened. But the ego cannot organize against environmental failure in so far as dependence is a living fact.

In other words, we are examining a reversal of the individual's maturational process. This makes it necessary for me briefly to reformulate the early stages of emotional growth.

As has been Winnicott's habit throughout his writings, he affirms Freud's contribution, saying that it may be valuable, in cases of simple neurosis, to analyze what may be an underlying castration anxiety.

But Winnicott is talking here about a different and more profound level of underlying anxiety, which he characterizes as more "psychotic." What Winnicott is addressing is the patient's fear of coming apart at the very core of his own ego—what Winnicott calls the breakdown of the "unit self."

The "unit self" in Winnicott's writing indicates the point at which an infant is able to distinguish "me" from "not me," is able to see the mother as other than himself, and "can begin to create an external world at the same time as he is acquiring a limiting membrane and an inside," some time around the fifth through the twelfth month. Winnicott describes this as "the point at which the centre of gravity of being in the environment-individual set up can afford to lodge in the centre [of the baby], in the kernel rather than in the shell" and can become localized in the baby's body (1952, pp. 99–100).

OK. So if the "unit self" were to break down, that would mean that a person would devolve into a state wherein his very being—his sense of "me" versus "not me," would be somehow shattered into disorganized fragments.

He then says that the ego—which denotes the infant's inherent tendency to organize and integrate experience—organizes defenses against its own breakdown. Organizing defenses is part of the job of the ego. But in this feared breakdown, the ego's organization—and its organizing function—is threatened. Then he says this arresting thing: "the ego cannot organize against environmental failure in so far as dependence is a living fact." What's he saying here? It seems that he's speaking in both past and present tenses. In the infantile past, the incipient ego cannot organize itself while dependence is absolute—is "a living fact"—if the maternal environment is failing to provide ego support to that infant. This is because that infantile ego is wholly dependent on the maternal environment in order to be able to integrate experience and to proceed toward an organized, differentiated self.

Ok. That's in the past tense. And in the present tense, the ego of the patient cannot remain organized if this infantile dependence comes forward into the therapeutic relationship (into the transference) and the therapeutic relationship fails to provide an adequate holding environment. This earliest of states can be replicated in the transference such that a therapeutic misstep or failure is not merely a mistake; it is felt by the patient to be a failure in the holding environment, which is catastrophic, and is experienced as annihilating.

He now expands this thought by elaborating early emotional growth.

Emotional growth, early stages

The individual inherits a maturational process. This carries the individual along in so far as there exists a facilitating environment, and only in so far as this exists. The facilitating environment is itself a complex phenomenon and needs special study in its own right; the essential feature is that it has a kind of growth of its own, being adapted to the changing needs of the growing individual.

He's simply saying here that each of us is born with a maturational tendency, which can unfold optimally if and only if there exists a facilitating maternal environment, meaning all the things involved in early infant care—holding, handling, reading tensions and urgencies, responding, protecting, object presenting—all of these things. He has addressed this perfect-followed-by-good-enough-maternal-environment in many former papers.

The individual proceeds from absolute dependence to relative independence and towards independence. In health the development takes place at a pace that does not outstrip the development of complexity in the mental mechanisms, this being linked to neurophysiological development.

Hmm. He's implying here, but not stating outright, that in healthy development, there is a pacing that is important. He has explored this in other papers, most notably, "Mind and its relation to the psyche-soma" (1949). His argument in that paper is that when an infant is forced to use mental mechanisms too soon—in order to compensate for a not-good-enough environment—the mind develops in a hypertrophied way, and comes to dominate rather than to serve the psyche-soma (the body/emotional center/soul) of the individual.

The facilitating environment can be described as *holding*, developing into *handling*, to which is added *object-presenting*.

In such a facilitating environment the individual undergoes development which can be classified as *integrating*, to which is added *indwelling* (or *psychosomatic collusion*) and then *object-relating*.

This is a gross over-simplification but it must suffice in this context.

OK. Let's pause. There are several forward developmental movements which occur in the infant. One major movement is *integration*: s/he first locates and integrates a sense of space and of time for him/herself. The infant is protected from gravity and *held* in *space*. And s/he experiences events that repeat in *time*, over, over, over again.

S/he is *handled* by the mothering person. S/he begins to identify, differentiate, and integrate experiences related to the body. S/he begins to locate her/himself in the body—to *indwell* her/his body, and to imaginatively elaborate his/her bodily experiences. This elaboration is the formative process that underlies the development of the infant's psyche. The infant begins to "know" that her/his hunger is not merely disruption of a going-on-being state, but is a specific sensation to which there is a specific remedy. S/he begins to discover that her hand is attached to a motor mechanism over which s/he discovers she has control. All of this is the work of *indwelling*—of identifying, differentiating, and integrating bodily experience.

As the infant does this, s/he moves in development to the place wherein s/he identifies the body as the location of his/her *being*. S/he begins to integrate disparate experiences over time to the point where s/he is able to feel what it feels like to have a consistent me who inhabits a consistent body.

So, indwelling precedes recognizing there is a me and, a not me. When there is an "indwelt" infant, s/he can begin to recognize that there is an inside and an outside, a "me" and a "not me." This recognition sets the stage for *object relating*—for receiving ministrations that are *(object)-presented* from outside of him/her. It sets the stage for being in relationship with persons who are psychically recognized by the infant as distinct from himself, as outside himself.

It will be observed that in such a description forward movement in development corresponds closely with the threat of retrograde movement (and defences against this threat) in schizophrenic illness.

OK, what's this? In schizophrenic illness, there is the process of going backward in development—losing one's relationship to others (object relating), losing one's sense of indwelling in the body, losing one's sense of the integration of sensory and motor sensations, and of one's place in time and space. In schizophrenic illness, some of the oddities that appear from the outside to be purposeless are instead the individual's attempt to generate defenses that will keep their being from completely flying apart into fragments and being out of control.

Absolute dependence

At the time of absolute dependence, with the mother supplying an auxiliary ego-function, it has to be remembered that the infant has not yet separated out the "not-me" from the "me"—this cannot happen apart from the establishment of "me".

OK. We follow him here. The "me" versus the "not me." But now he is about to skip to the discussion of primitive agonies, which are the features of the feared breakdown of personal integration that is the main focus of this paper. He does this transition without really orienting us to what he is doing. He's talked about the fear of breakdown in some patients but not in others, about what it is that breaks down, about the early stages of emotional growth, and briefly about the stage of absolute dependence.

So next, he catapults us into a discussion of primitive agonies—without making the bridge explicit. The bridge is this: in the beginning months of life, an infant is absolutely dependent on his maternal environment for everything that pertains to him. If there are compromises in the quality and quantity of maternal care, an infant experiences states of anxiety—Winnicott would say states of *agony*—that are excruciatingly real and that play a formative role in that person's psyche as s/he moves forward into further development. These are the states that are reactivated in adult patients' fear of breakdown. They are the signature features of the feared breakdown.

He begins to elucidate these features by simply listing them for us. Many writers speak of these as "primitive anxieties," but Winnicott feels this is too weak a word to describe the degree of fear and suffering inherent in these states. He lists for us the primitive agonies suffered by babies and feared by adults, and in each case he lists the defense that is employed to attempt to defend against a full drop into these states.

Primitive agonies

From this chart it is possible to make a list of primitive agonies (anxiety is not a strong enough word here). Here are a few:

1. A return to an unintegrated state. (Defence: disintegration.)

OK. Babies are able to be integrated in one moment and then to drop into unintegration the next. This is the nature of being a baby. But once we have achieved integration and are no longer in an absolutely dependent and maternally ego-supported state, the specter of losing our integration—of losing the center of our being, losing our relationship to space and time, losing our sense of indwelling our own bodies, losing the coordination of our five senses, losing our volitional motor control, losing our access to language—these are indeed deeply frightening to anyone who is not a baby. Disintegration differs from unintegration in that the latter is a resting state for a baby, the former is a deeply terrifying state.

Its defense, as Winnicott lists, is simply to collapse into the disintegration—not to attempt to master it. He has observed in other writings that voluntary surrender into disintegration is psychologically preferable to being forcibly taken over by it.

> 2.   Falling for ever. (Defence: self-holding.)

Falling forever. Winnicott identifies two sensations that are brand new to a newborn: breathing and gravity. The sense of not being held securely enough and of being in the sway of gravity's endless pull downward are indeed frightening to think about, and infinitely more frightening to experience. This fear is the basis of amusement park rides that give us the feel of falling—but not of falling forever.

Winnicott notes that those babies who are not held develop the defense of holding themselves. They do this via patterns of autistic-like movements, repetitive rocking, stiffly holding themselves, and so on. These efforts can be observed from the outside, as are painfully evident in the Spitz (1947) films of orphaned babies.

> 3.   Loss of psychosomatic collusion, failure of indwelling. (Defence: depersonalization.)

Loss of the indwelling of one's own body. Our indwelling of our own body is what makes us feel alive and human. A dead body is no longer indwelt by the spirit of the person. A dissociated human is no longer located in his/her own body. This is a violent event. The ripping of the spirit, which is meant to dwell in the body until its demise, out of the body is an unthinkable event. And yet, Winnicott lists it as one of the primitive agonies that some babies suffer and that some patients realistically fear.

The defense he notes that babies and patients employ is that of depersonalization—the escape into the feeling of not being real or feeling disconnected or detached from one's body.

> 4.   Loss of sense of real. (Defence: exploitation of primary narcissism, etc.)

Derealization is a state that some people experience in the context of acute anxiety and trauma. They feel that the things about them have become not real.

A defense against this is the feeling that one has created everything in the world around them and therefore has control, which is an exercise of primary narcissism.

> 5.   Loss of capacity to relate to objects. (Defence: autistic states, relating only to self-phenomena.) And so on.

The loss of capacity to relate to objects is a frighteningly alone state. It includes not being able to make oneself understood by others.

Defenses against this utter aloneness include autistic, self-contained states, and schizoid states—in other words, a shut down of the impulse to even reach for objects and relationships.

Psychotic illness as a defence

It is my intention to show here that what we see clinically is always a defence organization, even in the autism of childhood schizophrenia. The underlying agony is unthinkable.

Here Winnicott has just said something pivotally important. We who interact with a patient encounter the patient's *defense* against experiencing the underlying state, no matter how disfiguring or befuddling the defense may seem. The defense is there to protect the person from what underlies it, which Winnicott refers to as the "underlying agony," which, in his words, is so intense as to be "unthinkable."

It is wrong to think of psychotic illness as a breakdown, it is a defence organization relative to a primitive agony, and it is usually successful (except when the facilitating environment has been not deficient but tantalizing, perhaps the worst thing that can happen to a human baby).

OK. Winnicott is saying that psychotic illness is the attempt to prevent a complete breakdown and catastrophe. It is a defensive organization that is usually in some ways successful in keeping a person protected from experiencing the underlying primitive agonies that he would fall into without the protection of his psychotic symptoms. The self of the schizophrenic person is not utterly annihilated; it is preserved in some form due to its defense.

He comments, however, in his paper "Ego distortion in terms of True and False Self" (1960) that it is possible to destroy the infant's capacity to defend and preserve even a hidden True Self within. He says that this dangerous situation pertains in cases where the mother is alternatively good and bad "in a tantalizingly irregular manner." This mother would be expressing a need (as part of her own mental illness) to cause confusion and muddle in those in her world, including her child. This would threaten, and perhaps even cause, the effective annihilation of the core True Self in the child because of the destruction of the infant's capacity to defend against it, which, according to Winnicott, is "perhaps the worst thing that can happen to a human baby."

OK. Now, having given us enough preamble, he shifts to his main theme.

Statement of main theme

I can now state my main contention, and it turns out to be very simple. I contend that clinical fear of breakdown is *the fear of a breakdown that has already been experienced*. It is a fear of the original agony which caused the defence organization which the patient displays as an illness syndrome.

This is it! This is Winnicott's central insight in this paper: that the "clinical fear of breakdown is the fear of a breakdown that has already been experienced." OK. Let's hear him explain this!

This idea may or may not prove immediately useful to the clinician. We cannot hurry up our patients. Nevertheless, we can hold up their progress because of genuinely not knowing; any little piece of our understanding may help us to keep up with a patient's needs.

We can retard the progress of our patients by not knowing or not understanding what their defenses are so strongly defending against, or by being in a hurry to get to something we define as a goal.

There are moments, according to my experience, when a patient needs to be told that the breakdown, a fear of which destroys his or her life, *has already been*. It is a fact that is carried round hidden away in the unconscious.

I'll stop Winnicott mid-paragraph for emphasis. There are moments when patients need to be told that their fear of breakdown, either explicit to them, or hidden away from their consciousness by their symptoms—their defenses—is the fear of a breakdown that has already occurred. They fear that it will come upon them as they do the work of therapy. But their fear of it as a future event is actually their fear of an event that has already occurred in their past. He then continues.

The unconscious here is not exactly the repressed unconscious of psychoneurosis, nor is it the unconscious of Freud's formulation of the part of the psyche that is very close to neurophysiological functioning. Nor is it the unconscious of Jung's which I would call: all those things that go on in underground caves, or (in other words) the world's mythology, in which there is collusion between the individual and the maternal inner

> psychic realities. In this special context the unconscious means that the ego integration is not able to encompass something. The ego is too immature to gather all the phenomena into the area of personal omnipotence.

Winnicott references momentarily Freud's and Jung's conceptions of the unconscious, and makes the point that this fear of breakdown makes use of a different facet of the unconscious. This way of being unconscious is neither repression nor a participation in the collective. Instead, it is a state of being wherein the ego, whose job it is to integrate experience into the area of personal omnipotence, was and is not able to do this integrating. He'll explain this more clearly as he continues.

> It must be asked here: why does the patient go on being worried by this that belongs to the past? The answer must be that the original experience of primitive agony cannot get into the past tense unless the ego can first gather it into its own present time experience and into omnipotent control now (assuming the auxiliary ego-supporting function of the mother (analyst)).

Ok. This is a wow from Winnicott! The patient fears his own breakdown either explicitly or implicitly—via his defenses, expressed as symptoms—even though the agonies that would be involved in such a breakdown of the ego are already past. Why? Winnicott's answer is that an experience cannot make it into the past if it's never been fully experienced in the present. And this (feared) experience was too big for the incipient ego of the child to handle—to experience and to integrate—in part due to the insufficient ego support of the mother back then. So it haunts the patient, unconsciously, and cannot make it into the past "unless the ego can first gather it into its own present time experience and into omnipotent control now." In other words, it must be experienced to be let go of, and that experiencing cannot happen unless the analyst/therapist provides the kind of ego support necessary to hold the experiencing of such agonies in the present. Such primitive agonies cannot be experienced and integrated by the self alone. He'll explain this in more detail.

> In other words, the patient must go on looking for the past detail which is *not yet experienced*. This search takes the form of a looking for this detail in the future.
>
> Unless the therapist can work successfully on the basis that this detail is already a fact, the patient must go on fearing to find what is being compulsively looked for in the future.

OK. So part of the work of the therapist is to discern that a patient is fearing that some things, some details, that are psychically dreadful may happen to them in the future. The patient is on the alert for this; s/he guards him/herself from it by every means possible.

> On the other hand, if the patient is ready for some kind of acceptance of this queer kind of truth, that what is not yet experienced did nevertheless happen in the past, then the way is open for the agony to be experienced in the transference, in reaction to the analyst's failures and mistakes.

This is key, so let me interrupt here. Winnicott says this: that "what is not yet experienced did nevertheless happen in the past" and calls this a queer truth. This is indeed a "queer truth"! But, is it possible to be a participant in an event or a feeling without *experiencing* it? This is exactly what he is saying. And this is exactly what happens in dissociation. A physical or psychic event occurs, but we escape the experiencing of it. We go away. We freeze. We go dead. Current polyvagal theorists have provided neurophysiological models of exactly this state. Under great stress or trauma, we as humans have the capacity, indeed the proclivity, to go with our most primitive neural systems via the dorsal vagus nerve, and to put ourselves into an opossum-like state, dead to pain, terror, experience in general.

OK. So if the patient can accept this "queer truth" "that what is not yet experienced did nevertheless happen in the past" then, Winnicott says, the door opens to their experiencing replicas of such experience with us as therapists in the intimacy of our relationship with them in the present—in the context of our failures and mistakes with them. For instance, we make micro-errors of imperfect attunement (mis-wordings, mis-timings, "off" interpretations, forgettings, ends of sessions, vacations, illnesses, family obligations, etc.) that have *macro*-emotional effects on our patients in their transferential relationship with us. These simulate and stimulate past traumas. The difference between these mis-attunements and the ones they experienced as dependent infants is both in degree *and in the fact of the holding/ego-support environment that was missing in their original environment that is now present for them in the relationship with the therapist.*

> These latter can be dealt with by the patient in doses that are not excessive, and the patient can account for each technical failure of the analyst as countertransference. In other words, gradually the patient gathers the original failure of the facilitating environment into the area of his or her omnipotence and the experience of omnipotence which belongs to the state of dependence (transference fact).

OK. At this point, we have to understand what Winnicott is saying about omnipotence. Early in life the infant, who is absolutely dependent on the maternal environment for life, sustenance, and attunement, inhabits a subjective world which is characterized by the illusion of his own omnipotence. It is the infant who "creates" the mother, the breast, the world. He has no capacity to know the world that exists outside of his creation—his "omnipotence." Ideally, the infant is allowed to develop for a while in this subjective world where the world of objective reality does not insist itself; does not impinge. Everything that happens in his world becomes, from the infant's point of view, a creation of the infant. For a while, his treatment is dictated by the infant's rhythms and derives as a response to his spontaneous gestures. A good-enough (responsive) maternal environment preserves the infant's continuity of being, and allows him to progress on his maturational trajectory to the point where he can transition from subjective, omnipotent reality to objective, external reality; from the world of entirely "me" to the world of, well, "not me."

So when Winnicott says that the patient can deal with the failures and mistakes of the therapist by gathering them into the area of his omnipotence, he is saying that the patient is free, in the context of the trusting dependence of the transferential relationship with his therapist, to make *subjective* sense of the impact of the therapist's technical failures—without having to account for the objective reality or scale of the mis-attunements. As this happens in the pre-sent relationship—in doses that are not excessive—the patient can, in parallel fashion, gather into his "area of omnipotence" the original failures of the past maternal environment. In other words, the patient can freely feel the impact of the lack of attunement in the therapist, and can thereby predicate and elaborate what may have been the pain of his experience as a young dependent child.

> All this is very difficult, time-consuming and painful, but it at any rate is not futile. What is futile is the alternative, and it is this that must now be examined.

This is Winnicott's summary comment on doing this work of examining micro-misattunements in the therapeutic relationship and relating them to the original agonies: "very difficult, time-consuming and painful, but ... not futile." He now will move on to what *is* futile in working with patients whose "future" breakdown is feared.

Futility in analysis

I must take for granted an understanding and acceptance of the analysis of psychoneurosis. On the basis of this assumption, I say that in the cases I am discussing the analysis starts off well, the analysis goes with a swing;

> what is happening, however, is that the analyst and the patient are having a good time colluding in a psychoneurotic analysis, when in fact the illness is psychotic.

OK. So Winnicott is distinguishing between neurosis and psychosis—in terms of the patient's thinking and experiencing process. He is saying that we can mistake the level of a patient's developmental injury and thus can carry out a therapy that is falsely predicated on a higher level of mental health than actually exists in our patient.

> Over and over again the analysing couple are pleased with what they have done together. It was valid, it was clever, it was cosy because of the collusion. But each so-called advance ends in destruction. The patient breaks it up and says: So what? In fact, the advance was not an advance; it was a new example of the analyst's playing the patient's game of postponing the main issue. And who can blame either the patient or the analyst (unless of course there can be an analyst who plays the psychotic fish on a very long psychoneurotic line, and hopes thereby to avoid the final catch by some trick of fate, such as the death of one or other of the couple, or a failure of financial backing).

So here Winnicott playfully describes how clever and cozy a therapy can feel from the therapist's side, while simultaneously missing the entire point of what brought this person into the therapy—that there is the looming fear of a breakdown, one that Winnicott says has already occurred.

> We must assume that both patient and analyst really do wish to end the analysis, but alas, there is no end unless the bottom of the trough has been reached, unless *the thing feared has been experienced*. And indeed one way out is for the patient to have a breakdown (physical or mental) and this can work very well. However, the solution is not good enough if it does not include analytic understanding and insight on the part of the patient, and indeed, many of the patients I am referring to are valuable people who cannot afford to break down in the sense of going to a mental hospital.

OK. This is clear. The feared thing must be experienced in order for the therapy to be of real value in the life of the patient.

> The purpose of this paper is to draw attention to the possibility that the breakdown has already happened, near the beginning of the individual's

life. The patient needs to "remember" this but it is not possible to remember something that has not yet happened, and this thing of the past has not happened yet because the patient was not there for it to happen to. The only way to "remember" in this case is for the patient to experience this past thing for the first time in the present, that is to say, in the transference. This past and future thing then becomes a matter of the here and now, and becomes experienced by the patient for the first time. This is the equivalent of remembering, and this outcome is the equivalent of the lifting of repression that occurs in the analysis of the psychoneurotic patient (classical Freudian analysis).

OK. This is the nub of the paper, all in one paragraph! Some important parts and pieces are presented:

1. That the fear of breakdown is the fear of something that has already happened in the patient's past;
2. That the occurrence of the feared agonies in this patient's life happened near the beginning of his life;
3. That it is crucial that the patient remember these agonies in order to be free of them;
4. That the patient cannot use the ordinary powers of memory to remember these agonies because the patient in some way absented himself from the events—in Winnicott's words, the patient "was not there for it." This means that the patient's psyche in some way left the scene, so to speak, because the experience was too much to bear;
5. The only way for the patient to remember this past thing is to experience it in the present in the transference—in the relationship with the therapist;
6. This past thing that is feared to be a future thing thus becomes a present thing, and can now actually be experienced for the first time;
7. This here-and-now experiencing is the equivalent of remembering the past event;
8. The outcome is the lifting of the veil of repression that has hidden the past agonies from the patient (and deposited them into the future).

Further applications of this theory

Fear of death

Little alteration is needed to transfer the general thesis of fear of breakdown to a specific fear of death. This is perhaps a more common fear, and one that is absorbed in the religious teachings about an after-life, as if to deny the fact of death.

> When fear of death is a significant symptom the promise of an after-life fails to give relief, and the reason is that the patient has a compulsion to look for death. Again, it is the death that happened but was not experienced that is sought.
>
> When Keats was "half in love with easeful death" he was, according to the idea that I am putting forward here, longing for the ease that would come if he could "remember" having died; but to remember he must experience death now.

Here Winnicott is helping us see one of the various extensions of the fear of breakdown: the fear of death. He says that some patients are not even consoled by their belief in an afterlife because for these particular patients the fear of death is a proxy for their fear of breakdown. They fear a "death" that they have already experienced in their distant developmental past.

> Most of my ideas are inspired by patients, to whom I acknowledge my debt. It is to one of these that I owe the phrase "phenomenal death". What happened in the past was death as a phenomenon, but not as the sort of fact that we observe. Many men and women spend their lives wondering whether to find a solution by suicide, that is, sending the body to death which has already happened to the psyche. Suicide is no answer, however, but is a despair gesture. I now understand for the first time what my schizophrenic patient (who did kill herself) meant when she said: "All I ask you to do is to help me to commit suicide for the right reason instead of for the wrong reason." I did not succeed and she killed herself in despair of finding the solution. Her aim (as I now see) was to get it stated by me that she died in early infancy. On this basis I think she and I could have enabled her to put off body death till old age took its toll.

OK. So Winnicott is giving us one way in which to look at those who chronically consider suicide. It is, perhaps, a making real of a death that has already happened to their psyche. And he recounts the death by suicide of one of his patients, who, he thinks in retrospect, needed him to recognize that she had suffered psychic death in infancy.

> Death, looked at in this way as something that happened to the patient but which the patient was not mature enough to experience, has the meaning of annihilation. It is like this, that a pattern developed in which the continuity of being was interrupted by the patient's infantile reactions

to impingement, these being environmental factors that were allowed to impinge by failures of the facilitating environment. (In the case of this patient troubles started very early, for there was a premature awareness awakened before birth because of a maternal panic, and added to this the birth was complicated by undiagnosed placenta praevia.)

Winnicott has written about the topic of annihilation in others of his papers. The infant has a fundamental need for a continuity of being that can only be provided by an attuned maternal environment. Lacking that attunement, a baby suffers serious impingements on his going-on-being, which accrue to the point wherein he experiences the annihilation of his incipient self. In the case of the patient whom Winnicott lost to suicide, her difficulties started in utero via the mother's panic (which we now know suffuses the fetus with toxic cortisol), and in the birthing process via placenta previa (which potentially causes dangerous bleeding in the delivery process and is a risk to both infant and mother).

Emptiness

Again my patients show me that the concept of emptiness can be looked at through these same spectacles.

Here Winnicott is helping us see another of the various extensions of the fear of breakdown: the experience of emptiness.

In some patients emptiness needs to be experienced, and this emptiness belongs to the past, to the time before the degree of maturity had made it possible for emptiness to be experienced.

Once again, Winnicott is invoking the concept that something happened to a developing little one—or, in the case of emptiness, that did *not* happen, wherein the child could not be present for something, and must carry the non-experiencing forward into their life.

To understand this it is necessary to think not of trauma but of nothing happening when something might profitably have happened.

It is easier for a patient to remember trauma than to remember nothing happening when it might have happened. At the time, the patient did not

> know what might have happened, and so could not experience anything
> except to note that something might have been.

In the case of emptiness, there was the absence of something necessary to the child's development. There was a lack that left them with something missing, which, of course, they cannot identify because it was an absence rather than a presence.

Example

I render Winnicott's case examples less closely because the narrative has to develop. So let's hear this case re: emptiness.

> A phase in a patient's treatment illustrates this. This young woman lay uselessly on the couch, and all she could do was to say: "Nothing is happening in this analysis!"
>
> At the stage that I am describing, the patient had supplied material of an indirect kind so that I could know that she was probably feeling something. I was able to say that she had been feeling feelings, and she had been experiencing these gradually fading, according to her pattern, a pattern which made her despair. The feelings were sexual and female. They did not show clinically.
>
> Here in the transference was myself (nearly) being the cause now of her female sexuality fizzling out; when this was properly stated we had an example in the present of what had happened to her innumerable times.

OK. I'll break in here. Here is an example of how Winnicott let the patient hold him responsible for the fizzling out of her sexuality. Objectively, Winnicott was not the cause of this, but subjectively (in her "omnipotence") he was. He was that figure to her, transferentially, who was a present-tense example of something she had experienced repeatedly in her life. He worked with her to be able to state accurately her subjective reality.

> In her case (to simplify for the sake of description) there was a father who at first was scarcely ever present, and then when he came to her home when she was a little girl he did not want his daughter's female self, and had nothing to give by way of male stimulus.

Her own father was the original source of this emptiness for her, but she would not have been able to get in touch with this had she not experienced his absence in the transference with Winnicott.

> Now, emptiness is a prerequisite for eagerness to gather in. Primary emptiness simply means: before starting to fill up. A considerable maturity is needed for this state to be meaningful.
>
> Emptiness occurring in a treatment is a state that the patient is trying to experience, a past state that cannot be remembered except by being experienced for the first time now.

OK, this is an important tip to therapists: emptiness in a treatment is a state a patient is trying to experience. We should not get in the way by trying to fill up the emptiness, but rather, we should let it occur and make meaning of it. (This is a mistake that young therapists are prone to because they often feel "the need to be helpful".)

> In practice, the difficulty is that the patient fears the awfulness of emptiness, and in defence will organize a controlled emptiness by not eating or not learning, or else will ruthlessly fill up by a greediness which is compulsive and which feels mad. When the patient can reach to emptiness itself and tolerate this state because of dependence on the auxiliary ego of the analyst, then, taking in can start up as a pleasurable function; here can begin eating that is not a function dissociated (or split off) as part of the personality; also it is in this way that some of our patients who cannot learn can begin to learn pleasurably.

The only way a patient can tolerate feeling what they actually feel, in this case, emptiness, is because of their dependence in their relationship with the therapist, who acts as an auxiliary ego for the patient, just as a good-enough mother acts as an auxiliary ego for an infant. Nested within the care and presence of the therapist, the patient can afford to feel and experience things that would otherwise have been beyond them before this point. In the case of emptiness, a patient can afford to tolerate feeling truly empty. Winnicott sees emptiness as the precursor for the act of taking in pleasurably.

> The basis of all learning (as well as of eating) is emptiness. But if emptiness was not experienced as such at the beginning, then it turns up as a state that is feared, yet compulsively sought after.

Non-existence

Here Winnicott is helping us see another of the various extensions of the fear of breakdown: the search for non-existence.

> The search for personal non-existence can be examined in the same way. It will be found that non-existence here is part of a defence. Personal existence is represented by the projection elements, and the person is making an attempt to project everything that could be personal.

What is he saying here? Non-existence—to make a subject into nothing—can be considered within the context of annihilation. It amounts to a total destruction or a complete obliteration of a subject. The person is attempting to rid himself of everything that is personal; in essence, to aspire to a feelingless state.

> This can be a relatively sophisticated defence, and the aim is to avoid responsibility (at the depressive position)...

Right. If we are not really here and substantive, then there is no such thing as responsibility for my impact on the other...

> or to avoid persecution (at what I would call the stage of self-assertion, i.e. the stage of *I am* with the inherent implication *I repudiate everything that is not me*). It is convenient here to use in illustration the childhood game of "I'm the King of the Castle—You're the Dirty Rascal".

Right. If we are one with God or King of the universe, then you are my subject, and I can so invalidate you that I am not accountable to you because you don't count. Nothing of what I do can be judged or evaluated. I am beyond being controlled by or harmed by you.

> In the religions this idea can appear in the concept of oneness with God or with the Universe. It is possible to see this defence being negated in existentialist writings and teachings, in which existing is made into a cult, in an attempt to counter the personal tendency towards a non-existence that is part of an organized defence.

If I disappear into oneness with God, my existence is mere illusion. I therefore embrace my own non-existence.

> There can be a positive element in all this, that is, an element that is not a defence. It can be said that *only out of non-existence can existence start*. It is surprising how early (even before birth, certainly during the birth

process) awareness of a premature ego can be mobilized. But the individual cannot develop from an ego root if this is divorced from psychosomatic experience and from primary narcissism. It is just here that begins the intellectualization of the ego-functions. It can be noted here that all this is a long distance in time prior to the establishment of anything that could usefully be called the self.

Winnicott ends his paper in a kind of philosophical reflection on our very beginnings as a human: "only out of non-existence can existence start." He ends by asserting that our root as a human has its proper ground in psychosomatic existence, and that the need to summon up premature ego functions, particularly via intellectualization, subverts the developmental process, and can and does begin surprisingly early. This is, of course, the best an infant can do—it is compensatory and, thus, by definition, defensive, because the environment of the primary caretaker is failing to hold and facilitate the infant's growth in fundamental ways.

Summary

I have attempted to show that fear of breakdown can be a fear of a past event that has not yet been experienced. The need to experience it is equivalent to a need to remember in terms of the analysis of psychoneurotics.

This idea can be applied to other allied fears, and I have mentioned the fear of death and the search for emptiness.

Author references

Chapter 1 Mind and its relation to the psyche-soma

Cordon, I., Pipe, M., Sayfan, L., Melinder, A., & Goodman, G. (2004). Memory for traumatic experiences in early childhood. *Developmental Review*, 24, 101–132.

Fairbairn, W. R. D. (1944). Endopsychic structure considered in terms of object-relationships. *International Journal of Psychoanalysis*, 25, 70–93.

"Lobotomy," (n.d.). Wikipedia.

Nelson, C. (1995). The ontogeny of human memory: A cognitive neuroscience perspective. *Developmental Psychology*, 31(5), 723–738.

Pert, C. (1997). *Molecules of emotion: The science behind mind–body medicine*. New York: Touchstone Publishers, Simon and Schuster.

Chapter 2 Primitive emotional development

Ogden, T. (2001). Reading Winnicott. *Psychoanalytic Quarterly*, 70, 299–323.

Chapter 3 Hate in the counter-transference

Freud, S. (1910). The future prospects of psycho-analytic theory. *The standard edition of the complete psychological works of Sigmund Freud, volume XI (1910): Five lectures on psycho-analysis, Leonardo da Vinci and other works*, 139–152. London: Hogarth Press.

Grob, G. (1994). *The mad among us*. New York: Free Press.

Winnicott, D. W. (1945). Primitive emotional development. In *Through paediatrics to psycho-analysis: Collected papers* (pp. 145–156). Levittown, PA: Brunner Mazel, 1992.

Winnicott, D. W. (1965). The effect of psychosis on family life. In *The family and individual development* (p. 88). London: Routledge.

Chapter 5 The antisocial tendency

Bowlby, J. (1944). Forty-four juvenile thieves: Their characters and home life. *International Journal of Psychoanalysis*, 25, 19–53.

Bowlby, J. (1969). *Attachment. Attachment and loss: Vol. 1. Loss*. New York: Basic Books.

Bowlby, J., & Robertson, J. (1952). A two-year-old goes to hospital. *Proceedings of the Royal Society of Medicine*, 46, 425–427.

Winnicott, D.W. (1936). Appetite and emotional disorder. In *Through paediatrics to psycho-analysis: Collected papers* (pp. 33–51). Levittown, PA: Brunner Mazel, 1992.

Winnicott, D.W. (1941). The observation of infants in a set situation. *International Journal of Psycho-Analysis*, 22, 228–249.

Winnicott, D.W. (1945). Thinking and the unconscious. In C. Winnicott, R. Shepherd, & M. Davis (eds.) *Home is where we start from: Essays by a psychoanalyst (1986)* (pp. 169–171). New York: Norton.

Winnicott, D.W. (1950). Aggression in relation to emotional development. In *Through paediatrics to psycho-analysis: Collected papers* (pp. 204–218). Levittown, PA: Brunner Mazel, 1992.

Winnicott, D.W. (1956). Primary maternal preoccupation. In *Through paediatrics to psycho-analysis: Collected papers* (pp. 300–305). Levittown, PA: Brunner Mazel, 1992.

Winnicott, D.W. (1958). The observation of infants in a set situation. In *Through paediatrics to psycho-analysis: Collected papers* (pp. 52–69). Levittown, PA: Brunner Mazel, 1992.

Winnicott, D.W. (1969). The use of an object. *International Journal of Psycho-Analysis*, 50, 711–716.

Chapter 6 Primary maternal preoccupation

Hartmann, H. (1939). Psycho-analysis and the concept of mental health. *International Journal of Psycho-Analysis*, 20, 308–321.

Hartmann, H. (1964). *Essays on ego psychology*. Oxford: International Universities Press.

Palombo, J., Bendicsen, H., & Koch, B. (2010). *Guide to psychoanalytic developmental theories*. London: Springer.

Winnicott, D.W. (1949). Mind and its relation to the psyche-soma. In *Through paediatrics to psycho-analysis: Collected papers* (pp. 243–254). Levittown, PA: Brunner Mazel, 1992.

Winnicott, C. (2016). D.W. W.: A reflection. In: R. Ades (ed.) *The collected works of D. W. Winnicott: Vol. 12, Appendices and bibliographies*. New York: Oxford University Press.

Chapter 7 Ego distortion in terms of True and False Self

American Psychiatric Association (1980). *Diagnostic and* statistical manual of mental disorders, 3rd ed. Washington, DC: American Psychiatric Association.

Sechehaye, M. A. (1951). *Autobiography of a schizophrenic girl; with analytic interpretation by Marguerite Sechehaye* (Grace Rubin-Rabson, Trans.). New York: Grune and Stratton.

Winnicott, D.W. (1949). Mind and its relation to the psyche-soma. In *Through paediatrics to psycho-analysis: Collected papers* (pp. 243–254). Levittown, PA: Brunner Mazel, 1992.

Winnicott, D.W. (1956). Primary maternal preoccupation. In *Through paediatrics to psycho-analysis: Collected papers* (pp. 300–305). Levittown, PA: Brunner Mazel, 1992.

Chapter 8 The aims of psycho-analytical treatment

Winnicott, D.W. (1949). Hate in the counter-transference. *International Journal of Psycho-Analysis*, 30, 69–74.

Chapter 9 Notes on ego integration in child development

Freud, S. (1923). The ego and the id. In J. Strachey et al. (Trans.) *The standard edition of the complete psychological works of Sigmund Freud*, Vol. XIX. London: Hogarth Press.

Sechehaye, M. A. (1951). *Autobiography of a schizophrenic girl; with analytic interpretation by Marguerite Sechehaye* (Grace Rubin-Rabson, Trans.). New York: Grune and Stratton.

Winnicott, D. W. (1956). Primary maternal preoccupation. In *Through paediatrics to psycho-analysis: Collected papers* (pp. 300–305). Levittown, PA: Brunner Mazel, 1992.

Chapter 10 Mirror-role of mother and family in child development

Winnicott, D. W. (1949). Mind and its relation to the psyche-soma. In *Through paediatrics to psycho-analysis: Collected papers* (pp. 243–254). Levittown, PA: Brunner Mazel, 1992.

Chapter 11 The use of an object

American Psychiatric Association (1980). *Diagnostic and statistical manual of mental disorders*, 3rd ed. Washington, DC: American Psychiatric Association.

Winnicott, D. W. (1953). Transitional objects and transitional phenomena—A study of the first not-me possession. *International Journal of Psycho-Analysis*, 34, 89–97.

Winnicott, D. W. (1968). Playing: Its theoretical status in the clinical situation. *International Journal of Psychoanalysis*, 49(4), 591–599.

Chapter 12 Fear of breakdown

Spitz, R. A. (1947). Grief: A peril in infancy. In K. M. Wolf (ed.) *Psychoanalytic research project on problems of infancy.* University Park, PA: PennState Media Sales.

Winnicott, D. W. (1949). Mind and its relation to the psyche-soma. In *Through paediatrics to psycho-analysis: Collected papers* (pp. 243–254). Levittown, PA: Brunner Mazel, 1992.

Winnicott, D. W. (1952). Anxiety associated with insecurity. In: L. Caldwell, & T. Robinson (eds.) *The collected works of D. W. Winnicott: Vol. 4, 1952–1955* (pp. 99–100). Oxford: Oxford University Press, 2016.

Winnicott, D. W. (1960). Ego distortion in terms of true and false self. In *The maturational processes and the facilitating environment: Studies in the theory of emotional development* (pp. 140–151). London: Karnac, 2007.

Index

Note: Figures are shown in italics. Footnotes are indicated by an "n" and the footnote number after the page number e.g., 88n11 refers to footnote 11 on page 88.

abnormality, double 141
absolute dependence 128–129, 130–131, 172, 180, 189, 225, 226–227
accidental happenings 8, 68
active adaptation 6, 7, 9, 11, 13–14, 17, 88
acute anxiety 53, 228
adaptation: active 6, 7, 9, 11, 13–14, 17, 88; False Self 154; graduated failure of 9; reality 40
addiction 81, 96
adult maturity 5
affectionlessness 102
aggression 80, 168, 216, 217–218; and primary maternal preoccupation 97, 105, 106, 107, 108, 114, 115
ambivalence 28, 30, 33, 52, 57, 164–165
anaclitic relationships 120
analysis of resistance 163–164
analyst's love 55, 57–58, 59
analytical psychology, Jung's 47n7
anencephalia 171, 184–187, 188–189
anger 66, 104, 120, 164, 213–214, 218
annihilation 17, 44, 80, 136, 139, 148, 166, 218; and fear of breakdown 229, 236–237, 240; and primary maternal preoccupation 125, 126, 127, 128, 130, 131
antidepressant and antipsychotic medication 21, 53, 54
antisocial personalities 56
antisocial tendency 97–116, 168
anxiety 17, 26, 29, 32, 39, 84, 227; acute 53, 228; archaic 126, 178, 180, 185; castration 223–224; chronic 53; counter-transference 61–63; defence against 77–78, 164; depressive 77–78; infant 184; and persecution 181; psychotic 51, 52, 56, 61, 63, 185, 206;

primitive 125; reactive 63; unthinkable 126, 178, 180, 185
apperception 74–75, 194–195, 197–198
archaic anxiety 126, 178, 180, 185
artistic creation 37n3, 40, 81
attachment 72–73, 75, 80, 83, 102, 103–104
attunement 6, 7, 122, 178, 190, 194; and antisocial tendency 110, 112; and ego distortion 145, 156; and fear of breakdown 232–233, 237; and primitive emotional development 36, 37, 42; and psycho-analytical treatment 166, 168
autism 123, 184, 187, 228, 229
auto-eroticism 49, 76–77, 79, 89
average expectable environment 118, 119
awake self 39–40

Bacon, Francis 197–198, 200, 200n4
bad environment 6; *see also* impingement
bad objects 88n11, 104
bedwetting 108, 112, 115
bipolar disorder 56–57
birth experience 15, 16
body schema 2, 3, 18, 20
borderline cases 57, 58, 134–135, 169, 206–207
Bowlby, John 31, 102, 103, 103n1, 104
brain 3–4, 19, 20–21, 22, 54, 187; *see also* anencephalia
breakdown, fear of 221–241
British School of Object Relations 52

capacity to relate to: external reality 152; objects 207, 219, 228–229
Caretaker Self 137–138, 186
castration anxiety 223–224
cataloguing 14, 17, 20, 22, 183

cathexis 146, 207–208, 218
chance events 8, 68
character disorders 204
child development 88, 117; ego
    integration in 170–189; mirror-role in
    190–202
chronic anxiety 53
coincidences 8, 57, 58, 68, 165
compliance 11, 130, 133, 147, 153, 154
compulsions/compulsiveness 49, 236,
    239; and antisocial tendency 99, 101,
    106, 109, 110, 111, 112, 113, 114–115
conflict-free area in ego 124
confusional states 11, 14
constitutional factors 130–131
contempt 31
continuity of being 143, 144, 179, 233,
    236–237; and mind 6, 8, 13–14, 15, 22
control, of the therapist 31
countertransference 28, 29, 54–55, 59, 60,
    65, 162, 232; anxiety from 61–63
creativity 24, 71, 81, 91, 93, 109, 150; of
    the patient 201, 202; in playing 204;
    primary 73, 81, 90, 91, 105, 151, 154,
    155
cross-identifications 208
cultural life 154, 168

death, fear of 235–236, 241
deep sleep 38, 53
defence mechanisms 40, 130, 158, 223,
    229, 230; antisocial 97; against anxiety
    77–78, 164; against betrayal of True
    Self 139; against depersonalization 182;
    against depression 26–27, 30, 31; False
    Self 136, 154; against insecurity feelings
    49; against loss of object 49; oneness
    with God as 240; primitive 130;
    against primitive anxieties 49; against
    threat of loss of psycho-somatic union
    182; psychotic illness as 229; of self-
    holding 186; against a tantalizing early
    environment 10; against unintegration
    180; against the unthinkable 147–148
delinquency 46, 97, 102
delusion 95, 96, 144–145n1, 165, 176,
    215
dependence 11, 12, 111, 119, 120, 169,
    199, 216; absolute 128–129, 130–131,
    172, 180, 189, 225, 226–227; and ego
    distortion 135, 138, 143, 156; extreme
    156; and fear of breakdown 223, 224,
    232, 233, 239; relative 166, 189

depersonalization 35, 38, 63, 174–175,
    182, 184, 207, 228; *see also*
    personalization
depression 26–27, 28–29, 30, 31, 78, 197,
    199–200; therapist's own 24
depressive anxiety 77–78
depressive position 33, 45, 56–57, 103,
    104, 240
deprivation 65, 78, 168; and antisocial
    tendency 97, 102–104, 103n1, 107,
    108, 109, 110, 111, 112, 113–114
deprived complex 100, 101, 109, 110
derealization 207, 228–229
destruction/destructiveness 104, 105,
    112, 214, 219; object 219–220; reactive
    213–214
development: early 3, 5–6, 15, 34, 36,
    41, 105–106, 119, 131; emotional *see*
    emotional development; normal 3,
    142, 153, 165; ontogenetic 142; of a
    personal pattern 76; *see also* integration;
    personalization; realization
developmental compromises 10
developmental processes 34, 126, 131,
    143, 241
developmental stages 3, 5
Diagnostic and Statistical Manual of
    Mental Disorders (DSM) 135, 206
disease 4, 9, 187, 188, 207
disillusionment 68, 88, 89–90,
    92–93
disinhabiting, of one's body 63, 186,
    207
disintegration 113, 164, 165, 179, 180,
    206–207, 227; and primitive emotional
    development 35, 36, 37, 38, 46
disorders 4, 41, 52, 53, 61, 187, 188, 204
dissociation 39–40, 46, 107, 141, 232
double abnormality 141
double helix 114
dreams 39, 40, 62, 163
drives 97, 101, 107–108, 171, 174–175,
    185
DSM (Diagnostic and Statistical Manual
    of Mental Disorders) 135, 206

early development 105–106, 119,
    131; and mind 3, 5–6, 15; and
    primitive emotional development
    34, 36, 41
early maternal environment 118
Egas Moniz, António 21–22, 53–54
ego: definition of 170; nature of 171

ego development 110–111, 131, 171, 173–174, 175, 176, 177, 178, 184, 190
ego distortion 133–159
ego establishment 126
ego immaturity 106, 131
ego independence 166, 167
ego integration, in child development 167, 170–189
ego maturity 104, 113, 131, 152
ego needs 9, 109, 110, 126, 136
ego organization 128, 153, 184, 186, 224
ego support, mother's 35–36, 177, 180, 187, 224, 231; and antisocial tendency 109, 110, 116
ego-coverage 170, 178
ego-experience 183
ego-relatedness, between mother and baby 127
ego-strength 165, 166, 167, 189
electroconvulsive therapy 53
emergent self 20
emotional development 10, 22, 24–50, 97, 189, 190–191; and first not-me possession 79–80, 88, 95; and hate in counter-transference 54, 56, 62; primitive 24–50
emotional growth 212, 224, 225, 227
emotionally attuned environment 7
emptiness 237–238, 238–239, 241
encopresis 40
environment: bad 6; emotionally attuned 7; facilitating 204, 210–211, 225, 229, 232, 237; good 7, 12; good-enough 22, 117, 118, 129, 130; perfect 6, 8, 9, 10; psychologically attuned 7
environmental adaptive failure 14
environmental care 87, 98–99
environmental deficiency disease 9–10
environmental failures 10, 24, 58, 113, 116, 188, 224
environmental influences 165–166
environmental provisions 90, 129, 130, 191; and antisocial tendency 104, 113, 116; and ego integration 181–182, 189
erratic behaviour, of the mother 9
evacuated child case study 66–67
experiencing 81, 96, 171, 191, 193, 195, 232, 234, 238; the de-fused object-seeking part of the double helix 114; of a good-enough early environment 23; here-and-now 235; id phenomena 183; intermediate area of 74; of

ourselves as physical beings 1, 4, 5; of primitive agonies 229, 231; of stimuli 152; the underlying state 229
explicit memory 13
"exploitation" versus "use" 219
external reality 233; and ego distortion 145, 149, 151–152, 155; and first not-me possession 73–74, 74–75, 89, 91, 94; and primitive emotional development 40–43, 44–45, 46–47, 49–50; and use of an object 204, 211, 213, 214, 218, 219
external relationships 13–14, 28, 30, 44
extreme dependence 156

facilitating environment 204, 210–211, 225, 229, 232, 237
failure of the mother 1, 10, 88–89, 88n11, 125, 128, 141, 186, 195
falling forever 186, 207, 228
false entity 3
false localization 3, 19, 21
False Personality 140, 155–156
False Self 15, 130–131, 133–159
family, mirror-role of 190–202
fantasy 74, 77, 212, 218; and primitive emotional development 26, 27, 43–44, 45; and psycho-analytical treatment 160, 162, 165; unconscious 25, 62, 168, 212
fear: of breakdown 221–241; of death 235–236, 241; of madness 168
fecal incontinence 40
feeding satisfaction 185
fetishism 81, 87, 95–96
fever therapy 53
first not-me possession 71–96
flight to sanity 122
fragmentation 177, 178–179
free association 27–28, 162
Freud, Anna 31, 117–118, 119–120
Freud, Sigmund 3, 75, 95, 97, 110, 164, 169, 216–217; and ego distortion 134, 142, 149; and ego integration 171, 177, 183, 189; and fear of breakdown 224, 230–231, 235; and hate in counter-transference 53, 55, 67–68; and primary maternal preoccupation 119–120, 122, 124, 125; and primitive emotional development 26, 27–28, 41, 43
frustration 88–89, 119–120, 126, 127, 128, 136, 183

going-on-being 35
good enough mother 8–9, 104, 143–144, 172, 175, 176–177, 184, 239
good environment 7, 12
good objects 88n11, 104
good-enough care 129, 184, 185, 186, 196
good-enough environment 22, 117, 118, 129, 130
graduated failure of adaptation 9
greed/greediness 36–37, 108–112, 239
guilt 28, 29, 56–57, 60, 115, 124

hallucinations 41, 80, 89, 144, 145, 146
handling 76, 176–177, 181–182, 188, 191, 192, 225
Hartmann, Heinz 117, 118, 124
hate, in the counter-transference 51–70
healing dreams 62
healing properties 11
here-and-now experiencing 235
history-taking, value in 85
holding, maternal 35–36, 181, 210
homeostatic equilibrium 118, 119
hope, lack of 101–102
hydrotherapy 53
hyperkinesis 179
hypochondria 21–22, 26, 27, 148–149, 165, 168–169
hypo-mania 56–57

id desires 110
id experience 26, 36–37, 119–120, 130, 131
id phenomena experiencing 183
id-drives 174–175
ideal/loved object 29
identifications 201, 207; with the analyst, 51; analyst's personal 55, 60; cross- 208; with the crushing mechanism 17; with the dependent individual 11, 12; with the environmental aspect of dependent relationships 11, 12; and false self 139–140; male 122; of mother and baby/infant 7, 118, 119, 129, 148, 149, 150; primary 88; social 123–124
id-needs 109, 110–111, 136
id-satisfactions 136, 174, 175, 183
ill parental figure 168
illusion 41, 42, 43–44, 44–45, 71, 75, 88, 88n11, 89, 90, 91–93, *91*, *92*, 94, 95–96, 145
imaginary companions, of childhood 38

imaginative elaboration 74, 77, 126, 151, 177, 192; and mind 1, 2, 4, 5, 19–20, 21
impingements 80, 107, 152, 155, 237; and mind 6, 13–14, 17, 22, 23; and primary maternal preoccupation 125–126, 127, 128, 129, 131
implicit memory 7, 13, 14
inability to concentrate/inattentiveness 179
indwelling 181, 225, 226, 227, 228
infant anxieties 184
infant care 9, 11, 58, 89, 108, 225; and ego integration 170, 179; and primitive emotional development 36, 37
infantile dependence 169, 199, 224–225
infantile neurosis 118
infantile schizophrenia 184, 187
infantile sexuality 162
infant–mother relationship 42, 118, 170, 172, 178, 186; and ego distortion 135, 137, 142
inhabiting the body, process of *see* personalization
initial solipsism 75
innate developmental tendencies 124
inner reality 151, 152
inner world 20, 26, 27, 66, 74, 209
insanity 222
insecurity 49
instincts 27, 67, 71, 106–107, 114, 134, 136, 175; and primary maternal preoccupation 124–125, 129–130, 131
instinctual aggressiveness 218
instinctual drives 171, 185
instinctual experiences 25, 26, 27, 36–37, 38, 119–120, 130, 131
instinctual tensions 9, 91, 136
insulin shock therapy 53
integration: psychic 36; in space 174; in time 174
intellect/intellectual approach 18, 21, 88, 141, 142, 153, 162, 171, 187
intellectualization, of the ego-functions 241
intelligence quotient (I.Q.), and release of the mother 9
intermediate area of experience 71, 73, 74, 76, 90, 93–94, 96, 155
internal objects 95
interpersonal relationships 74
interpretations: making of 205–206; postponement of 63

introjection 73, 109, 131, 147, 164, 165, 168
introversion 47
I.Q. (intelligence quotient), and release of the mother 9
irreducible mental elements 1–2

Jung, Carl 47n7, 140, 230–231
justified hate 65

Klein, Melanie 1, 56–57, 103, 104, 117, 143, 213, 216–217; and first not-me possession 87, 90n12, 91, 93; and primitive emotional development 26, 27, 28, 29, 33

Lacan, Jacques 190–191, 200–201
latent schizophrenia 184, 187
later-expressed pathologies 170, 179
laws of reality 44
leucotomy 21, 53–54
libido 97, 105, 106–107, 107–108, 113–114, 115
lobotomy 21, 53–54
localization 26, 27, 34–35, 188, 223, 224; and mind 2, 3, 4, 12, 13, 19–20, 21, 22
love 28–29; analyst's 55, 57–58, 59; mother's 67–68; mouth 106–107, 113–114; primary 111; primitive 48, 58, 106, 109, 110, 111, 218

madness, fear of 168
magical laws, of fantasy 44
maladaptation 1, 12
management, of patients 51–52, 53, 58, 98, 100, 101, 102
marvellously good mother to others 11
maternal care 69, 111, 137, 152, 226, 227; and ego integration 175, 176–177, 179, 184, 186, 188; and first not-me possession 90, 90n12, 94; and mind 9, 10, 22; and primary maternal preoccupation 122, 129; *see also* mother's breast
maternal coverage 178
maternal environment 71, 91, 109, 118, 142, 143, 180; and fear of breakdown 224, 225, 227, 233, 237; and mind 1, 7, 10–11
maternal failure 1, 10, 88–89, 88n11, 125, 128, 141, 186, 195
maternal holding 35–36, 181, 210
maternal object 29, 33, 104, 182

maternal phallus 95, 96
maternal preoccupation, primary 7, 117–131, 148–149
medications 21, 53, 54
melancholia 104
memory 15, 97, 103, 104, 121, 124, 152, 235; implicit 7, 13, 14; narrative 13, 14–15
mental activity 7–8, 9, 14, 22, 89
mental development 22, 23, 192
mental functioning 9–10, 11, 13, 14, 17, 19, 20, 22, 23, 34; *see also* mind
messiness 108, 110, 111, 112, 115
metapsychology, of Winnicott 89–90
metrazol therapy 53
mind, and the False Self 141–142; and the psyche-soma 1–23; *see also* mental functioning
mind-psyche 11, 12–13, 141, 142
mirror-role, of mother and family in child development 190–202
modified analysis 167–168
moods 11, 32–33
mothering *see* maternal care
mother's breast 41–42, 81, 86, 90, 95, 209, 216; *see also* maternal care
mother's ego support 35–36, 224, 231; and antisocial tendency 109, 110, 116; and ego integration 177, 180, 187
mother's love and hate 67
mother's therapy 111, 112
motility 106–107, 113–114, 124, 125, 131, 143
mouth love 106–107, 113–114
multiple projections 158
multiple selves 40

nail-biting 48
narcissism, primary 177, 228, 241
narrative memory 13, 14–15
near-normal child 97
need-anticipated-by-and-met-by-the-mother-repeatedly 42
negative experiences 217
negative transference 163, 164, 166
neuropeptides 3
neurosis 100, 112, 206–207, 224, 234; and hate in counter-transference 53, 57, 61, 62, 64; infantile 118; and psycho-analytical treatment 161, 168, 169; *see also* psychoneurosis
neurotransmitters 3

non-conformity, to cultural/familial laws and norms 98
non-existence, psychological 139, 157, 158, 188–189, 239–240, 240–241
non-I objects 173
normal child 46, 93, 97, 115
normal development 3, 142, 153, 165
normal illness 122
not-good-enough mothering 184
not-knowing 17, 18, 19
not-me objects 173
not-me possession 71–96, *84, 91, 92*
nuisance value, of the antisocial child 107–108

object destruction 219–220
Object Relations 74
object relationships 16, 27, 45–46, 46–47, 49, 73, 143
object retaliations 164, 165, 168–169
object usage 203–220
object-finding 58
objective counter-transference 55
objective hate 65
objective reality/objectivity 59, 154–155, 212, 233; and first not-me possession 81, 90–91, 94; and primitive emotional development 24, 42–43, 45
object-presenting 176–177, 182, 188, 191, 225
object-relating 207–208, 210, 211, 212, 219, 225; and ego integration 175, 176–177, 182
object-seeking 104, 105, 106–107, 114
obsessions 56, 59, 81, 118
Oedipus complex 165
offense 217
Ogden, Thomas 24
omnipotence 42, 57, 58, 160, 167, 192, 195; and antisocial tendency 105–106, 108, 110; and ego distortion 140, 143, 144, 145, 151, 152, 154–155; and ego integration 171, 172–173, 180, 182; and fear of breakdown 231, 232–233, 238; and first not-me possession 71, 73, 80, 81, 86, 88, 89–90, 91; and use of an object 203, 204, 208, 209, 210, 211–212, 213, 214, 215, 216–217, 219
ontogenetic development 142
oral eroticism 106–107, 113–114
oral erotogenic zone 71–72
ordinary castration anxiety 62, 63
ordinary devoted mother 122

ordinary good mother 7, 117–131, 148–149
outer reality 71, 74, 75, 93

paranoia 30, 31, 87, 165, 181
paranoid-schizoid position 28, 29, 31, 33, 45, 104, 165
pathological super-ego 115
patient attacks 215–216
patient's interpretations 205
penis envy 122
perceptions 18, 27, 113, 164, 175, 176, 210, 213; and first not-me possession 74–75, 81, 90, 94; and mirror-role of mother and family 194–195, 197–198
perfect environment/perfection 6, 8, 9, 10
persecution 29, 30, 31, 87, 165, 181
personal actuality 179
personal pattern, development of a 76
personality disorders 52, 61, 188
personalization 63, 151; and ego integration 170, 173, 174–175, 176–177, 181–182, 189; and primitive emotional development 24, 34, 35, 38, 45; *see also* depersonalization; disinhibiting the body
phantasy *see* fantasy
physical experience 1, 2 4, 5, 22
play 14, 31, 32, 46, 69–70, 109, 204; and ego distortion 145, 156, 157; and first not-me possession 71–72, 81, 93
pleasure-principle 88
positive transference 163, 164
possession, first not-me 71–96, *84, 91, 92*
post-mature infants 33
postnatal infants 124
postponement of interpretation 63
pre-concern, stage of 45, 46n6, 115
pre-depressive position and relationships 28, 29, 31, 33, 45, 104, 165
premature infants 33
preoccupation, maternal 7, 117–131, 148–149
primary creativity 73, 81, 90, 91, 105, 151, 154, 155
primary identification 88
primary love 111
primary maternal preoccupation 7, 117–131, 148–149
primary narcissism 177, 228, 241
Primary Process 1, 140, 151, 163
primary unintegration 46

primitive agonies 227–229, 231
primitive anxiety 125
primitive emotional development 24–50
primitive love 48, 58, 106, 109, 110, 111, 218
primitive needs 11, 169
primitive, pre-depressive relationships 28, 31
primitive relationships 27, 30
primitive retaliation 46–47
primitive ruthlessness 45, 46n6, 115
projection 26, 56, 70, 73, 152, 240; and psycho-analytical treatment 164, 165, 168–169; and use of an object 207–209, 213, 214, 215, 216
prostration attacks 38
proto-thinking *see* imaginative elaboration
psyche-soma, and the mind 1–23
psychic integration 36
psycho-analytic research 59
psycho-analytical treatment, aims of 160–169
psychological disorders 53
psychologically attuned environment 7
psychology, after conception 33
psychoneurosis 52, 206, 223–224, 233–234; *see also* neurosis
psychosexual stages of development, of Sigmund Freud 87, 125
psychosis 9, 10, 52, 58, 100, 135, 206, 234; and primitive emotional development 25, 34, 38; and psycho-analytical treatment 161, 168
psychosomatic collusion 181, 225, 226, 227, 228
psychosomatic disorders 4
psychosomatic illness 21–22
psychotic anxieties 51, 56, 61, 63, 185, 206
psychotic disorders 41, 53
psychotic illness, as defence 229
psychotic process 37, 38, 186

reactive anxiety 63
reactive destruction 213–214
reality: inner 151, 152; laws of 44; objective 42–43, 45, 90–91, 94, 154–155, 212, 233; outer 71, 74, 75, 93; self-created 49
reality adaptation 40
reality orientation 24, 42–43, 59, 81, 91, 94

reality principle 88, 109, 161, 173, 210, 213–214, 217, 218
reality-sense 85
reality-testing 74–75, 86, 90, 92
realization, of realities 34
recidivism 101
recovery 107, 122, 123, 127, 128, 131
re-experiencing 16, 19
regression 96, 108, 112, 115, 199; and ego distortion 135, 138, 156, 157; and mind 14, 15, 16, 19; and primitive emotional development 30, 32, 35, 44
relational worlds 162, 203
relationships: external 13–14, 28, 30, 44; object 16, 27, 45–46, 46–47, 49, 73, 143
relative dependence 166, 189
religious feeling 81
re-parenting 67
repression 30, 53, 55, 60, 80, 231, 235
resistance 163–164, 166, 214–215, 218
restlessness 98, 155, 179
retaliation 46–47; and psycho-analytical treatment 164, 165, 166, 168; and use of an object 214, 215, 216, 217
rhythmic pleasures 120
ruthlessness 29, 45, 46, 110, 114

sanity 32–33, 37, 37n3, 38, 52, 53, 122, 222
satisfaction 42–43, 44, 44n4, 45
schizoid personality 49, 184, 188–189
schizophrenia 21, 184, 185, 187, 229
Sechehaye, Marguerite 144, 144–145n1, 175–176
secondary narcissism 196
Self: Caretaker 137–138, 186; False 15, 130–131, 133–159; True *see* True Self
self-analysis 205–206, 214, 215
self-created world, of fantasy 43, 47n7, 49
self-cure 106, 114
self-discovery 204
self-establishment 204
self-esteem 62
self-holding, defense of 184, 186, 228
self-phenomena 228
self-representation 20
sense of existing 177, 178
sense of real 228
sensitivity 36, 121–122, 124, 125, 172
separation 31, 102, 103–104, 107
six-month marker, of development 29, 31–32

sleep, deep 38, 53
sleep-walking 40
social identification 123–124
solipsism, initial 75
somatic experiences 1, 15, 21, 22, 23, 241
soma-to-psyche-to-mind development 12
somnambulism 40
spatialization 151
special orientation 7, 117–131, 148–149
splitting 26, 57, 164, 165
spontaneity 21, 109, 129, 130, 195; and ego distortion 143, 145, 146, 147, 154
squinting 40
stage of concern 33, 45, 56–57, 103, 104, 240
stage of pre-concern 45, 46n6, 115
standard analysis 161–162, 166, 167
stealing case study 98–100
stimuli 130, 151, 152
strong male identification 122
subjective object 171, 173, 192, 208, 213, 219; and psycho-analytical treatment 160, 161, 162
subjective reality 57, 238
subjectivity 86, 91, 94, 206
sucking, of fingers and thumbs 47–50, 72, 76–77, 84
suicide 17, 139, 207, 236, 237
superego 26, 115, 124
survival: of the analyst 215, 216; of the infant 7, 29; of the infant's initial attempts at destruction of the breast 217; of the object 211, 212, 214–215, 216, 218, 219–220
symbiotic relationship 118, 119
symbol formation 146
symbolic realization 144, 144–145n1, 175–176
symbolism, relationship of the transitional object to 81
symbolization 82
symbol-usage 146

tantalizing maternal environment 10–11, 148, 229
temporalization 151
tensions, instinctual 9, 91, 136
theory of mind 5

therapeutic relationship 29, 64, 116, 162, 205, 224, 233
transference: negative and positive 163, 164, 166; unconscious 61, 160, 166
transference neurosis 161, 168
transference–countertransference 28, 162
transitional objects/transitional phenomena 71–96, *84*, *91*, *92*
trauma 103, 160, 167, 185, 201, 202, 216; and ego distortion 136, 152, 153; and fear of breakdown 228, 232, 237–238
triumph, over the therapist-object 31
truancy 66, 108, 112, 113, 115
True Self 15, 22; and ego distortion 133, 138–139, 140, 143, 144, 145, 147–148, 150–151

unconscious, the 21, 26, 30, 230–231
unconscious compulsion 114–115
unconscious co-operation 163, 168; *see also* resistance
unconscious destruction 216, 219
unconscious drives 101
unconscious fantasy 25, 62, 168, 212
unconscious guilt 115
unconscious hate 64
unconscious motivation 113
unconscious transference 61, 160, 166
unintegration 52, 143, 179–180, 227; and primitive emotional development 35, 36, 37, 38, 39
unit self 177, 178, 181, 221, 224
unit status 74, 178
unreality, feeling of 16–19
unthinkable anxiety 126, 178, 180, 185
use of an object 203–220
"use" versus "exploitation" 219

verbalization 162
vigilance, of the psyche-soma 8–9, 10

weaning 83–84, 83n9, 93
whole-person-to-whole-person relationships 33
willful non-conformity, to laws and norms 98
withdrawal 103, 146, 157, 195–196
Wulff, M. 82n8, 86, 87, 94–95

zone-dominance 124–125, 129–130

Printed in the United States
by Baker & Taylor Publisher Services